A Cop's Tale—
NYPD The Violent
Years

A Cop's Tale— NYPD The Violent Years

A Detective's Firsthand Account
of Murder and Mayhem

DETECTIVE SERGEANT
JIM O'NEIL (RETIRED) WITH
MEL FAZZINO

BARRICADE

Published by Barricade Books Inc.
185 Bridge Plaza North
Suite 308-A
Fort Lee, NJ 07024
www.barricadebooks.com

Library of Congress Cataloging-in-Publication Data

O'Neil, Jim.
    A cop's tale : NYPD the violent years : a detective's firsthand account
of murder and mayhem / by Jim O'Neil with Mel Fazzino.
        p. cm.
    Includes bibliographical references and index.
    ISBN 978-1-56980-372-1
    1. O'Neil, Jim. 2. Police--New York (State)--New York--Biography.
3. Police--New York (State)--New York--History. I. Fazzino, Mel. II.
Title.

HV7911.O44O44 2009
363.2092--dc22
[B]   2009004432

ISBN 13: 978-1-56980-372-1
ISBN 10: 1-56980-372-2

10   9   8   7   6   5   4   3   2   1

Manufactured in the United States of America

DEDICATION

This book is dedicated to the love of my life, my wife, Peggy O'Neil.

TABLE OF CONTENTS

CONTENTS

Acknowledgments

Many thanks to Melissa Stanton. Her support and advice was appreciated.
To Ed Schneider, my old partner, for his encouragement and suggestions.
To Tim Herlihy, my nephew and a successful co-writer of many movies with Adam Sandler. Tim's encouragement and advice on certain additions and changes to the manuscript were heeded, implemented, and appreciated.
To my family, for all the times I was not there during my career and for the encouragement received during the writing of this book.

Note

The story you are about to read is true. The characters depicted all existed, and the incidents described actually took place. Some names have been altered to protect the identities of victims, as well as the confidential informants whose identities I promised never to reveal.

To leave the world a bit better . . . to know even one life has breathed easier because you have lived. This is to have succeeded.

—*Ralph Waldo Emerson*

CHAPTER ONE

This Ain't Russia, Baby

The sunlight was slowly fading and with it the heat of the day began to dissipate. Some of the residents were preparing to trade their daylight masks of civility for ones that mirrored their darker side. A side that would turn them into roving marauders, preying on their neighbors.

They were basically a moral people but as the darkness drew them out into the streets they lost their individual identities and became one with the mob. Four thousand strong they were and as dusk approached they readied themselves for a night of violence. Nobody planned it but the looting was inevitable.

First came the yelling, then the screaming out at social injustices, and just as the mob was gathering a feeling of invincibility a low almost imperceptible sound was heard. Not a random street sound but one with a purpose. A word repeated over and over like some barbaric chant. As the mob strained to hear, the sound grew louder; it was getting closer. But as realization spread that the sound was being chanted by only forty cops there was a collective sigh of relief. After all, what could so few do against the awesome might of four thousand angry, oppressed citizens? The relief was short-lived, however, as the cops lined up into an inverted "V" flying-wedge formation brandishing axe handles and chanting their mantra. With every step the flying wedge took it uttered the word as each cop reassuringly slapped an axe handle into the palm of his hand. The mob stood its ground, waiting to see what the cops hoped to do against such a formidable foe.

They didn't have long to wait.

The word grew louder and clearer, and as the first of the mob lost consciousness from the blow of an axe handle the word was finally understood. It seemed to echo off the tenement walls and all at once the four thousand heard it. At first the crowd froze in disbelief; after all, this was not Russia, this was good old Brooklyn, U.S.A., and it was 1964. "KILL . . . KILL . . . KILL . . . KILL."

The chant's effect was twofold, emboldening the cops and injecting fear into the mob. Now the forty felt like four hundred as axe handles separated teeth from jaws, broke noses, shut eyes, and bashed heads. The mob had just been introduced to the NYPD's Shock Troops—the Elite Tactical Patrol Force.

This was NYPD riot suppression 1964-style and my first taste of an escalating disregard for the law that ushered in some of the department's most violent years.

CHAPTER TWO

To the Academy

Today New York City is the safest big city in the country, largely due to the New York Police Department's (NYPD) proficient use of modern information technology, statistics, and forensic sciences. But it wasn't always that way.

When I joined the force as Patrolman James O'Neil in 1963 the crime rate was at an all-time high. Criminals roamed the streets of certain neighborhoods, almost at will, as violence continued to escalate. Back then it was bare-knuckle law enforcement with cops getting as down and dirty as the criminals. There were no computers, forensic science was in its infancy, cell phones hadn't been invented, and walkie-talkies were a luxury.

My two-decade journey beginning in 1963 was carved out of the NYPD's extremely violent and corrupt years. During that time, the Department transformed into one of the most honest forces in one of the safest large cities in the country, as my career morphed from patrolman, to detective, to sergeant, to Internal Affairs investigator, to boss of the Homicide Task Force, and finally to head of the Senior Citizens Robbery Squad. This book is as much a testimony to cops who serve New York City today as it is to those who came before them. It is my fondest desire that you read on and enjoy, and when you finish the words put down here you will have a newfound admiration for those who are sworn to protect and serve.

It was July 4, 1936, and fireworks filled the sky as people reveled in the streets. That was the day I was born into the O'Neil family. I was so disappointed on my fourth birthday when I found out it wasn't my birth being celebrated but that of our nation. That day I became just another kid growing up in Ridgewood, New York.

Ridgewood was a hodgepodge of one- and two-family homes interspersed with some light industry and made up of poor to middle class working people. Being a New York City fireman put my father near the top of the neighborhood's social strata.

The area was predominately German so it was no surprise that the remaining Irish and Italian populace gravitated toward each other, both socially and for protection from ethnic strife.

Life was simple back then with almost no crime. Families left their doors unlocked and spent time together. I fondly remember nights gathered around the radio, which was twice as tall as I was, listening to Fibber McGee and Molly. The Great Gildersleeve, and occasionally, Gangbusters. Afternoon radio shows such as Superman and Jack Armstrong—The All American Boy left me indelibly infused with the idea that, in the end, good always triumphed over evil.

Throughout the neighborhood, a bevy of vendors hawked their wares from horse-drawn carts. My favorite was the milkman. I loved his horse, Anna. She knew the route and would stop at each house while her master went door to door exchanging empty bottles for full ones. And Anna loved me, probably because I used to steal sugar cubes from home and feed them to her.

World War II came and went leaving very little imprinted on my young mind. No surprise there, since I was embroiled in my own war. Being a skinny, laid-back kid with a stuttering problem made me the target of bullies, but when I was twelve that suddenly stopped.

My biggest nemesis was Frannie Sommers, who lived a block away from me. One day, shortly after my twelfth birthday, he began pushing me around to the point where I had to fight or run for the safety of my home. I chose to fight and we stood toe to toe for ten minutes trading punches. I remember Frannie's mother leaning out the window yelling, "Kick his ass, Frannie." That was right before I landed a good one that caught him square on the nose and drew blood. He let out a scream and ran home. My life suddenly improved as the bullies sought easier targets.

The cop on the beat, Big George, knew every kid in my school by name, and when report cards came out he insisted on seeing them. He'd praise those who did well, and encourage the rest by saying, "I want you to get those grades up or you could turn out like me."

I was a mediocre student in high school, spending more time holding a stickball bat than a pencil, and even Big George couldn't change that. His encouragement fell on deaf seventeen-year-old ears, and I left during my senior year to enlist in the Navy.

That's where I met my first drinking buddy, Gino Barraca. We were both eighteen and on shore leave in Havana when, one night, Gino got ossified. I still had plenty of party left in me, so I put him in a cab and sent him back to the ship. When Gino got in the back seat of the cab he discovered that someone had left a half-finished pint of whisky there, which he quickly stashed under his belt. When he reached the ship he staggered up the gangplank and managed a salute to the Officer of the Deck (OD) who asked, "What's that bulge under there, Barraca?"

Gino swayed as he answered, "Nothing sir."

"Lift up the jumper now, sailor."

Gino complied and the OD saw the pint. He was one of the few decent officers on board and he gave Gino a chance. "I'm going to turn my back Barraca and I better hear a splash."

There was a splash and Gino was told, "Come aboard, sailor."

He got fifteen feet before the OD realized Gino was only wearing one shoe and that the splash wasn't made by a bottle. Gino got ten days in the brig for that and had to pay for a new pair of shoes.

We were inseparable right up to the night we had a head-on collision with a drunk driver. Gino suffered a broken wrist. The six skull fractures, six jaw fractures, smashed cheekbones, pulverized nose, and handful of broken teeth that I sustained almost killed me. And on the front page of the Norfolk Virginian my death was greatly exaggerated. The bone between my eyes, which I was told is the hardest bone in the human body, was broken into an inverted "V" shape and had punctured my brain sac, causing spinal fluid to leak out my nose. I almost died several other times during my ninety-six-day stay at Portsmouth Naval Hospital. I lost much of my sense of smell, which would turn out to be a real asset in my future career.

I returned to active sea duty and finished my hitch. The Navy and I parted company four days before my twenty-first birthday.

I knocked around in retail management for the next five years until a buddy of mine asked me to go with him to take the police department's entrance exam. I hesitated until he accused me of being afraid that I would score lower than he would. The gauntlet had been thrown down and a bet was made.

Five months later, on February 15, 1963, I was standing at attention inside the old police academy with 144 strangers. I got called, my buddy didn't, and I won the bet. For a brief second a little voice inside was saying, "This is a mistake."

Thank God I didn't listen.

The training was demanding with all classroom work being done at PS 2, a four-story abandoned public school on Manhattan's lower West Side built in the mid-1800s, reclaimed by the city, and pressed into doing duty as the police academy.

Physical training was conducted at the Brooklyn Armory, an evil-looking building made of solid stone, with fort-like parapets, boasting large, tall windows on all sides.

Sessions at the outdoor firing range at Rodmans Neck in the Bronx were a weekly obligation. I can still hear Sergeant Dylan O'Day's booming voice shouting instructions and cautioning us, "Become proficient in the use of your weapon for someday you may be called upon to make a split-second decision whether or not to fire that weapon." Pointing his trigger finger at us and mimicking the firing of a gun, he'd say, "Just remember once you pull the trigger only the hand of God can take that bullet back."

Then he would give us the unofficial department policy, "Never shoot to wound, always shoot to kill." Then the statistic, "A nationwide FBI study found that the average distance between a cop and an adversary during a gunfight was twenty-one feet." A dramatic pause and O'Day continued, "So why aren't there more dead cops? Proficiency lads, proficiency." Eyes squinting, and again pointing that lethal finger at us, O'Day would pose the question, "And whose job is it to make you proficient in the use of your weapon?" He'd pause, scan the lot of us, and answer, "It's your job."

I took his words seriously and practiced every night for at least an hour developing a smooth trigger squeeze. I'd place a dime on the flat portion of my empty .38's gun barrel and practice dry firing it. The idea was to squeeze the trigger so smoothly that the dime stayed on the barrel. Sometimes I would get up to twenty dry firings before the dime fell. I became extremely proficient in the use of my weapon, but experience would teach me that being proficient wasn't always good enough.

Experience taught me best and my first arrest, while still at the academy, opened my eyes to the way things really worked. At the end of April 1963, Danny Mazza, a friend of mine and a fellow rookie cop, said he had some information on a guy selling tons of illegal fireworks near the Cross Island Parkway in Rosedale, Queens. When we found the guy he was selling out of a station wagon loaded with fireworks from floor to ceiling. We bought some, and as soon as money went from our pockets to his hands, we cuffed him. I called the local precinct, told them that two off-duty rookie cops had an arrest for a large amount of fireworks, and requested a car with a couple of uniformed cops be sent to our location.

In less than a minute we began hearing sirens wailing from all directions. I couldn't believe the response. With roof lights flashing and sirens at full pitch, police cars careened the wrong way down one-way streets, driving over lawns, and dangerously cutting across the median of the adjoining Cross Island Parkway. More than a dozen cars screeched to a halt within feet of the criminal's station wagon. The uniformed cops leapt from their vehicles and took charge as they informed us of the serious danger of an explosion with so many fireworks packed into one vehicle. They broke the contraband down into smaller quantities, and each of the cars took an equal amount to transport back safely to the precinct house. Danny and I were so proud of ourselves for making an arrest while still attending the academy. Brimming with pride we got into one of the cars with our prisoner and headed off to book him and start on what we figured would be hours of paperwork vouchering the enormous amount of illegal fireworks as evidence. Boy, what schmucks we were. Imagine our surprise when we arrived at the station house to find that most of the evidence had mysteriously disappeared. There were only two small boxes of cherry bombs left to be vouchered. It was a cold shower of reality that the job was not on the level, and the first of many lessons to be learned in the years to come about what was and wasn't acceptable behavior for "The Good Guys." Welcome to the NYPD of 1963.

Graduation was less than two months away when we were asked if anyone was interested in applying for possible assignment to the Tactical Patrol Force (TPF) upon graduation. The TPF was a roving band of police squads that were rotated into any precinct where the crime rate was accelerating. Their job was to reduce crime in that precinct dramatically and quickly. They did their job very well and earned the nickname "Ass-Kicking Squad."

To be considered for the TPF you had to be over six feet tall, in great physical condition, have above average intelligence, and be highly motivated. There were a few exceptions due to unwritten "contracts." A contract is police jargon for you scratch my back and I'll scratch yours. If you do something for someone and then you need a favor at a later date you call in the contract and collect your favor.

No one was going to put in a contract for me but I did meet the elite TPF criteria, so I volunteered and two weeks later I was interviewed by the commanding officer of the TPF, Inspector Michael J. Codd. The man's bearing impressed me. He was well over six feet, slender but broad at the shoulders, with a full head of neatly combed gray hair, and blue eyes that cut the air like cold sharpened steel.

I didn't know it then but he was one of the finest cops ever to wear the uniform. The interview lasted fifteen minutes and in that short time I knew I wanted to work for this man. He stood up and shook my hand, saying, "Officer O'Neil, it was a pleasure meeting you. I wish you luck in all your endeavors."

I thanked him and remembered thinking, "Shit, I didn't make it."

On June 28, 1963, as they announced names followed by assignments I heard, "Police Officer James O'Neil assigned to the TPF—12th Squad." Outwardly I showed no emotion but inside I was doing cartwheels. I was going to be part of an elite, ass-kicking, crime-fighting, gut-busting squad and I couldn't wait to get started.

CHAPTER THREE

Feathers

Two days after graduation I reported to the 4th Precinct on Erickson Place over on Manhattan's lower West Side. It was an old four-story cement building built in the early 1900s. Large wooden double-hung windows adorned the first three stories with smaller metal-framed windows on the top floor. Large black letters painted on the frosted glass semicircle above the massive entrance doors proclaimed this building to be the 4th Precinct and underneath it in small but proud gold letters, were the words, "Home of the TPF."

My arrival into the 12th Squad brought their strength up to fourteen men. I was partnered up with a twenty-three-year-old, six-foot-five, two-hundred-ten-pound wild man by the name of Jimmy Crean. A good partner but someone I considered unorthodox even for those times. My gut feeling was that sooner or later he would come under the scrutiny of the bosses and get thrown off the job. When Jimmy retired he was the captain of a Bronx detective district and today he's a very successful lawyer. Go figure.

As we were assigned to the highest crime areas in the city, we always walked our post with a partner. A post could be two to four blocks long. Back then we didn't have walkie-talkies, there were no cell phones, and you couldn't count on being near a call box when trouble erupted. If you needed help you would take your nightstick and bang it hard on the sidewalk several times. It made a very distinctive sound and would easily carry to the next post. Every TPF cop who heard it would come running to your location—primitive but very effective.

If you made an arrest one partner would take the prisoner to the station house and the other would stay on the street.

The first time I was left alone on post it was in Harlem on a warm summer night. I was standing on the corner of West 129th Street and Lenox Avenue across the street from a bar that had no air conditioning, so the front door was wide open and I was able to hear a disturbance coming from inside. I began crossing the street to see what was causing the ruckus, but before I made it to the other side a dirty gray 1959 Chevy pulled up in front of the bar. Three huge black cops in uniform slowly emerged from the vehicle. Between them there must have been at least a thousand pounds of cop on the hoof. As the last cop exited the car I reached the corner and noticed that the volume of the disturbance had increased. Some guy was standing at the end of the bar, with his back to the door, yelling obscenities at the bartender. One of the monster cops slowly walked into the bar and came up behind the screamer, balled his hand into an enormous fist, and brought it down on top of the guy's head in a pile driver-like motion. The guy's knees buckled and he crashed to the floor unconscious.

The cop waved to the bartender and exited the bar. As he passed me he nodded and said, "If you want him, kid, take him, he's your collar." The three of them got back in the car and drove off. I got the hell out of there myself, not wanting to get involved in what was sure to be a lengthy write-up about a questionable police action. Later when I saw my sergeant I told him what I had seen, stressing the size of the cops. He laughed, "You were just introduced to The King Cole Trio. There isn't a person in Harlem who doesn't know them. They're famous up here and probably do more to keep the peace than all the other cops in the precinct combined." Somewhere in the back of my mind an admiration for the kind of instant justice meted out by The King Cole Trio began to take hold.

Two months later on an autumn afternoon Jimmy made an arrest and again I was alone, this time on a foot post near 82nd and Broadway. Across the street was the Ansonia, a luxury residential hotel that once was home to the likes of Enrico Caruso and Babe Ruth. It was there the Chicago White Sox conspired to throw the 1919 World Series. But the migration of thousands of poor Hispanic immigrants during the mid-1900s had changed the neighborhood into what were now the tough, gang-ridden streets portrayed in West Side Story. With her luster gone and her grandeur forgotten this once proud structure had become just another old fleabag. Seventeen stories high and made of masonry, she had been collecting dirt on her facade since 1904. The small windows that dotted each floor were so filthy you couldn't see through them; that was probably a good thing.

There were storefronts on either side of her entrance. One of the stores was a Kent Cleaners and standing in front of it was this skinny black woman in her late sixties, apparently drunk, waving her cane in the air and yelling at the manager, "You motherfucking bastard, who do you think you're fucking with?"

The manager, Tommy Rice, a small black man in his forties, pointed his finger at her and yelled back, "Get away from my store you crazy old witch. Get out of here before I call the cops."

I started walking toward the two of them and as soon as she saw me coming she smashed the head of her cane through the cleaner's plate glass window, shattering it into a thousand pieces. When the manager saw me, he started shouting, "Officer, officer arrest her, arrest her. I want her arrested."

Waving her weapon of glass destruction menacingly in the air, she screamed, "Call the cops on me will ya, you little shit nigger motherfucking bastard. I'll bring you more trouble than a barrelful of motherfuckers."

I grabbed her as she started to lunge at Tommy. "You're under arrest. I'm taking you in."

I front-cuffed her and she made no effort to resist, still too busy laying down a barrage of obscenities at Tommy. I summoned a radio car and rode with her in the back seat to the 20th Precinct. Leaning on her cane, she hobbled up the six steps to the entrance of the station house; an old dilapidated three-story wooden structure. I escorted her through the entrance, across the dirty wood floor, past the desk, and into the muster room where I handcuffed her to a cast-iron radiator.

I left her there while I went to the one twenty-four room, so named because section 124 in the patrol guide stated that there must be a room in every station house adjacent to the desk for the purpose of administration, record keeping, and providing all forms necessary for processing arrest reports. After getting the necessary paperwork, I started back to my prisoner when I heard off to my left, "Whose prisoner is that handcuffed in the muster room?"

I turned and recognized a captain in the TPF who was a real ball-buster and hated by everyone. I continued walking, and said, "She's mine, captain."

He shot a stern look my way, "Oh she is, well, she shouldn't be left unattended like that."

We were standing next to the old lady and he was still busting my balls when the little darling took her cane and slipped the handle around the back of the captain's ankle and gave it a tug, sending him ass over teakettle. He hit the floor with a loud thud, turned beet red, and said, "Fuck her, leave her there until you finish your report." He turned abruptly and stormed out of the room. Without even looking back he shouted, "And have maintenance turn that fucking heat way up."

I must admit that I felt a warm glow for this seemingly helpless old woman who had managed to take this arrogant captain down a peg and remember thinking, "I'm going to like this job." I left her handcuffed while I went to the deli next door. I came back with an ice-cold bottle of beer and handed it to the old lady, "Here, sweetheart," I said to her. "You did good."

About two weeks later Jimmy and I were assigned the Columbus Avenue post again. We were doing car stops when we got a hit on a stolen plate. It was Jimmy's turn at bat so he took the collar and I was left alone on post.

Shortly after he left I became an assault victim. I had just reached the corner of West Eighty-second Street and was standing under this very large maple tree. I was unaware of the perp's presence until I felt something hit me across the visor of my hat, the left side of my uniform coat, and pants. My lightning fast reflexes took over and I caught sight of the perp as he flew away. Covered in pigeon shit I let go a shower of profanity. I hate pigeons—fucking winged rats. I walked across the street to Kent Cleaners, saw Tommy Rice, and said, "Tommy, I need a favor."

He took one look at me and broke out laughing.

"Not funny, Tommy."

"I know but it's ironic."

"Ironic?"

"That old lady you arrested two weeks ago for breaking my window, know what they call her?"

"No."

"The bird lady."

When Jimmy returned he found me in the back room of Kent Cleaners wearing nothing but my underwear and gun belt. I swore him to secrecy. When my uniform was cleaned I went to join him on post. I saw this heavyset old lady on a stoop next to the cleaners laughing hysterically and I asked her, "What the hell are you laughing at?"

Her answer inspired me to write a poem for an English composition course I was taking at New York Tech. I called it:

"The Blue and White Suit"

As I a rookie proud and neat
Diligently patrolled my beat
An old woman on a stoop nearby
Beckoned to me—It caught my eye
I approached and asked what could I do
She said, I'd just like to talk to you
I'm old and lonely—my friends all gone
So we talked—It went on and on
During this time unbeknown to me
A pigeon landed in a tree
The branch was directly overhead
You get the picture—enough said
Why oh why did that tiny bird
Hit me with that liquid turd
He must have shit with all his might
It changed my uniform from blue to white
The old lady laughed, I started to curse
With what she said I'll end this verse
She said, Sonny, calm down don't curse or cry
Just be grateful that elephants don't fly
P.S. what the hell
It made her laugh brought out her wit
And that wasn't the first time I'd been full of shit.

My professor gave me an "A" so something good did come from the incident. And after a month the police artist sketches of the offending pigeon stopped turning up on my desk, in my locker, and on the windshield of my car.

Summer bled into fall, and winter kicked up its snowy heels while Jimmy and I continued suppressing crime. As spring was approaching I recall being alone on post and becoming privy to the birth of an expression that cops still use to this day.

We were required to write a certain number of traffic tickets per month. This was never referred to as a quota, which was and still is illegal. No quotas allowed but guidelines were certainly permissible. I needed to issue one more summons to make my guideline for the month. It was around seven in the evening, the light was fading, the sky was cloudless, a radio somewhere nearby was playing "Love Me Tender" by Elvis, and a gray 1961 Ford van was coming toward me going the wrong way on a one way street.

I motioned the driver to stop and said, "Pull over to the curb sir and let me see your driver's license and vehicle registration."

The driver obeyed and as he jolted to a stop I could hear what sounded like the cackling of a few chickens. His first name was Moishe and he had a full, round face with puffy red cheeks. Flaming red hair in cascading curls sprouted from under a black fur hat and his long unkempt beard was the same color as his hair; very unusual for a Hasidic Jew. "Officer, is something wrong?" he asked. "Did I do something wrong? I'm a law-abiding citizen. Officer, I wouldn't break a law."

"You're driving the wrong way on a one-way street. Didn't you see the arrows?"

"Officer, I didn't even see the Indians. Only kidding, just making a joke, no disrespect meant."

I managed not to laugh and just as I was about to let him go with a warning I heard from behind me, "Hey Jim, what's up?"

It was Barry Stein, another TPF cop who was working the foot post next to mine. Barry was six-one and heavily muscled. "Just a traffic stop, nothing heavy." Lowering my voice I whispered to Barry, "I was just going to let him go, seeing as the street was just changed to a one-way last week."

Shaking his head Barry asked, "He's a landsman of mine, okay if I take this one?"

I gave Barry the license and registration and he walked

back to Moishe. "Sir, please step out of the van."

Moishe did as he was told. "Oh my God, officer, what's wrong?"

Barry flipped open his ticket book and with pen at the ready he said, "You're getting a ticket for driving the wrong way on a one-way street."

Visibly sweating now, Moishe pleaded, "Officer, please don't give me a ticket, I'm just a poor chicken purveyor working hard to support my family. Just give me a good scare, you know, scare me good, but no ticket." Then Moishe said it, and a new way of describing an offered bribe was added to the police vocabulary: "Don't be a schmuck . . . Take a chicken." Moishe reiterated, "take the chicken" as he put his hand on Barry's shoulder and pushed. Big mistake.

Barry grabbed him, forcibly spun him around, cuffed him, and literally threw him into the back of the van. I drove, and as we headed off with Moishe and the chickens to the station house Barry yelled, "And now you're under arrest."

I glanced to my right and said in a low voice, "I got a bad feeling about this, Barry."

We parked in front of the 94th Precinct, which happened to be right next door to a Hasidic school. As we walked Moishe up the precinct steps we heard people yelling out the windows of the school, "They got Moishe, hey look, they got him handcuffed."

An angry crowd of about thirty people from next door filled the precinct lobby shouting, "What are you doing arresting Moishe, he's a good man, a law-abiding man. So you're anti-Jewish, is that it?"

Barry turned, faced the crowd, reached inside his shirt, and pulled out the Star of David he wore on a chain, saying, "See that, I'm Jewish."

Unsatisfied with Barry's gesture someone in the crowd screamed, "Yeah you're Jewish, but you don't like the beards."

We booked Moishe for assaulting an officer, the crowd

was dispersed, and that night a captain came in and voided the arrest.

Up to now my career had been interesting, even amusing, inasmuch as I was getting a flavor for those citizens I had been tasked with protecting. I was learning the job in a relatively safe environment but that was soon to change—thank God.

CHAPTER FOUR

Super Jew and Me

In May of 1964, Jimmy was ordered to show the ropes to a kid fresh out of the academy. I said my good-byes and went in search of a new partner. I knew Davy "Super Jew" Katz had just lost his partner so I asked him if he would like to hook up with me. Davy was six-two, well built with thinning hair, and when his gout acted up he walked with a slight limp that worsened in direct proportion to the amount of beer he consumed. It wasn't his appearance that earned him his nickname but the Superman t-shirt he wore under his uniform. To the chagrin of many a handcuffed perp Davy would unbutton his shirt and fling it open to reveal the large "S," saying, "See that, you street scum? Tell your kids you weren't fucking with any run of the mill cop. Oh no, you had the misfortune to tangle with Super Jew."

Before he agreed to become my partner he imposed a condition. "All I want out of this job is to become a detective," he told me. "Are you up for that Jim?"

"Hell yes, partner."

Davy was a great partner and over the next two years we made more arrests than the twelve other cops in our squad combined. We worked our asses off, frequently pulling twelve-hour shifts for eight hours pay. Back then there was no such thing as paid overtime or time given back. If you wanted to spend extra time on a case it was on you, unlike the contracted set-in-stone rules governing today's police force with respect to compensation.

Sometimes catching criminals, especially junkies, was like shooting fish in a barrel. The barrel was two old, rundown, six-story, red brick buildings at East Third Street and Avenue C on Manhattan's Lower East Side. The buildings were attached and stood alone on the corner surrounded by vacant lots.

The first time we were assigned to that foot post we observed a lot of people carrying bottles of water going into one of the buildings. That was the tip-off that they were going to be shooting up heroin. They would take a bobby pin and wrap it around the outside of the bottle cap and then mix the heroin and the water together in the cap. Using the bobby pin as a handle, they would hold the cap over an ignited book of matches to heat up the heroin. Placing a cotton ball in the cap they would use a needle to draw the heroin through the saturated cotton. The idea was to use the crude filter to prevent any uncooked lumps of heroin from being drawn into the needle and clogging it up. In drug lingo the crude filter was known as "satch cotton," short for saturated cotton.

A firehouse made that foot post even more desirable. A cop could go to any firehouse in the city around dinnertime and get a great meal. With the price of a complete meal as little as eighty cents, but never more than two dollars, the cost of the dinner was split evenly among everyone at the table.

One time I made an arrest on my way to the firehouse and, not wanting to miss dinner, I took the perp with me; it was steak night. I handcuffed him to the pole the fireman slid down when hurrying to answer an alarm. I went upstairs, had my meal, then gathered up my prisoner and took him into the precinct for processing. Good thing for him there were no fire alarms during dinner.

The roll call officer assigned foot posts randomly every month. Not wanting to leave our foot post assignment to chance, Davy and I gave, as was the unofficial custom, half a hat to the roll call officer at the beginning of each month.

The expression "a hat" was around long before I came

on the job. It seems to have started when illegal gamblers, wanting to show their gratitude, would walk up to a detective, stuff a twenty in his shirt pocket, and say, "Why don't you take this and buy yourself a hat." It was more of a thank you than a bribe.

With the East Third Street and Avenue C foot post ours, the games began. We staked out the building for two days to familiarize ourselves with the junkies' comings and goings. It wasn't long before Davy and I figured out that the never ending procession of dirty, emaciated men and women were shooting up on the sixth floor roof landing. The plan we came up with was Machiavellian in nature, but simple in execution.

"Okay, Jim, how do you want to handle this?"

"I'll sneak up the stairs hugging the wall until I reach the fifth floor. Once there I'll move away from the wall so I can be seen, and I'll start shouting 'Police, you're all under arrest!' That'll roust them."

A smile slowly crept its way across Davy's face, "And I'll come up through the adjacent building, cross over, and be waiting outside the door to the roof, trapping them between us. Just like shooting fish in a barrel."

In the next year we made over two hundred arrests in that building and not one of the junkies ever caught on to how we were doing it. People would ask me all the time, "Jim how do manage to catch so many bad guys? What's your secret?" I would tell them, "It's no secret. These assholes are stupid."

From time to time we would be sent to the 23rd Precinct in Spanish Harlem. It was a real tough area with a high crime rate and wall-to-wall drugs, mostly heroin and cocaine; designer drugs were yet to come into vogue. East 100th Street was considered the most dangerous in the city. On a 6 PM to 2 AM tour they would assign four TPF cops just to that block. When an arrest was made, which often was the case, another cop would be reassigned from a different post to cover for the arresting officer who had to process the bad guy.

One day Davy and I worked a 10 AM to 6 PM, covering a parade. The parade ended early and we were sent to the Twenty-third to finish out our tour. We ended up on East 100th Street at three in the afternoon where we found a beat cop patrolling by himself. He was a vertically-challenged Greek who probably just made the minimum height requirement for the job. But what he lacked in height he made up for with one of the biggest pair of balls on the job; this was one tough son of a bitch. We were at the opposite end of the block when we saw him get into a confrontation with a big Hispanic male at least six inches taller than himself. We walked over to him in case he needed assistance. We should have saved our energy because by the time we got there he had backed the guy up against a brick wall, with the tip of his nightstick under the guy's nose. Whenever he wanted to emphasize his words he would push up hard with the nightstick. This would make the guy's head bang against the wall. "I told you to stay the fuck off my street, asshole," the little cop snarled.

"This is a free country, why do I gotta stay off this street?"

A push and a bang.

"Hey, that hurt."

A push and a bang.

"I know my rights and you can't do this."

"Listen, fuckbag, you don't know shit. This is my street and when I tell you to stay the fuck off it you do what I say."

A push and a bang.

"And you know why you're gonna do what I say?" A push and a bang. "I'll tell you why. Because I'm the gorilla and you're the monkey."

We smiled and went back to the other end of the block. God I loved the job back then, when a cop could be a cop without fear of being accused of police brutality.

Most of the time it was pretty routine, walking a post, busting junkies, making arrests for an assortment of crimes, and breaking up fights. I remember one we broke up in the Irish Harp, one of the many Irish bars sprinkled throughout Washington Heights. We were two doors down when we heard yelling and the sounds of a fight in progress. I turned to Davy and said, "Here we go again."

We took out our axe handles, which were longer, heavier, and better in a fight than our nightsticks—hey only dumb animals don't use tools. Fairness was not in our creed but winning on the street was. Instilling fear in the bad guys was what kept you and other cops alive and by extension the good citizens in your charge

Officially we only carried department-issued nightsticks but unofficially, when it came to choice of weapons, the department always looked the other way for the TPF. Of course this was pre-civilian review board, when a cop didn't have to worry about being brought up on charges for exerting a little necessary force. We rushed inside the Irish Harp and it took a few seconds for our eyes to adjust to the smoke-filled, sunlight-deprived room. On our left the barstools were empty--all the patrons were clustered around the pool table at the back of the bar. There were two large, sweaty Irishmen on the pool table pummeling each other. As soon as they noticed us standing there in our blues they stopped kicking the shit out of each other and turned their attention toward us.

"Which one do you want, Super Jew?"

"Ladies' choice, Jim, why don't we let them pick."

And pick they did. The larger of the two went after Davy, the other one came at me. It didn't last long and half an hour later we were booking two battered and bloody Irishmen.

My partner felt bad for the guy he fought with, so the next morning he brought him a bacon and egg on a roll and a large coffee. He limped over to the holding cell (the gout was on him again) and went in. The Irishman was lying down on a cot and when Davy offered him breakfast the guy looked up through swollen eyes and stared at the food. Then through swollen and bruised lips he mumbled, "You fat, bald, gimpy-legged, Jew bastard, take that fucking sandwich and shove it up your fucking ass."

I started to laugh out loud and Davy beat the shit out of the guy all over again.

Davy asked me, "Jim, is there a full moon tonight or something?"

"I think so," I answered. "Why?"

"The day is just beginning and I tried twice to do something decent and both times . . . Aww, forget it."

"Twice?"

"Yeah, I'm driving to work this morning on Long Beach Road where I saw this guy walking with a small suitcase. As I got close to him he stuck out his thumb so I stopped and he got in. I asked him where he was going and it turns out he was on his way to work in the Jewish section of the 94th Precinct. I told him he was lucky because I was passing right by there. I could tell he was Jewish from the way he was dressed so I mentioned that I was also Jewish. We were having a nice conversation when he asked me what I did for a living. I told him I was a cop. He commented on how wonderful that was and what this city needed was more nice Jewish boys to become cops; he seemed like a good guy. When he asked me what department I was with I told him it was the Tactical Patrol Force. He looked at me, his face screwed into a grimace, and he started yelling at me. He called me a fascist pig, a bastard, and then he ordered me to stop my car and let him out. I started to slow down but before I could come to a full stop he opened the door and jumped out. I had no idea what had just happened but I knew I should just keep driving. I looked in my rearview mirror and he was shaking his fist in the air and jumping up and down."

"You said he was Jewish?"

"Yeah."

"Hasidic by any chance?"

"Well, yeah."

"Did he have red hair and a red beard and a chubby face with reddish cheeks?"

"Right again. You know this guy, Jim?"

"You ever hear the story about Barry Stein and Moishe the chicken purveyor?"

"Sure, 'Don't be a schmuck—take a chicken.'"

"Well, the guy you picked up had to be Moishe."

CHAPTER FIVE

All Hell Breaks Loose

Davy and I spent some more routine weeks on the streets and then on the twenty-fifth of July during a 6 PM to 2 AM tour all hell broke loose as New York's first major race riot of the civil rights era blossomed. Two days prior to that was the Lieutenant Gilligan incident in Spanish Harlem, and we had been expecting trouble. A fifteen-year-old black kid wielding a knife in one hand and holding a garbage can cover as a shield in the other decided to bag himself a cop. He charged and Gilligan drew his weapon, firing only once. The bullet tore through the cover and pierced the kid's heart.

The next day professional agitators were out stirring up demonstrations on 125th Street saying that the kid never had a knife. Many in the community were listening and racial tension hung heavy in the air. Posters with Gilligan's picture were stapled to telephone poles all over Harlem announcing, "WANTED FOR MURDER." I still have one of the posters and to this day I have no idea how they got his picture.

It was around 8 PM on July twenty-fifth when a radio motor patrol car (RMP) came speeding down the street with its light flashing. That was a signal for all TPF cops to mobilize at the precinct house. Remember, we still didn't have walkie-talkies.

"That's us, Jim," Davy yelled.

We both took off and ran the three blocks to the station house. When we got there a uniformed sergeant was barking out commands through a megaphone. "Listen up TPF, rioting has spread all along Eighth Avenue between 115th and 135th streets. The precinct cops aren't trained in riot suppression so the department pulled them out of there. You're going to take their place and meet the monster head on. The First, Seventh, and Twelfth Squads are mobilizing to West 125th Street and Eighth Avenue. You'll be joined by motorcycle police from every precinct in the city. When you get there form up around Inspector Codd, he'll tell you what to do. Good luck men, it's rough out there."

Between the three squads there were forty-two of us. We grabbed our protective riot gear, which consisted of a white air raid warden's steel helmet and nothing else. Unlike today's well dressed riot cop, we had no bulletproof vests, full helmets with shatterproof face plates, handheld shields, or high laced combat boots. We were stuffed into commandeered patrol cars and as soon as one filled up it took off with lights flashing and sirens wailing. Inside, faces showed no emotion, mouths spoke no words, and blank eyes stared straight ahead as we sped along Riverside Drive. I don't know what anybody else was thinking but I was wondering if tonight was going to be the first time I would fire my service revolver in the line of duty. I glanced over at Davy and as the flashing red light split the darkness it cast a surreal glow on his profile. It only took a few minutes to get to the scene of the rioting, but it seemed longer.

My inexperience shielded me from the fear of what I was about to encounter. It was dark as we approached West 125th Street and we could see the glow of what appeared to be several small fires in the distance. When we got to West 125th and Eighth we saw Inspector Codd standing there. Behind him we could see that there were fires all up and down Eighth Avenue and there was rioting and looting in progress. As soon as the last of the TPF had formed up around the Inspector he began speaking, "Now gentlemen let me apprise you of the situation. The rioting is to the left and right of us all along Eighth Avenue. First and Seventh Squads work your way downtown on Eighth Avenue and Twelfth Squad work your way uptown. You're here to suppress looting, discourage and suppress rioting or unruly demonstrations. Now go get them."

That was the extent of the coordination we got. Today there would be a fully-staffed command center; cops would be decked out in full riot gear and would be wearing headsets to maintain constant contact with their commanders.

Inspector Michael J. Codd was our command center and he was in the thick of it with us. I never saw anyone else over the rank of sergeant on the streets of Harlem until after the riots were squashed. I don't know where the hell they were but they weren't with the troops.

Eighth Avenue was lined with one-story storefronts and multi-story tenements. The 12th Squad began moving uptown where we ran into a barrage of assorted garbage, bottles, and Molotov cocktails. We even started taking some sporadic gunfire. Davy and I took cover in a tenement doorway. We began shooting in the general direction of anything being thrown at us and returned fire when fired upon. That seemed to discourage most of them but there were those stubborn few who were intent on doing us bodily harm.

One guy on the roof of a four-story tenement on West 125th Street kept popping up at irregular intervals and lobbing bricks at us. A sergeant I had never seen before, covered in soot from head to toe, was yelling at the top of his lungs, "Would somebody shoot that fuck's head off?"

Baby-faced Jimmy Denton, six-feet-seven with a full head of dark wavy hair, was an expert marksman.

"Hey Sarge," said Jimmy, "I'll get him."

He aimed his gun at the spot where the guy kept popping up. Must have been about forty seconds before a head reappeared. Jimmy let go one round and the guy vanished. No brick was thrown that time.

"Shit, I think I got him. I think I got him," screamed Jimmy.

The soot-covered sergeant was the first cop on the roof. Jimmy, Davy, and I were right on his heels. We found the guy lying next to a large pile of bricks with a bullet right between his eyes; we all cheered. Shortly after we got there Inspector Codd arrived and joined us around the body. "Gentlemen," he asked, "who's responsible for this?"

"Um . . . it was me, Inspector."

"What's your name, son?"

"Jimmy Denton, sir."

"Good job, Jimmy. I'm going to have a uniformed officer wait with you until the M.E. arrives." Turning to the sergeant, he said, "Assign an officer to stay with Jimmy, and tell him to bring some sandwiches and beers for the both of them. Here's ten dollars—my treat." Turning to us, he ordered, "Gentlemen, let's get back to the streets."

It would turn out to be the only death officially listed as occurring during the riots. The rash of floaters pulled out of the waters surrounding Manhattan, in the weeks following the end of the riots, was obviously a very large coincidence.

Davy and I returned to 125th and Eighth and started working our way up toward 135th Street. While we had been up on the roof, the 12th Squad had suppressed the rioting along Eighth Avenue up to 127th Street so Davy and I hurried to catch up with them.

We'd enter any store that had broken windows and if we found anyone inside we would beat them to the ground with our axe handles, then move on to the next store without making any arrests. No need to, when you're dispensing well-deserved instant justice.

I didn't find it necessary to shoot any of the looters but I did see a few get shot. I remember a short black woman in her forties, a little on the heavy side, running out of a shoe store carrying several pairs of shoes. I heard someone shout, "Police, stop or I'll shoot."

She probably didn't believe that a cop would shoot her

over a lousy bunch of shoes so she kept running. A shot was fired and she was left bleeding in the street. Bleeding all over those shiny new shoes. I kept moving and formed no opinion about what I had witnessed.

Just as Davy and I hooked up with Jimmy Crean and a motorcycle cop on 129th Street, six guys came running out of a mattress store. They weren't carrying anything but when they saw us they took off. We chased them down an alley where they ran through a thick wooden door, slamming it shut behind them. We could hear them laughing and we shouted for them to open the door and come out.

"Suck dick assholes, if you want us come and get us." More laughter.

That seemed to really piss off the motorcycle cop and as he fired six rounds through the door he screamed, "Suck on these." The laughing stopped and he headed off in search of his unit. We moved on without a thought as to who was dead or alive on the other side of the door.

Shortly after that Jimmy and Davy managed to get caught on film. The picture showed two looters running, their shirts in tatters and fear deeply imprinted on their faces, looking back at the two pursuing cops. Jimmy's nightstick was on a downward arc inches from making contact with the head of one of the suspects. Good thing they didn't get Davy's axe handle in the picture. That was the New York Press Photographers' action photo of the year for 1964.

It was around 2 AM when the riot intensified. Jimmy had gotten separated from us when we fell back to 125th Street as Davy and I began taking constant small-arms fire. We ducked into the recessed doorway of a storefront on 125th Street and began returning fire.

Davy turned to me and asked, "Jim, how many rounds you got left?"

"I got one left and how about you?"

"Three. Here, take one and save it for yourself. I don't

think they're taking any prisoners."

Just then we saw a patrol car with two uniformed officers inside. It was creeping down 125th Street with its flashing light turned off. We could see the officers leaning out the windows and saying something to every cop they passed. When they reached us the one riding shotgun leaned out and said, "Hang in there, an ammo truck from the Rodmans Neck range is five minutes behind us."

About ten minutes later we saw a silver-colored step-van slowly coming up the middle of 125th Street. Both rear doors were tied back to keep them wide open. Cops were running out of doorways and disappearing behind the van. They reappeared with boxes of ammo in their hands and ran back for the cover of the doorways. When the van got to Davy and me we ran behind it. A uniformed range officer threw out boxes of .38-caliber ammo, fifty rounds to a box. Two cops carrying Thompson submachine guns flanked him on either side. I caught four boxes of ammo and so did my partner. When we got back to the relative safety of our doorway we reloaded our service revolvers, filled up our bandoleers and our dump pouches, and went back to war.

Our replacements came by at 4 AM. By then most of the rioters temporarily had lost the desire to be unruly. We went home and twelve hours later we were back.

It was relatively quiet along Eighth Avenue between 119th and 132nd Streets. There were considerably fewer looters and rioters on the streets but it was still daylight. Most of the fires were out and ambulances had evacuated the injured to area hospitals. As darkness approached we began to hear sporadic gunshots and could feel the fragile peace begin to shatter. More garbage was being thrown off the rooftops and it was yesterday all over again. The last of the sunlight had faded and in the distance I heard an RMP's siren.

I asked Davy, "You hear that?"

"Yeah," he answered, "I wonder what's up."

I turned toward the sound of the approaching siren and saw that the flashing light was on. As it got closer we saw a megaphone protruding out of the passenger side window, and a stern voice shouted, "One, Seven, and Twelve Squads form up at the bus barns on the double." That was six blocks away over on Third Avenue. We sprinted all the way there.

When Davy and I arrived we saw TPF cops being loaded onto a large green school bus. We joined up with them and when we were all seated, a small elderly gentleman, all dressed in black, got on the bus, stood next to the driver, and faced us. It was Monsignor Dunne, one of the most feared men attached to the NYPD. If he thought you had a drinking problem he could have you sent to the farm, and nobody wanted to go to the farm. That was thirty days to dry out, thirty days without a single drink.

All attention was on the monsignor as he raised his hands and gave everyone a general absolution. "All your sins are forgiven in the name of the Father, of the Son, and of the Holy Ghost. May God be with you."

"What about me, Monsignor, I'm Jewish," piped up Super Jew.

"Son, tonight you're Catholic."

Monsignor Dunne left as quickly as he had appeared, the bus door closed, and we pulled out of the yard. By the time we reached the East River Drive we were doing seventy miles an hour and had picked up two police cruisers as escorts. They were strung out about one hundred feet ahead of us with their lights and sirens on. There wasn't much traffic on the road and what little there was got the hell out of our way. Captain Quenton was a good boss and the men respected him. He was sitting in the front seat when all of a sudden he stood up and turned to address us. "All right, men, listen up. The riots are much worse in Brooklyn and that's where we're headed. Tonight you'll get a chance to put into practice what you learned about riot control. We're being sent in to break the back of the riot. I can tell you we're looking at an estimated four thousand rioters. Keep your heads, remember your training, and you'll make it through the night."

Nobody said a word. The captain turned and sat down. From somewhere in the back of the bus I heard what sounded like an axe handle being banged on the floor, again and again. Then more axe handles picked up the rhythm—bang, bang, bang. Then everyone was keeping the beat. The captain never even turned around. Somebody started chanting "KILL" every time the axe handles hit the floor, over and over, louder and louder until everyone was repeating it. "KILL . . . KILL . . . KILL" again and again, over and over, louder and louder, like a deadly mantra.

Suddenly we were at Fulton and Nostrand about one block from the main riot. The bus stopped, the chant stopped, the door opened, and the captain stood up. "Remember, keep your heads and keep your guns holstered," he warned us. "Good luck, men."

We exited the bus, directly into a barrage of bottles, rocks, bricks, and Molotov cocktails. Every cop was slapping leather and firing off rounds into the surrounding buildings. My revolver was empty before I even made it to the cover of a doorway. I started reloading and was looking around to see if my partner was okay. I didn't see Davy but across the street in another doorway was Captain Quenton reloading his weapon.

Between the three TPF squads and the captain we must have gotten off three hundred rounds within ninety seconds, before restoring peace to the area. One of the buildings had so many holes in it that on a windy day you'd probably hear it whistle "Dixie."

The captain had us form up into a column of twos, ordering, "Follow me, we're going over to Fulton and Bedford to the main riot."

He took off at a trot and we stayed close on his tail. As we got closer we passed the precinct cops who were pulled back out of range of all the flying debris.

The main riot was in the business district on Fulton, almost exclusively one-story storefronts. There must have been four thousand rioters concentrated on one block. It was wall-to-wall chaos, with looting everywhere. There was some screaming and the sounds of breaking glass but I was surprised how relatively quiet the four thousand were. Just then a short man in a gray suit and tie, wearing that ridiculous TPF-issued steel helmet, came walking toward us. He was Phil Walsh, a three-star chief of detectives, a rank equivalent to a lieutenant general in the Army. "All right, TPF, get over here, you're working for me now."

He turned toward the riot and clasped his hands above his head to create the shape of a pyramid. That was the signal for us to form up behind him into an inverted "V" flying wedge formation. Walsh took the point position and ordered, "Let's get those sons of bitches."

As soon as we formed up we were no longer individuals. We were one unit, with one purpose. And that purpose was to break the back of the riot as quickly as possible. With that in mind we methodically pressed on, marching up Fulton Street, in unbroken formation. With axe handles at the ready, we started the chant again, and with each step the wedge took it uttered, "KILL."

The rioters seemed oblivious to our presence until the wedge hit them. With axe handles flailing and rioters falling we began kicking some serious ass. It was then we grabbed their attention. Bravado changed to fear as they began trampling each other in an attempt to flee. Many of them ran into buildings, but a hell of a lot of them were beaten down with axe handles and trampled by the wedge. Ten minutes later we reached the end of the block. We turned to survey what we had done. The street and sidewalks were covered with bodies, some unconscious, and some writhing in pain, bleeding and moaning. Others were staggering off somewhere to lick their wounds.

That's how forty TPF cops put down four thousand rioters and broke the back of the Brooklyn riots.

All that was left now were a couple of nights of mop-up operation to suppress sporadic looting and occasional mayhem. We spent the next two days, six TPF cops to a radio car, riding around and stopping whenever we spotted looters. We would get out of the car, kick the shit out of them, get back into the car, and move on.

We were told to disregard all radio calls except for a 10-13, "officer needs assistance," and a 10-30, "robbery in progress against a person." Of course any shots being fired got our immediate attention and were never ignored.

When we were pulled out of there and I had time to think, I realized that I had never been afraid. Fear was a luxury you couldn't afford. You just reacted and trusted the men you served with.

CHAPTER SIX

Wedding Bells and Malignant Melanomas

It was 1964—cold, bleak, nighttime, and January. The wind was howling but it couldn't drown out the big band sounds coming from the ballroom at the Hotel Taft. The closer I came to the entrance the louder the music got and the warmer I felt. The Jersey Shore Club Dance Band played Sinatra as I made my way to the coat check. Coatless, I joined three of my TPF buddies who were already seated around a table and ogling the women. I hadn't had time to get a drink when Jimmy Crean said, "Check out those two coming out of the ladies room. I'll take the blonde and you take the redhead."

He got no argument from me as I walked right up to the prettiest woman I had ever seen. Tall, about five-foot-eight, with long flaming Maureen O'Hara red hair, wearing a black turtleneck sheath dress and standing on three-inch stiletto heels. I smiled and said, "Hello, my name is Jim O'Neil".

"I'm Peggy Herlihy."

"Would you like to dance, Miss Peggy Herlihy?"

"I'd like that."

As I held her in my arms and moved slowly around the dance floor I saw Jimmy Crean dancing with Peggy's blonde girlfriend. I looked at Jimmy and mouthed the words "Thank you." He offered a "You're welcome" smile and turned away. I got a table and some drinks for Peggy and me and we talked the night away. So it was no surprise when she agreed to see me again.

A snowy week after I first held Peggy in my arms, I was driving my 1963 gold Ford Galaxie 500 XL convertible, a veritable tank by today's standards. I was headed to Albany Avenue in Flatbush, Brooklyn, where Peggy lived. She was waiting when I got there and after a quick set of parental introductions we were on our way to the Chateau Madrid in Manhattan, a hundred-dollar-a-plate, fancy schmancy restaurant-club. The main roads were plowed and to this day Peggy has no idea why she told me to take a side street but she did and I complied. What was I thinking? The side street hadn't been plowed but I could see two ruts in the snow where other cars had already gone down the street. I say down because it turned out that the street had a fifteen-degree slope. But I had a heavy car and the extra weight would hold me in good stead. Wrong. The ruts had been packed down so much that they were solid ice and once I got in them and applied the brakes I began to pick up speed. Obviously not a good development for either me or the guy stopped at the bottom of the street. When I hit him he was catapulted into the intersection and into the side of a passing taxi. The police came and because nobody was injured, the accident report didn't take long to fill out. All right, it was a new car and the front was damaged but it was drivable and I was with Peggy and we were again on our way to dinner. As I adjusted my rearview mirror I realized the guy behind us was picking up speed. You guessed it—BAM—now the back of my car was damaged.

We completed our trip to the Chateau Madrid with very little small talk and no more incidents. When I handed the parking valet the keys and told him to be careful with my new car, Peggy broke out laughing. She had an infectious laugh that spread to me but stopped at the confused valet. The food was great, the flamenco dancers who danced atop the tables were amazing and the conversation filled ride home was delightful. When Peggy told her mother about the evening she remarked, "You'll never see that guy again." That was only the first of many times the elder Mrs. Herlihy would be wrong about me.

Five months later, Miss Peggy Herlihy agreed to become Mrs. Peggy O'Neil and I was thrilled to have something soft in my life. The date was set for May 8, 1965, and the world seemed rosy, right up until a growth on the back of Peggy's leg was diagnosed as skin cancer; the price an Irish girl paid for trying to look as tan as her Italian girlfriends. Dr. William Pancke, a tall, thin, confident man, removed the growth and the biopsy showed it was a malignant melanoma—a particularly aggressive cancer with a 5 percent survival rate. Marriage had an 80 percent survival rate so we went with the odds and got married at St. Therese of Lisieux on Avenue D in East Flatbush. We got pregnant almost immediately and Peggy took on a glow that radiated new life. Then three months into her pregnancy it was back to Dr. Pancke with a lump in her groin. Our worst fears were surpassed when the good doctor informed us that the malignancy had spread to Peggy's lymph glands, some of which were resting on her uterus. If the glands were removed she would have a chance but the baby wouldn't. Peggy chose life for our baby. The doctor tried to change her mind but she told him, "I would rather die than kill my baby." Dr. Pancke removed all the glands except the ones on the uterus and cautioned us to get back to remove those as soon as was prudent after the delivery.

I'm not a particularly religious man but I won't dispute the power of prayer and the part it played in our lives. Her courage became the topic of sermons, and masses were said throughout Brooklyn, parishioners prayed, and entire Catholic schools took time to pray for her. To be honest all the prayer didn't stop me from being a nervous wreck but it helped Peggy and I was grateful for that. She had God for support and I had Davy Katz and my other TPF partners.

After giving birth and recuperating, Peggy had the remaining glands removed and to this day is cancer-free. She had beaten overwhelming odds and today my eldest son Jimmy is serving as a Suffolk County police officer. If it weren't for the courage of his mother and, yes, okay, the power of prayer, he might never have drawn a breath, and for that I thank Peggy and God.

CHAPTER SEVEN

Plain Clothes–Hell No, I Won't Go

Several months after the riots of '64 were put down, I was asked if I wanted a transfer to a plainclothes division. I respectfully declined the very lucrative position.

Everyone knew about the corruption on the job and I'm not talking about a free cup of coffee or a meal on the arm. I'm talking about enormous amounts of money. The average uniform cop didn't see much of it but that was not the case with the guys and gals working the plainclothes divisions. Each division was made up of several precincts, with undercovers (UCs) working in plain clothes monitoring public morals. Cops known as "The Pussy Posse" rode herd over prostitution while the rest of the plainclothes cops enforced the laws against gambling. In those days plainclothes units were cash cows.

I knew of one lieutenant who insisted on getting 20 percent of everything his guys got under the table. Nothing slipped past this guy so when he found out that one of his squad accepted a carton of cigarettes he demanded two packs for himself. Lieutenant "Puffs" didn't even smoke.

I could have used the extra money but I wanted nothing to do with what I considered a house of cards. It was only a matter of time before those on the take would be brought to task. My decision to stay clean had nothing to do with my having high moral standards and everything to do with my fear of ending up in jail.

Some divisions, especially those in the ghetto, brought

in enormous amounts of hush money from numbers operations each month. In ghetto parlance these operations were known as "writing the digit," where for as little as ten cents you could venture a guess at what the last three numbers of the total amount bet that day at a selected racetrack would be. This hush money was quietly referred to as the "monthly nut" and was considered by numbers operators as a normal cost of doing business.

A black friend of mine, Gene Doughty, was assigned to the Sixth Division Plainclothes, which covered three Harlem precincts. He drove a new Mercedes Benz and owned several houses, all paid for on a cop's salary of $10,000 a year. One night we were knocking down a few drinks, on the arm, at an after-hours club and I asked Jerry, "What's the nut in the Sixth Division?"

"I'll tell you but you'll find it hard to believe. The nut for each member in the Sixth Division is $3500 a month and any scores you make on your own you can keep."

I almost fell off the barstool. "Damn," I said. "I believe you but I had no idea it was that much."

I heard similar numbers from a friend of mine who was a detective in the old Police Commissioners Confidential Investigative Unit (PCCIU). Once a month he would go to a sixth floor bathroom in the Police Headquarters Annex at 400 Broome Street in Manhattan. He never went there empty-handed, always carrying a paper bag with $10,000 in it. He would walk into the bathroom, place the bag in an empty toilet stall and wait until a headquarters detective he knew only by sight would retrieve the bag. No words ever passed between the two men, even though they had been repeating the same scene every month for over a year. The money supposedly was for the chief of the department.

Most precinct commanders had their own "bag man" who was responsible for tabulating gross revenues from illegal gambling and after-hours operations so the monthly nut could be assessed properly. He would collect and then deliver said monies to the proper contacts within the Department.

Every so often a scandal would erupt and the shit would hit the fan. A few sacrificial lambs would get locked up and soon after that the bag man was back to his old tricks, as the Blue Wall of Silence prevailed. Although most cops were honest and hard-working they tended to look the other way and keep their mouths shut; whistle-blowers were marked men and could get hurt.

Bart Behan, a retired lieutenant who left the job in the 1930s, loved to tell me stories about the corruption in the job during the early part of the last century and how it extended all the way to the top. Now in his eighties, and the former bag man for Manhattan East during Fioriello LaGuardia's administration, Bart would say, "Jim, LaGuardia, known as The Little Flower, had a reputation for honesty and I can vouch that he never touched a corrupt dime. Once a month I would take a satchel full of money and enter the mayor's residence at Gracie Mansion. I would see The Little Flower and he would say, 'How are you Bart? Just put the bag on the mantel.' Then I would leave and never once did I see him touch that bag."

Davy and I managed to skirt the outer edges of corruption while continuing to make record numbers of arrests. Being in the TPF was a prerequisite for becoming a detective and that, along with our arrest records, ushered us into that elite position. In late 1966 Davy was assigned to the 9th Detective Squad out of the East Village and I tried in vain to get into narcotics. Inspector Ira Bleuth, who interviewed me, said, "Jim you have an impressive record, highest in arrests, three medals for valor, and you seem highly motivated but I can't use you in narcotics. You're too tall, too white, and you don't speak Spanish. You'd be made the minute you hit the street."

"I understand. Thanks for being up front with me inspector."

Extending his hand and firmly gripping mine, he said,

"Good luck to you, Jim."

I thanked him and headed straight for a small neighborhood bar on Merrick Road in Laurelton. The bar was called Harry Sterry's, and it was owned by one Harry Sterry, sixty-two years old, on the slim side, with a full head of gray hair, and a face as Irish as the Blarney Stone. You could name any drink and Harry, a great mixologist, would make it to perfection. I don't know whether it was Harry's vaudevillian sense of humor (he had worked in vaudeville with Jimmy Durante) or the drinks, but the bottom line was I always felt better after a stop at Harry's. It was late in the afternoon when I walked into the bar, and he said, "Good day to you, Jimmy." He never called me Jim. "What'll be your pleasure?"

"A tall cold one from the tap."

I threw a five-spot on the bar and downed the first of several beers.

"So tell me, Jimmy, what's got you in here so early on this fine day?"

"I just got turned down for a detective's spot in narcotics."

"That sucks. Hey, you know who you should talk to?"

"No, who?"

"Bill Friel, he might be able to help you out there, Jimmy boy."

I had met Bill at Harry Sterry's almost six months before and we became friends. We would knock down a few and talk about everything under the sun, but I never got around to asking him what he did for a living. I took Harry's advice and a week later when I ran into Bill I told him about my dilemma. It turned out that he was president of the United Republican Clubs of Queens County.

Right after I spoke with him he called Nat Hentel, who was the DA at the time. "Nat, you're up for re-election soon and I swing seventy thousand votes," Bill told him. "If you want me to swing them your way you'll give my friend Jim O'Neil a good job."

One month later I was assigned to the Queens DA squad—a detective's dream job. I was there about a month when my CO, Captain Kissain, called me into his office and said, "Detective O'Neil, you're to report to the mounted unit stables by Columbus Avenue. Be there this afternoon no later than three and ask for Dr. Kelso. He's the police veterinarian and he's going to give you a lesson on animal anatomy."

"Why animal—?"

"Don't ask any questions. I can't tell you more than what I've already told you."

I got to the stables at three sharp and found an anxious Dr. Kelso waiting for me. He had a horse brought out to the practice ring and began explaining the animal's musculature to me. "Now, Detective, if you were going to tranquilize this animal with a dart rifle you would want to shoot him in the flank. That's the safest place to shoot this or any other similar animal. Understood?"

"Yes, Doctor." I left without asking any questions.

Two weeks later I was on my boat in the Great South Bay when I got caught in a sudden windstorm and was driven onto the beach. I waited out the storm, couldn't call home, didn't have a marine radio, and cell phones weren't invented yet. It was one in the morning before I got towed off the beach and another hour before I made it back to the canal behind my house. While tying up at my dock I heard Peggy saying, "Thank God you're all right. Captain Kissain called twice. He wants you to call him as soon as you get in."

I called right away. Two rings and, "DA squad, Detective Kelly speaking, how can I help you?"

"Kelly, it's me, Jim."

"Where were you? Kissain's been looking for you."

"Shipwrecked . . . I'll tell you all about it later. Let him know I'm on the line."

Ten seconds later I heard, "Where were you?"

"I was shipwrecked, Captain."

"Yeah, well I don't give a fuck if you were stuffed and mounted over the mantel. All I wanna know is how long before you can get in here?"

"An hour, hour and a half at the most."

"Too long, I'll send someone else upstate."

"Upstate?"

"All right, leave now and get here as soon as possible. No later than 5 AM or you'll miss the party. We're working with the Treasury Department's Alcohol Tobacco and Firearms people to form a joint ATF-NYPD task force that will be hitting seven locations simultaneously at 6 AM. You'll go with one of the teams hitting Queens. See me when you get into the squad, and don't spare the horses."

I hung up the phone, changed, kissed Peggy, ran out the door, jumped into the car, and drove like a maniac to the squad. It was 4 AM when I entered the parking lot behind the Queens Criminal Court building where the DA's squad had a suite of basement offices.

As soon as I entered the squad room I heard a deep growl of a voice, "O'Neil let's go, the briefing is just getting started." It was Bucko McDonald, a uniformed officer assigned to handle the squad's clerical duties, and he was gesturing toward the conference room.

"Thanks, Bucko."

When I got there I saw about thirty people in chairs facing the empty podium so I figured I wasn't late. There were detectives from our squad as well as agents from the ATF. I took a seat and a minute later Captain Kissain came in carrying several sealed manila envelopes. He placed them on the podium and looked around the room.

"Good morning," Captain Kissain said. "Most of you have no idea what you're here for so let me enlighten you." He went on to tell us for the past year, the task force had been gathering information on a militant right-wing organization and through a series of wiretaps was able to identify seven locations where it was believed illegal weapons were being stockpiled. At 6 AM all of these locations were going to be hit. The teams in this room were going to be moving on the Queens locations and other teams were en route to an upstate location.

These self-declared patriots were called the Minutemen, a heavily armed, extreme right-wing group of fanatics, very secretive, and considered very dangerous. Captain Kissain told us if we do our jobs this morning, the Minutemen would cease to be dangerous by lunchtime. He began handing out envelopes to the assigned team leaders. Inside were the names of their team members along with the address of the location they would be hitting, pictures of the suspects, warrants, telephone numbers, and other pertinent information.

My team was made up of two other detectives from the DA squad and me, with an ATF agent named Carl Lynde in charge. Our target was a private house owned by a former Green Beret, now a New York City fireman, named Bill Keller. My father was a lieutenant when he retired from the fire department after thirty-six years of service and arresting a fireman didn't sit well with me.

We stopped at Goldie's Diner, three blocks from our target, for coffee and had just gotten out of our car when I noticed a yellow cab parked in the southwest corner of the parking lot. It was the cab used by the DA Squad for surveillance and I recognized the guys inside from this morning's meeting. Carl nudged me and without looking at the cab whispered, "Jim, I think Goldie's is being staked out by some of our task force."

"It is. I made them too."

"What do you think—get back in our car and take off or go inside and order some coffee to go?"

"If the suspects see us getting back in the car and leaving it might look suspicious."

"I agree, Jim, let's get the coffee to go."

When we entered the diner I noticed six suspicious

guys sitting at a back table; I made like they weren't even there. We left with our coffee and no one was the wiser. At about the same time we were rousting Bill Keller, the cuffs were being slapped on six Minutemen at Goldie's.

Bill was on his way to the diner when we arrested him. According to information gleaned from wiretaps these seven were going to drive upstate, where a plane was waiting. They planned to load up with weapons and parachute into the Adirondacks near a secluded leftist training camp believed to be full of Communist sympathizers who wanted to overthrow the government. Once on the ground they were going to set up positions around the camp and start shelling it with mortars. Parachutes and automatic weapons were found hidden in cars owned by two of the Minutemen arrested at Goldie's; these guys were not fucking around.

When we searched Bill Keller's house we found some shotguns and rifles as well as a Green Beret knife. The knife was definitely illegal; the guns were questionable. We overlooked the knife; after all, this guy was a fireman and a vet, not some mutt off the street. I took Bill into custody but didn't cuff him—call it professional courtesy. The rest of my team stayed at the house cataloguing the seized weapons.

I didn't know how many days Bill would be in the system so I offered to drive him to his firehouse, affording him the opportunity to arrange for a "mutual." A mutual is when you ask someone to cover your tours so you can take off. When you come back you cover an equal number of their tours. It was done all the time and the bosses would have no reason to suspect anything.

He was very appreciative. "That's damn decent of you," he said. "But why are you doing it?"

"Well, my father was a fireman and I'm sure he would have approved."

When we got to his firehouse, I went inside with him while he arranged for his mutuals and ten minutes later we arrived at the 108th Precinct; the reporters and the photographers were waiting for us. Next day on the cover of the *Daily News* was a picture of me leading Bill Keller up the precinct steps. Bill had pulled his shirt up over his head so you couldn't see his face. But I, on the other hand, was easily recognizable.

My uncle, who was a dyed-in-the-wool conservative, recognized me. He communicated his feelings to me by cutting out the picture, taping it to a roll of toilet paper, and mailing it to me with a note that read, "This is what I think of you."

The entire operation went off without a hitch. Well, if you don't count the dead dogs from the upstate raid. Manny Babone, aka "The Baboon," was the detective who took my place on the team. He was an excellent shot but lacked my recently acquired knowledge of animal anatomy, so when The Baboon was asked to tranquilize the two rottweilers guarding the Minutemen's estate he darted both dogs in the head; two excellent but fatal shots. The Minutemen sued and the ASPCA condemned the killings. Like I said—almost without a hitch.

When the Minutemen were brought into arraignment court they were in good spirits and were singing "God Bless America" at the top of their lungs. Bill Keller saw me, smiled, and threw a salutary nod my way.

A month later Nat Hentel lost his bid for re-election and when the new DA took over he replaced the entire squad with his own detectives. There were a lot of contracts being filled that day.

CHAPTER EIGHT

Fort Zinderneuf—73rd Precinct

Located in the Brownsville Bedford-Stuyvesant section of Brooklyn, the 73rd Precinct covered one square mile. It was affectionately known as Fort Z, short for Fort Zinderneuf, the last outpost of the French Foreign Legion in the classic film *Beau Geste*.

Numerous schools were sprinkled throughout the precinct. Several factory areas were in operation, and two hospitals administered to the local citizenry. One of those hospitals was "Lutheran," which had the dubious honor of being my birthplace. A few streets were lined with private homes but the large majority of residences were six-story tenements built around the turn of the century. There were a few of the ever present city housing projects that seemed to breed criminal behavior. And then there were the numerous bars whose patrons held a wealth of information—information that could not be forced but once trust was gained could be finessed.

The main shopping area was on Pitkin Avenue. Only blocks away were two marketplaces with stores and street vendors boasting a cornucopia of edible goods. Both markets were named after the avenues on which they were located. The Belmont market had a preponderance of storefronts coexisting with numerous street vendors. The Prospect market, on the other hand, was all six-story tenements, or "taxpayers" as they were otherwise known. The Prospect buildings were drab and dingy, falling into disrepair, a scene reminiscent of a turn-of-the-century black-and-white photograph of Manhattan's Lower East Side. Small hole-in-the-wall stores, mostly Jewish mom and pop operations, occupied the ground floor of these taxpayers. Pushcarts lined both sides of the street and customers flooded the market. It was controlled consumer chaos. The area had once been heavily Jewish, housing mostly European Jews who had been immigrating since the late 1800s. As they moved to more affluent communities, homegrown immigrants and poor southern blacks, all searching for jobs and a better life, rapidly replaced them.

I was transferred here from the DA's squad in January of 1967 and would spend the next five years as a 73rd Precinct detective. In those days detectives were responsible for investigating every crime committed in their precinct. There was no such thing as a homicide detective, or a robbery detective. Specialized squads that would cover multiple precincts wouldn't come into being for at least another five years.

The precinct house was an imposing structure built around the turn of the century with an all-stone façade and six wide stone steps leading up to a large solid oak door. On either side of the door were large green glass globes resting on top of ornate black iron poles. Painted on each of the globes, originally illuminated by gaslight, were the words "73rd Pct." Electricity had replaced the gaslight but almost everything structural was unchanged, from the wooden floors that creaked with every step, to the large round seal painted on the ceiling over the booking desk that should have stopped proclaiming the 73rd Precinct was in the City of Brooklyn when it came under the jurisdiction of the NYPD in the late 1800s.

The desk and adjacent one twenty-four room were on the right as you came through the entrance. The muster room, two holding cells, and the captain's office, with adjoining bunkroom, made up the rest of the first floor. A steel staircase leading to the second floor detective's squad room had endured so much foot traffic that the edges of the steps were rounded smooth. This uneven surface was listed as the cause of an occasional prisoner tripping and falling down the entire flight of stairs. At the top of the stairs was the detective's squad room with doors leading to an interrogation room, locker room, bunkroom, and bathroom. Throughout the squad room randomly placed gray metal desks sat covered in files, arrest report forms, telephones, and old Underwood typewriters.

Over in the far corner was an almost never-empty holding cage. Attached to the outside of the cage was an enclosed shelf that housed the fingerprint board. The squad room doubled as our lineup room. No two-way mirrors here, no blinding lights shining in the suspects' eyes, oh no, just a covered peephole the size of a half dollar in the locker room door. Witnesses were hidden in the locker room while suspects were lined up in the squad room. The cover on the peephole was lifted and witnesses were able to view the lineup. Each witness remained anonymous as only his or her eye was visible. It did however give new meaning to the term "eyewitness."

The 73rd was a veritable sweatshop where each detective caught over six hundred cases a year—an impossible caseload. That's why cases were prioritized into three piles. Pile number one: homicides, shootings, stabbings, stick-ups, and the occasional rape–investigate immediately. Pile number two: street muggings, commercial burglaries—investigate later. Pile number three: residential burglaries, purse snatches, larcenies and other low-level crimes—investigate never. Most pile number three cases went straight into the garbage; hell even if you had time to investigate them your chances of solving one was close to zero.

The 73rd was ranked third highest in crime out of the seventy-six precincts in the city. Only the 41st in the Bronx, known as Fort Apache, and the 28th in Harlem were worse. Carved out of the almost all-black 73rd Precinct was a three square block crime-free oasis. The area had been exclusively

Italian for more than a hundred years. The only calls you ever got there were an occasional black guy found dead with his dick cut off and stuffed in his mouth; the standard punishment for a black male who was stupid enough to make a pass at an Italian girl. No one ever accused the Italians of being subtle. You had a better chance solving a pile three case than a black homicide in the Italian section.

My first partner was Ronnie Schudde, a younger version of me. We were in the same class at the academy and it was nice to see a familiar face. About three weeks into our partnership I got a call from a uniform that there was a DOA on the elevated train tracks at East Ninety-eighth Street. I called to Ronnie, "Let's go, we gotta roll."

"What've we got?"

"Another DOA."

"You want me to drive, Jim?"

"Yeah, if the fucking thing starts."

"Amen to that."

We went downstairs to get the one and only car assigned to our squad; a beat-to-shit Plymouth sedan that refused go over forty because of a cracked carburetor. We used to stack a board and three bricks on top of the air cleaner and close the hood, thereby exerting enough downward pressure on the carburetor to seal the crack. Hey, it worked.

We were coming up on Strauss Street when the call came over the radio, "Seven-Three Precinct report of a man with a gun at 2052 Strauss Street."

"Ronnie, that's only two blocks from here. Do you want to run on this one?"

"Yeah, let's take it."

I picked up the mike, "Seven-three Squad to central, we will respond on that job." Central came back with, "Ten-four, Seven-three Squad."

I slapped the light on the roof and we gunned it. I think we hit forty that time. Less than a minute later we pulled up in front of 2052 where a thin black woman in her late sixties was standing on the curb motioning us to stop. We exited the car and identified ourselves. "I'm Detective O'Neil and this is Detective Schudde. What happ--"

"He just ran into the basement." She pointed to a door under the front steps and shouted, "And he's got a gun . . . And the motherfucker is crazy."

"Is there any other way out of the basement?"

"Yeah, around the back."

"You stay here ma'am."

There was a driveway on each side of the two-story semi-attached dwelling. We drew our guns, Ronnie took one driveway and I took the other. We got to the back of the house at the same time. One-story brick garages surrounded a small cement backyard. There were steps leading down to a closed basement door and while we were looking back and forth between the garages and the entrance to the basement the prick came through the door, gun drawn, and firing off rounds. He was no more than eight feet away from us when he ran out of bullets. It happened so fast that Ronnie and I didn't get off a shot until he had emptied his gun and was turning back toward the basement. We each got off a couple of rounds before he disappeared into the darkness. By then a radio car had arrived on the scene and the bastard was trapped between us. I looked over at Ronnie and he was doing the same thing I was, checking for bullet holes.

"You been hit, Ronnie?"

"No, you?"

"No, I'm ok. I can't believe he missed us. Shit he couldn't have been more than eight feet away."

We had no idea if we even hit the guy until fifteen minutes later when we found him cowering in a bedroom closet on the second floor. A bullet that nailed him in the ass, hit his hipbone, traveled down the thigh bone, and exited just above the knee where it was still attached to a long strip of flesh dangling from his leg.

"Great," I thought to myself. "There'll be a shitload of forms to fill out for this and we still gotta run on that dead body rotting on the tracks at Ninety-eighth Street."

We turned the wounded perp over to a couple of uniformed cops and were headed to our car when we heard, "Hey guys."

It was Joe Barone, a first-grade detective from our squad, a real nice guy but somebody who should have never been a cop. "What are you doing here, Joe?"

"I heard the "shots fired" transmission on the office radio, so I hitched a ride over in a radio motor patrol (RMP) car. Damn good thing I did too. Look at the both of you, your hands are shaking."

He was right. Ronnie and I were visibly shaken, but we were so hyped up we didn't realize it.

I spoke for my partner and me. "We'll be all right in a few minutes but right now we got a date with a stiff on Ninety-eighth Street."

"Your stiff ain't going nowhere. Both of you get in the car, I'll drive."

We did as instructed and Joe drove us to Red Jacks Bar. We walked in and occupied three stools at the end of the bar. Joe called out to the bartender, "Jesse, set up each of my friends here with a double of your finest scotch and when they're empty, fill 'em up again."

"Yes sir."

Good old Jesse. I liked him and that's why I felt bad when, two months later, as I was going through some wanted posters his face jumped out at me and I had to arrest him for bank robbery.

The scotch worked its magic and Ronnie and I stopped shaking. Today after a cop is involved in a gunfight, he gets sent to the Department shrink for trauma intervention. But back in 1967 the local bartender administered to us, and our trauma intervention came out of a bottle.

As we talked about how unbelievable it was that neither one of us had gotten hit I remembered a true story an instructor at the academy told us. Two undercovers from narcotics had set up a drug buy with two suspects. Even though it was winter the suspects insisted on conducting business at night in their car. Two perps in the front seat of a black 1960 Chevy Impala, two cops in the back seat, winter and all windows were closed when the cops were made. Everyone hit the floor as guns were drawn and without getting up perps and cops reached up and over the front seat and began firing until their guns were empty. The sound was deafening, the flashes of light were blinding, and smoke filled the car. Twenty-two shots fired and the score: cops zero, bad guys zero. Ten seconds of silence as it sunk in—nobody was hit. Then the perps were cuffed and hauled in, offering no resistance at all. Proficiency went out the window that night but Lady Luck didn't.

After we were cured we dropped Joe at the squad and finally headed out to the stiff on Ninety-eighth Street. We did what we had to do and then went home.

The next day they split Ronnie and me up. My guess was they figured we were both trigger-happy and shouldn't be together.

I became part of a four-man salt-and-pepper team, two white cops and two black cops. My white partner was Eddie Schneider and my two black partners were Ed Bailey and Fred "The Baby Lamb" Lambert. My first experience with my new partners was a fifteen-hour night tour. It was around 7 PM when Fred grabbed me and said, "Get the keys to the squad car, we're going to supper. There's something I gotta discuss with you."

I thought to myself, "What's up with this?"

We drove to a small restaurant on Lincoln Place for some shrimp and fries. In the middle of dinner Fred leaned over and said, "Look Jim, we're going to be kicking down doors and locking up some very dangerous badasses. Our lives may depend on how well we look out for each other. I want you to know that I'll die for you if I have to but I need to know that you'll do the same for me. After I tell you something if you feel that you can't give one hundred percent or don't want to work with me let me know and we'll get the boss to assign you to another team."

"Damn, Fred, what is it?"

"I'm married to a white woman."

"That's it?"

"Yeah Jim, that's it."

I extended my hand, "Shake, partner."

That was the start of a lifelong friendship with Fred and my other two partners. They would become the brothers I never had.

The first week all I did was observe my partners. One of the most important things I learned was when to wear my detective's hat, a classic felt fedora. You see, in a roach-infested tenement the critters would drop on you from the ceiling and wearing your hat would keep them out of your hair. If you wanted to keep them from crawling up your pants legs you made a habit of walking in place when talking to a witness. There were only a few Hispanic families in the almost exclusively black 73rd Precinct and for the most part their apartments were roach-free. Not that they were cleaner than the black families, it's just that the Hispanics all had chickens and chickens loved roaches.

By the second week my free ride was over and I began catching cases. There weren't enough hours in the day to handle them all, especially every two weeks on "Mother's Day," when the welfare checks were delivered and we would catch between eighty to one hundred robberies. Twice a month, junkies would follow the mailmen around and steal the checks out of the mailboxes, so what most people did was wait for the postman, get the check in person, and then cash it. A welfare recipient was allowed a maximum of two replacement checks a year to cover theft. Twice a year many recipients would claim that they were robbed right after cashing their check and would beat the State out of two welfare payments. My guess is that about 2 percent of the robberies were legitimate. Once a police report was filed the so-called victim would get a copy, present it at the welfare office, and a new check would be issued. The necessity of that report was the reason these pile three cases couldn't be thrown in the garbage.

However, we did the next best thing. We had a rubber stamp made that proclaimed:

"This matter was investigated by Detective _____, shield # _____. A canvass of the area was conducted attempting to obtain witnesses or information on this matter with no results. Complainant unable to identify perpetrator from photos. Confidential sources in the area were contacted in regard to this matter with no results. Case closed."

Of course there was no investigation done, no photos shown, and no confidential sources contacted, but the victims didn't care. All they wanted was that police report.

The area didn't get any worse on Mother's Day; it just got busier. It had gotten so bad that the garbagemen and the postmen stopped carrying any cash at all, paying for their lunch with personal checks.

With my first Mother's Day ordeal behind me I gladly listened when Ed Bailey observed, "Jim, you look swamped."

"Yeah, I'm up to my ass in alligators."

"Well, the alligators will still be here tomorrow. Right now it's time for a taste at the Highway Inn."

It was over on the corner of Dumont and Tapscott at the end of Kings Highway. One big room so dark you could hardly see the fifteen bar stools lining the long solid mahogany bar, the six tables with chairs surrounding a small dance floor, and an old unlit Wurlitzer jukebox that would trade six songs for a quarter. The RCA Victor black-and white TV sat on a high shelf behind the bar and was reserved for sporting events. At the back of the bar, just past the side entrance, was a short hallway leading to the bathrooms. You had to pass the kitchen and two recessed phone booths on the way to the bathrooms.

Ed introduced me to the owner, Abe, a small bald Jewish man in his sixties, only one of three white bar owners left in the precinct. Abe was very pleasant but seemed in a hurry to leave. It was getting late in the afternoon and he knew it wasn't safe for a white man to be in this neighborhood after dark.

I didn't know it then but my partners and I would log more hours in the Highway Inn than in our squad room. We were always working especially when we were sitting on a barstool. It was here we gained the trust of the good patrons of the Highway Inn. And that was the key to unlocking information that led to arrests. To the untrained eye we were drinking on duty when in reality we were on the job. Besides, knowing the local barkeeps came in handy when one of the desk sergeants or lieutenants asked you to get them a "flute" (a Coke bottle filled with whisky from a local bar) in exchange for a speedy arrest processing. If the desk officer was a nice guy he'd get a flute of the good stuff—not so nice and any rotgut was okay. Not that it cost anything for either one—a flute was always on the arm. Call it a small reward for protecting and serving.

We made many genuine friendships at the Highway Inn. One time a bunch of customers, in a mock ceremony, presented me with a "safe card" guaranteed to ensure my personal safety. It read, "In case of riot, the bearer of this card is an honorary Negro" and was signed H. Rapp Brown. I still carry that card in my wallet. One of the bartenders, Earl Bellow, loved fishing and had been on my boat many times. We'd fish all day and when we got back to my house we'd have the catch of the day for dinner.

I can't tell you how many times I would bring fish, clams, and shrimp to the Highway Inn and cook it up in the kitchen for everyone to enjoy. It became my home away from home.

We always stayed in pairs, even when at the Highway Inn, but on this particular night I was with Fred and he had to run on a personal matter. "I'll be back in about an hour," Fred told me. "You'll be fine, Jim, everybody in here loves you. To them you're a reverse Oreo, white on the outside and black on the inside."

"I know, and if anything happens I'll just flash my safe card."

Fred had been gone fifteen minutes, and I was sitting where I always sat, where all smart cops sat, on the last barstool farthest from the front door, when in walked three reasons why cops sit at the back of a bar.

That night I came very close to being shot. All the stools were taken and there must have been twenty people standing at the bar when three black guys I had never seen before walked in. One of them stayed at the front door, another one stayed at the front of the bar, and the third guy walked past me into the back. Thank God it was dark and crowded, and even though I was the only white face in the bar and the only one wearing a sports jacket he failed to notice me. I reached inside my jacket and unholstered my gun, but kept it concealed as he checked the bathrooms, the kitchen, and the phone booths. Luckily the third guy didn't find anyone and he started heading back my way. I was playing it out in my mind and knew what I needed to do. If he made a move I had to pop him in the head immediately. My snub nose .38 only held five rounds so I had to put him down with only one shot, leaving me with four rounds to be divided amongst his two pals. As soon as I fired, everyone in the bar would hit the ground, leaving the two scumbags and me the only ones standing. Two shots at each of the remaining guys and if I got them—end of story. If not I would duck into the hallway leading to the kitchen and reload my weapon.

The third guy was about to tell his buddies the coast was clear when he made me. He didn't know whether to shit or shout and almost tripped over his own feet. He saw my hand inside my jacket and knew I was carrying. If he had known I was the only cop in the bar it might have turned out differently but he couldn't take the chance that my partners weren't somewhere in the crowd, so he motioned for his buddies to leave.

As soon as they were gone everybody looked at me. Earl Bellow came over, put his hand on my shoulder and said, "You know that pasty face of yours just stopped them motherfuckers from robbing us?"

I held up my gun. "Brothers and sisters that asshole doesn't know how close he just came to having his brains blown out."

The house bought a round and we let out a collective sigh of relief. Meanwhile, two blocks away, three unknown black guys were sticking up the Bombay.

We frequented other neighborhood bars as well. There was Teddy's Happy House, which in 1969 would be the scene of one of the most bizarre murders I had ever come across.

Pacey's over on East New York Avenue and Bristol Street was owned by an old Jewish guy who had finally had enough and sold out to a Panamanian immigrant. The name of the bar remained unchanged and the barmaid Mozelle "Mo Mo" Brown stayed on. Mo Mo was in her thirties, dark skinned, stood about five-feet-eleven, and was a hell of a barmaid. The bowie knife openly displayed on her belt, as well as her readiness to use it, contributed to the lack of trouble on her watch. She was in the habit of telling a would be troublemaker, "Motherfucker, I'll cut you three ways—long, deep, and often." Nobody wanted to mess with Mo Mo especially after one memorable incident.

It was a damp Wednesday night and most of Mo Mo's customers were on their way to one of the many after-hours clubs that were so popular in Brownsville. I had just stopped in for a quick drink and was sitting in the shadows at the back of the bar sipping on a scotch when a large guy, who I guessed was in his early twenties, wandered in. I didn't recognize him, and from the concern on Mo Mo's face I figured she didn't either. She asked him what he wanted to drink and he put his left hand on the bar while pulling a knife with his other hand. By the time I had drawn my gun the would-be robber had been staked to the bar, with Mo Mo's bowie knife protruding from his left hand and his knife on the floor. My arrest record went up by one and Mo Mo's street cred had just gone off the Richter scale.

There were two guys there, Chino and Buddy, who made a good living off of writing the digit, where a correct guess got you a six hundred to one payoff. Your odds of winning were 999 to 1 but that didn't stop anyone from pursuing their dream of "hitting the number." Chino was Puerto Rican, a disabled vet and war hero and Buddy was a black guy with a nice disposition.

Writing the digit was no big thing. The way we looked at it a disabled war vet and his partner were entitled to make a decent living, and as long as they showed us the respect we deserved, by not conducting business in front of us, we left them alone. They put my partners and me on a number for fifty cents each day and even though we told them it wasn't necessary they insisted. It turned out their boss had ordered them to use a percentage of the profits for payoffs to the police. One week, two of my partners and I hit the number for $300 each, a lot of money back then.

The Date Room on East New York Avenue off of Howard Avenue was a regular weekly stop for us. The Trio on Saint John's Place was a less frequent stop and was reserved for those times when we were specifically looking for someone known to hang out there. We would also hit the Trio whenever we did a "full horn," our term for working every bar in the precinct. A modified horn was about eight bars and a light horn, one or two.

The Bombay on Livonia Avenue was a real bucket of blood. The people who hung out there didn't like cops and there was no chance of getting any information out of them, so even on a full horn we would skip the Bombay. The only time we went there was if we had to roll on a killing or an incident involving a cop. Once, we responded there on the call of a "shots fired" run involving two officers. When we got there we investigated and found that the two uniformed cops in a patrol car had stopped in front of the Bombay so one of them could get a pack of cigarettes. The cop riding shotgun got out and went inside, walked through the dark bar and stopped in front of the cigarette machine, where he began feeding it the fifty cents required for a pack of Marlboros. It was so dark that the cop didn't know he had walked into the middle of an armed robbery until he felt the barrel of a gun pressed into the back of his head and heard, "Me and my man are robbing this place."

It was at that moment he realized he should have quit smoking, like his wife wanted him to. Without turning around he said, "Take my wallet but not my gun or my shield. I get fined a week's pay if I lose them."

"I don't want your wallet."

"Tell you what I'll do. I won't try to stop you and I'll even give you a minute after you leave before I come after you. Just don't take my gun or my shield."

"You'll wait one minute after we leave before coming after us?"

"Yes, you have my word. I promise."

"Okay, it's a deal, Officer."

They continued robbing the bar and its patrons, and as they turned to leave two shots rang out. When the officer waiting outside came running through the front door he found his partner, standing over the two wounded crooks, gun in hand and venomously spitting out the words, "Still want that minute, assholes?"

By the time we got there all we could do was take

statements and make all the necessary notifications.

The remaining eight bars in the precinct would see us maybe twice a year unless we had a special reason for a visit.

I would say that 97 percent of the blacks in Brownsville were honest, hard-working people trapped there by circumstances and forced to raise their children in a very dangerous environment. My heart went out to them and nothing made me feel better than putting away some of the bad 3 percent. The law-abiding citizens liked the police, and wanted to see the bad guys behind bars, but until you earned their trust they wouldn't tell you squat. Once they knew that you wouldn't reveal where you got your information, they opened up.

Back then, there was no DNA, no CSI, and no computer databases—hell, running a single print could take a month. If you were lucky enough to get prints from nine or ten fingers, you might get a match in twenty-four hours. If the perp had never been arrested by the NYPD you couldn't get a match unless you sent the print, or prints, to the FBI in Quantico, Virginia. They had a print card for everyone finger-printed anywhere in the country, but you would never use the FBI unless it was a very heavy case.

In 1967, you solved cases by having your finger on the neighborhood pulse and your ass on a barstool.

CHAPTER NINE

A Little R&R and The Bigot

The 73rd was a pressure cooker and time off was a needed release. I lived on a canal just off the Great South Bay, which was located between Long Island's south shore and the sandy barrier islands of Fire Island and Jones Beach. Fire Island's inlet from the Atlantic Ocean was a veritable cornucopia of marine life, some of which would make their way to my dinner table. Nothing was more relaxing than spending a day on the boat drowning a few worms and killing some Budweisers.

I bought a used twenty-six-foot cabin cruiser that stretched my meager paycheck to its limits. Even with the additional $422 a month I got from the government for attending college it was a real financial burden, but my family loved the boat and the bay, so it was worth it. Most of my days off were spent on our boat with my growing family—we had another boy and were one step closer to the four boys and a girl that would complete us. Some of those days ended back in my kitchen with my partners, sometimes a neighbor, me, and always Johnnie Walker.

I remember a particularly hot July day in 1969 when Ed Bailey, his cousin John Payne, an undercover narcotics detective, and I had just returned from a day's fishing. We were all sitting around some Johnnie Walker Red exchanging small talk when there was a knock at my front door. It was a neighbor of mine from across the street, Vinnie Mollo. Vinnie, a tall, strapping fellow with a smile that would charm and a scowl that would intimidate, knew Ed but had never met John Payne. I introduced him to John as Detective Mollo and Ed broke out laughing. John was puzzled at his cousin's laughter until I explained that Vinnie wasn't a real detective and on occasion I would bring him into the city and give him my shield so he could interrogate perps and drink on the arm with us at the Highway Inn. Vinnie joined our circle and we again turned our attention toward Johnnie Walker and more small talk.

I asked Vinnie if he was still having trouble with his next-door neighbor, Charlie Palmer.

"Yeah, that bastard keeps calling unfounded complaints to town hall and they keep sending some pain in the ass inspector out to bust my chops."

Ed asked Vinnie to point out the offending neighbor's house and Vinnie indicated the white one next to his.

Ed suggested, "I think I should have a talk with this Charlie Palmer."

"I don't know if that's a good idea, my neighbor's a bit of a bigot and I don't think he likes black people."

"Oh, I gotta talk to this guy." Ed turned to me and asked for a teacup.

"Why do you want a teacup, you already have a glass?"

"Jim, just give it to me."

"Okay, partner."

We all gathered around the picture window in my living room as Ed walked out the door, teacup in hand. As he approached Charlie's house we could see that his normally lively gait had changed to an unsteady saunter. He paused at the front door, raised the cup above his head, leaned slightly backward, and began pounding on the front door until it opened. We couldn't hear what was being said but we were able to see Charlie's face change from normal to red and then to a ghostly pale white. His hand went to his chest as he staggered back into the house and slammed the door. As Ed came through my front door we all inquired, "What the hell did you say to him?"

"I just introduced myself . . . 'Hi mistah, eyes youse new neigh-boh, jus moved in upstairs next daw to ya. Kin eyes barrow a cup uh whi-i-ine?'"

Within a month, a "For Sale" sign went up in Charlie's front yard and three months later he was just a bad memory. I guess "Detective" Mollo liked his unofficial taste of law enforcement because a year after what will forever be known as the Charlie Palmer caper, Vinnie became a New York State Trooper.

The passing years would see lots of fishing trips and lots of capers. We'd pile into my boat, load up with bait and Budweisers, and head out for a day on the bay. One time stands out in my mind because of something John Payne did. Ed Bailey, his cousin John, Vinnie Mollo, Eddie Schneider, and I had just finished laying in the day's supplies and began pulling away from my dock when I realized we were painfully low on gas. I headed for a gas station that I rarely used on a nearby island. We made it there on fumes and were tied up for several minutes before the gas jockey finally appeared. He walked right past us and began pumping gas into a large cabin cruiser that had just pulled in. As he began exchanging pleasantries with the two white guys on board John turned to us and said, "Watch this."

I verbalized what everybody was thinking: "Uh oh."

John walked up behind the attendant, "What's your name?"

"Zach."

"Zach, you got a problem with colored people? We were here long before these white boys, but you decided to gas them up first. What are we, second-class citizens? Is this the headquarters for the Klan or something? I have a good mind to get a hundred Black Panthers out here tomorrow morning picketing this place in row boats, and don't think I can't do it."

We were having a hard time keeping a straight face and trying to appear seriously offended. The look on Zach's face didn't make it any easier but somehow we managed to hold it together. The poor guy looked like he was going to stroke out as he shut the pump off and hurried over to gas us up. After paying for the gas we introduced ourselves and began to laugh. Even the two guys in the cabin cruiser were smiling and winking their approval. No one was laughing as hard as Zach.

After that we always gassed up there and as soon as we tied up Zach would come running out yelling, "No Panthers, no Panthers—I'll be right there."

A lot of people today would say that our racial humor was politically incorrect but it was our way of saying, "I accept you as my brother, and as my brother I know there is no such thing as being politically incorrect." During the writing of this book, one of my brothers, Ed Bailey, passed away and I was asked to speak at his wake. His wife Maria requested that I relate any story I could about him—something funny, perhaps.

A smile creased my face as I told them about the night Ed came to go crabbing with Vinnie Mollo and me. By 7:45 PM Ed was fifteen minutes late so I decided to call the 73rd Squad to see how long ago he had left. When I found out that I had just missed him and it would most likely be around forty minutes before he got to my house I knew he was operating on "CPT." One of Ed's favorite expressions for describing anyone late for an appointment was to say they were operating on "CPT" (colored people's time). I figured it was TTTEAL (time to teach Ed a lesson), so we hatched a plan. Vinnie and I got two cloth diapers for each of us and stapled them together so they resembled two eyeless white hoods. Then we cut out holes for our eyes and waited for Ed to come. When we saw Ed's car pull up we put the hoods on and hid in bushes on either side of the path leading to my dock. As he approached, arms laden with foul weather gear, we leapt from our hiding places and grabbed him as we shouted, "We got you now, you black bastard!" Ed let out a loud whoop and threw all his gear into the air. Vinnie and I laughed so hard as we pulled the hoods off that we almost fell down. Ed had tears streaming down his face and was doubled over with laughter. This called for a few shots of Johnnie Walker Red before heading out. We toasted to good friends, good times, and good humor. Ed raised his glass and said, "If I could have gotten to my gun I'd have shot the both of you sons of bitches."

Everyone at the wake was smiling and Maria was as close to laughing as she could be under the circumstances.

CHAPTER TEN

A Bullet for Leroy—An Onion Sack for Frankie

It was 1969, warm for September 28th. The New York Mets were on their way to becoming the World Champion Amazing Mets and I was on my way into the squad when I caught a light at the corner of Hopkinson Avenue and St. Marks Place. On the south west corner was Teddy's Happy House, a local watering hole owned by a city corrections officer named Teddy Lassiter. I noticed two black guys arguing on the sidewalk across from Teddy's. Certainly nothing unusual about that, but what did strike me as strange was that the taller of the two was wearing a black-and-white checkered trench coat on a warm day. Something aroused the cop in me but before I could do anything, Trench Coat reached into the waistband of his pants, pulled out a gun, and fired. I heard the pop of a small-caliber pistol and saw blood and skin splatter from the victim's head. He put hands to head as he fell to the ground and the shooter took off at a gallop. I got out of my car and took off after the perp, who already had a big lead on me. He was wearing felony boots and began opening the distance between us.

I saw him duck into a building, but by the time I got there he was deep in the bowels of the tenement and had broken all the light bulbs in the hallway. I was a white cop chasing a black perp, with a gun, into a black hallway. This was not a situation I wanted to be in, especially without backup. I was standing in the entranceway with my gun drawn when a short, balding, rotund man in his fifties asked me, "Are you a cop?"

I gave him my standard answer. "No, I'm the garbage inspector checking for uncovered garbage cans. You see this gun, now who the fuck do you think I am?"

"Well I'm the super and I knew you was a cop. I figure you chased some brother in here and he broke the light bulbs as he ran in. I'm always changing them fucking light bulbs. Wish you guys would chase them into someone else's building."

"I'm Detective O'Neil, what's your name?"

"Everybody calls me Elgin, unless they're mad at me."

"Look, Elgin, call 911 and tell them that Detective O'Neil chased someone into the building and this someone just shot a guy in the head over at Hopkinson and St. Marks. Give them the address here and tell them I need backup right away. You got that?"

"Yeah, no problem."

Needless to say the call went out that Detective O'Neil was shot in the head at Hopkinson and St. Marks and somehow made his way to this building—officer down. I heard sirens from at least three different precincts and I knew Elgin fucked up.

Lights flashed, sirens wailed, car doors flung open, cops jumped out, and guns were drawn. At least twenty cops. Those who could fit into the entranceway were shouting, "O'Neil, you okay, are you okay? We heard you were shot in the head." Those who couldn't fit into the entranceway were outside shouting, "Is O'Neil okay?"

"I'm fine, the super made the call for me and he got it all screwed up."

I gave the description of the perp and told the uniforms, "He's probably gone, but search the entire building anyway. I have to get back to the crime scene and secure it."

In those days we didn't have CSI, so the responsibility of securing the crime scene fell on the detective's shoulders. I grabbed a ride with two uniforms back to the scene. When we got there I walked over to where the body should have been.

There were two young black kids kneeling around the large bloodstain left by the victim. When they saw me they stopped talking, stood up, looked at me, and said, "We didn't do nothing and we didn't see nothing, sir."

"Look I know you kids didn't do anything wrong. I saw the whole thing go down. Do you know what happened to the body?"

They both pointed across the street. "He got up and walked over there."

I couldn't believe my eyes. There he was sitting, ass on the curb and feet in the street. He was holding his head rocking back and forth, moaning, "My fucking head hurts."

I walked over to him and said, "I know you're hurt, and we're going to help you. What's your name?"

"Leroy Jones."

"Take it easy, Leroy, we'll get you to the hospital. No time to wait for an ambulance, let's get you into the patrol car."

He looked up at me and said, "I ain't going to no goddamn hospital and I sure as shit ain't getting into no motherfucking cop car."

"Look you're shot in the head, we're taking you to the emergency room at Saint Mary's."

"You ain't taking me to no motherfucking hospital, period."

"Period my ass, look, you're going. Easy way or hard way but you're going— period."

He went the hard way. We called for backup and it took six of us to get him into the patrol car but he was finally on his way. I stayed to secure the crime scene and as I watched the patrol car driving away with Leroy still struggling I thought to myself, "Leroy Jones, now there goes a tough piece of work."

Miraculously my car was still there. I drove to the squad and arrived just as Fred Lambert was rolling in. I filled him in on what had just gone down and we decided to peruse the periphery, as we use to say, and see if we could spot the guy who put a bullet in Leroy Jones's head. Fifteen minutes later Fred was driving while I peered out the window in the vicinity of the shooting and I'll be damned if we didn't see a tall black male in a checkered trench coat, walking a little white fluffy dog. It was the shooter, as sure as God made tomatoes.

"Hey Fred, that's the perp. Can you believe it, walking his dog in the middle of the day not two blocks from where he shot the victim?"

My partner smiled and said, "I can't believe how easy these assholes make our job."

I shook my head in agreement. "Let me out here, I'll come up from behind him, you drive around the corner, park the car and start walking toward him in case he tries to bolt."

I snuck up on him and he never even knew I was there until he felt the barrel of my gun pressed into his right ear. Did I mention I was part American Indian and that even as a kid I was good at sneaking up on people? Which is not a bad talent to have if you're a cop.

"Police, put your hands up."

"I can't, if I do I'll have to drop the leash and my dog will run away."

"If you don't put up your hands your fucking brains are going to run away."

He raised his hands, dropping the leash, and his dog took off. I cuffed the guy, turned him around and searched him. I found a .32-caliber pistol on him that had recently been fired and started to read him his rights. "You have the . . ."

"I told you, see I told you. Now how am I gonna get my dog back?"

"That's the least of your worries, pal, you're under arrest for the attempted murder of one Leroy Jones."

Forgetting about his dog and with his eyes bugging out of his head he asked, "What do you mean attempted murder? Is he still alive?"

"Shut up and listen." I Mirandized him then answered

his question. "Last time I saw him he was still breathing but that was over an hour ago. He's probably dead by now."

"Can you find out for me?"

"All of a sudden you're worried about him?"

"No, all of a sudden I'm worried about me." He got this look on his face like he had to shit but couldn't. "Man I didn't do nothing, I just heard about the shooting."

"What's your name?"

"I'm Frankie Giddens."

When Fred saw I had back-cuffed the suspect he returned to the car and brought it around to us. We threw Frankie into the rear seat, locked the .32 in the glove compartment, and took off for the hospital. I wanted to do what's known as a "show up," hopefully before Leroy Jones died. When a victim might not live long enough to make an ID in a lineup you can bring the suspect to the victim. If a deathbed ID is made during this show up, that becomes admissible and can be used as evidence in court.

From the back seat we heard, "Where are you taking me?"

Without looking back, I said, "The hospital. You were so worried about Leroy we figured you wanted to check up on him in person."

"Look, I don't really know the dude hardly at all, we don't have to go. Why don't you just take me to the station house?"

Fred yelled at him, "One more word and I'll make you wish it was you who got shot in the head."

Saint Mary's was built of solid-gray stone blocks in 1889. It looked more like a dungeon than a hospital but when you stepped inside she transformed herself into a modern-day facility staffed with dedicated doctors. Many a police officer is alive today because of Saint Mary's and her staff.

We parked in front of the emergency room and pulled a reluctant Frankie Giddens out of the back seat. Fred grabbed him by the handcuffs and lifted. That seemed to make him more pliable and as the expression on his face changed from fear to pain he came along willingly.

When we walked into the crowded emergency room I recognized one of the security personnel, an ex-uniformed cop from the 73rd by the name of Kelvin "The Kelvinator" Scott. Not a big man but tough as nails with the determination of a bulldog.

"Hey Kelvinator, what's up?" I shouted.

He turned fast and when he saw us he responded, "Well if it isn't Detective O'Neil hissssself and The Baby Lamb, what's up guys?"

I explained, "We're hoping to do a show up."

"Let me guess. Any chance your victim's a pain-in-the-ass brother with a gunshot wound to the head?"

"Yeah Kelvin, did he make it?"

"Can't say for sure, about a half an hour ago he was refusing to let them x-ray him so they paged me. By the time I got here he had pulled all the tubes and needles out of himself and had taken off. The doctor said your victim shouted something about hating fucking hospitals, as he staggered out."

"So this guy is gone?"

Smiling, Kelvin said, "Like yesterday's beer fart."

My partner and I headed back to the squad with Frankie Giddens in tow. From the back seat Frankie started up again, "Where you taking me, let me go, I didn't do nothing."

Fred made him pliable again with a smack to the head and Frankie didn't utter another word all the way back to the squad.

Vehicular traffic was light and we pulled up in front of the precinct house ten minutes later. Up the stone steps, through the large oak door, a quick wave to the sergeant at the booking desk, up to the second floor holding cells and Frankie Giddens was caged. I went to my desk and Fred headed to the bathroom. I noticed a young black girl about sixteen stop him, and pointing toward me he sent her in my direction. "Detective O'Neil," she said. "I'm Tyshell Jones, my brother is Leroy Jones and he told me to ask for you. He wanted you to know that he ain't going to press charges against nobody."

"Tyshell, if he doesn't press charges the shooter will walk away after almost killing him."

"I can only tell you what my brother said."

"Tell your brother all he has to do is come down to the station house, pick the guy that shot him out of a lineup and I'll take care of the rest."

"There is only one thing my brother hates more than hospitals."

"Let me guess, police stations."

She told me I was right, and I knew Frankie was going to walk on the attempted murder beef. But Frankie didn't know it. Always trying to turn a confidential informant (CI), I got Frankie and told him the situation, according to O'Neil. "Listen Frankie, I don't think Leroy is going to make a good witness so I spoke to the Assistant District Attorney [ADA] and if you plead guilty to illegal possession of a firearm he's willing to drop the attempted murder charge. If you cop to the possession charge you'll do nine months, otherwise the ADA goes after you for attempted murder which means you'd be looking at fifteen years. Do the math."

"I'll take the nine months."

"You made the right decision. One good turn deserves another so the day you get out you come to my office and I'll decide how you're going to pay me back.

Six months later I was knocking down some suds at Teddy's Happy House when this black guy came toward me and sat on the stool next to mine. He stared at me and said, "You don't recognize me, do you?"

"Can't say as I do."

"Give me your finger."

Intrigued, but still wary, I complied. He put the tip of

my index finger up to his forehead and I felt a lump under his skin. It was a bullet and I knew who it was.

"Now I remember you, you're Leroy Jones."

We bought each other a beer, drank them down, and went our separate ways. That was the last time I saw Leroy Jones alive.

Frankie Giddens did almost nine months to the day and as promised showed up at my office upon his release. He turned out to be a fountain of information and was an invaluable CI, responsible for helping us solve several homicides.

Whenever we turned up the name of a suspect we couldn't identify we would give Frankie a call. If he said he could help us we'd pick him up in a safe area and put him in the back seat with an onion sack over his head. He could easily see out through the wide mesh, while remaining unidentifiable to those on the street.

August 23, 1970, was an unusually comfortable seventy-five degree day. We had the street name of a suspect we wanted for a two-day-old homicide that went down in the vicinity of Teddy's Happy House. I called Frankie Giddens and said, "This is Detective O'Neil. You familiar with a guy whose street name is Tooth?"

"Yeah, his real name is Toby Booth."

"You can ID him for me?"

"Yeah."

"I like him for a homicide that went down near Teddy's. Think he's still around?"

"Last I heard Tooth was still breathing neighborhood air."

"Okay, meet you at the usual pick-up point in one hour."

My white partner, Eddie Schneider, and I picked him up and drove around the neighborhood surrounding Teddy's Happy House for about an hour without a Tooth sighting. We were passing Teddy's for the fourth time when we heard from the back seat, "Hey there's Fast Eddie," a guy we knew as Edgar Brown. "He killed a guy two weeks ago, three doors down from here, with a two-by-four—bashed his head in."

Eddie Schneider and I were up on everything going on in the precinct but neither of us recalled any homicide on this block in the last few weeks. After discreetly dropping Frankie off we headed back to the station house to do a records search. No homicides on that block in over a month, but what we found was the report of an accidental death fifteen days prior. It occurred a few doors from Teddy's Happy House. There were two eyewitnesses who stated that the deceased had fallen down a stoop and cracked his head on the bottom step. We kept reading and realized it was no accident—this was the homicide our CI was talking about.

"Son of a bitch. Eddie, take a look at who the witnesses are."

"I see. Edgar Brown—Edgar "Fast Eddie" Brown—and Robert Brown."

"What a fucking coincidence. I got an idea."

"Talk to me, Jim."

"We're going back to where we last saw Fast Eddie. Half a block before we get there you put the flashing light on top of the car and turn on the siren. If he's still there I'll bring us to a screeching halt. We'll jump out of the car and run at him yelling, 'Gotcha motherfucker.' Who knows we might get lucky and get a spontaneous statement out of him."

He was still there and I'll be goddamned if it didn't work. As soon as we ran up to him he blurted out, "Thank God it's over, I haven't been able to sleep for two weeks. I knew you guys would get me. I didn't mean to kill him, I just wanted to give him a good reason to stop screwing my girlfriend."

We Mirandized him and locked him up. An hour later he was giving his statement to an ADA and eventually he pleaded guilty to manslaughter. Oh, but our work was not yet done. We had to bust the balls of the detective who did the initial investigation and closed the case as an accidental death. We told him that if we ever wanted to kill someone and get away with it we would do it on his watch. Then we hurled the final insult, "You couldn't find Kate Smith in a phone booth." Now we were done.

Frankie had been helping us for about three months when he came into the squad and said he had to talk to me. He appeared to be very agitated and I asked him what was up.

"I got a question, Detective."

"So ask me."

"If a guy ... uh like hurts somebody else, then gets locked up and does time and ... uh like a year later that somebody else dies from the injuries could the guy who did it ... umm get charged with murder?"

Not wanting to scare away a valuable source I weighed my answer carefully, not honestly.

"Of course not. That would be double jeopardy."

"What a relief, I haven't been able to eat for two weeks."

I knew this had something to do with Leroy Jones but sometimes the smartest thing to do is to play dumb. This was one of those times.

"What do you mean, Frankie?"

"About two weeks ago Leroy Jones got drunk out of his goddamn mind at Teddy's Happy House. He walked outside, tripped over his fucking shoelaces and smashed his head into the curb. The bullet got pushed into his brain and he died instantly."

I couldn't help thinking, "Man, you can't even make this shit up."

CHAPTER ELEVEN

Two Notes in the Coop

About three weeks after the demise of Leroy Jones I decided to take a few well-deserved days off. When I returned to the squad the first thing I did was go to my coop to see if I had any mail. I found two notes from Lieutenant James "The Boat" Fulton.

The first note requested that I help Joe Wasser, referred to as Joe W., with a homicide he caught on one of my days off. He was a new detective and a hell of a good guy so I didn't mind helping him out.

The second note irritated me. The Boat wanted me to give Joe Barone, whom everyone referred to as Joe B., a hand with a homicide he caught while I was off. What bothered me was that this guy was two detective grades higher than me. He was a first-grade detective making the same pay as a lieutenant and I was a third-grade detective.

The guy rarely left the safety of the office. I remember one time, the Boat asked me to take Joe B. out and get him some drug busts to improve his arrest record. I took Joe B. with me to the roughest area in the precinct and pointed to four guys congregating on a corner. I told him to grab any one of them and he'd find drugs. He got out of the car but when they saw him approaching they scattered and Joe B. gave chase. He looked good in his role as a ghetto cop, right up until he tripped over an uneven section of sidewalk, fell on his face, and had to be rushed to Saint Mary's emergency room with a slight concussion.

I liked Joe B. ever since he had taken Ronnie Schudde and me for trauma intervention at Red Jacks Bar following a shooting incident back in 1967. But he should never have been a cop and wouldn't have been if it wasn't for his relation to a deputy chief inspector.

When Eddie and Fred got in I showed them the notes. They were glad to help Joe W. and made a disparaging comment about helping Joe B., but agreed to run down both homicides. Eddie and I saw some of our CIs and got them working on it while Fred agreed to stay at the squad to cover the phones. Fred called Louis Jeurs, an eighteen-year-old heroin addict who was the best CI we had ever come across, and told him what we were looking for. Before we got back to the squad Louis was on the phone with Fred. "Our guy is named Louis. He did both homicides and you can find him at 501 Howard Avenue, apartment 1C. Word is he's got his bags packed and he's leaving town, so you better hurry up and get over there."

Fred tried in vain to reach us on the radio so he ran downstairs and grabbed two uniformed cops in a radio car and headed off to round up the suspect. When they got there the guy had his suitcase all packed. Five minutes later and they would have missed him. He kept saying his name wasn't Louis, it was Eddie Beauchamp. When he was brought into the squad and searched we found a membership card in his wallet for an after-hours social club. The name on the card was Edzelle Lewis.

Our informant was right on. Louis Jeurs was still batting a thousand and both homicides were solved within two hours. We had just made Lieutenant Fulton's day.

I called Joe W. at home. "Good news," I told him. "We got the guy who did your homicide."

"What? Damn that was fast."

"We aim to please."

"Thanks Jim, I'll get dressed and come right in to process him. Thanks again."

Fred called Joe B. at home. "Joe, it's Fred. I wanted to let you know we just picked up the guy that did your homicide."

"What? Are you sure you got the right guy?"

"Yeah, I'm sure."

"How can you be so sure? I want to be positive you got the right guy before I come in on my day off."

"Look, the CI that gave us this guy is never wrong."

"You want me to come in on my day off because some CI fingered this guy? I don't know, Fred."

"Okay, hold on a minute."

Fred dropped the receiver on the desk and went over to the cage. He took Edzelle Lewis into the interrogation room and closed the door. About ten seconds later I heard yelling and screaming. It sounded like furniture was being overturned accompanied by smashing sounds. The thin metal walls were shaking as something softer than furniture was being thrown against them.

Fred came out rubbing his knuckles; Edzelle would be helped back later to the cage. Fred snatched up the receiver and yelled into the mouthpiece, "The motherfucker just confessed. Are you coming in now?"

As I mentioned before, Joe B. rarely ventured out onto the tough streets of Brownsville. So I was surprised when he asked, "Jim, would you mind going with me to Saratoga Avenue to pick up a suspect for questioning?"

Like I said, I liked the guy, so I responded, "Yeah, why not, my partners aren't in yet and this shouldn't take long."

I grabbed the keys to the squad's unmarked car and pointed the headlights toward Saratoga Avenue. "What's the address you got on your suspect?"

"It's 2341 Saratoga Avenue, apartment 3A."

We came up to a row of six-story tenements on Saratoga and parked in front of 2341. We went up to the third floor and Joe B. knocked on 3A. A sinister looking young black guy answered the door and snarled, "What you want?"

Joe B. hesitated, then asked, "Are you Willie Hyson?"

"Yes I am and who the fuck are you?"

"I'm Detective Barone and this is my partner Detective O'Neil. I got a beef on you and you have to come down to the station house so we can straighten it out."

Willie opened the door a little more so we could see his six friends sitting around the living room. "I ain't going nowhere with you honky motherfuckers."

Joe B. responded, "Now look, this is not a big deal but we need to clear it up. So what do you say, come with us and you'll be back here in an hour?"

"You fucking deaf or something? I ain't going anywhere you lily white motherfuckers."

Then his friends piped up, "Yeah he ain't going nowhere. Now get the fuck out of here."

I was thinking about reaching for my gun when Joe B. turned to me and said, "Let's go, Jim."

"What?"

"This is my case and I say we go."

I got sick inside but it wasn't my case. When we got to the car I threw the keys at Joe B. "Here drive back to the squad and don't ever ask me to go out with you again," I told him.

"What are you going to do?"

I pointed across the street and said, "See that pay phone? I hope it works because I'm calling the squad and have my partners come down here. That scumbag Willie is coming in one way or another and if any of his friends try to interfere I'll shoot them."

The phone worked and Fred Lambert and Ed Bailey were in. When I told them what had happened they fumed, "What the fuck, we'll be right there. No way the street ever gets wind that a 73rd Squad detective walked away from a fight."

No more than three minutes passed before my partners

were leaping from their car to my side. They were breathing fire and carrying baseball bats. Fred pursed his lips and said, "Lead the way my man."

I knocked on the now familiar 3A, and Willie answered the door. "Remember me, Willie? Turn around and put your hands behind your back or die."

He saw my two black partners and the baseball bats and he turned around. His loudmouth friends were quiet as I cuffed him. I started to leave with my prisoner when Fred stopped me. "Didn't you tell me that Willie's piece of shit friends said you weren't taking him anywhere and told you to get the fuck out of here?"

"Among other things," I answered.

In an instant Fred and Eddie were on the six, putting wood to bone. The six were running all around the apartment trying to elude the swinging bats, without much success. When it was over, there were six wise-asses lying on the floor moaning and writhing in pain. Eddie looked down and left them with this, "You ever disrespect a detective from the 73rd Squad again and we'll be back and finish the job. And no more Mr. Nice Guy. Oh, and if you want to continue breathing Brownsville air you won't even think of putting in a complaint. Remember we own these streets and you walk them because we choose to let you."

Willie didn't say a word, didn't even look at us. We turned him over to Joe B. for processing.

CHAPTER TWELVE

A&P Homicide

Twice a month the A&P on Ralph Avenue in the Brownsville section of Brooklyn would gladly cash my paycheck because it meant less cash on hand in case of a robbery. The only white employee was Jimmy Dunlop, the manager, who commuted from New Jersey. He was short, a little on the heavy side, thirty-two years old, had a wife and two kids, and was my friend.

I'd cash my check, Jimmy would grab two six-packs, get the meat and produce managers, and we'd go in the back room to kill some beers while bullshiting about all manner of things. We did this for about eight months until June 24, 1970, when Jimmy was murdered in a stickup that netted the criminals a whopping $65. Those bastards.

I wasn't catching when the case came in but I grabbed it anyway. I went off the chart, which meant I wouldn't catch any other cases, my current cases would go to my partners, and I would have no days off until the case was solved. This was personal and I wanted to nail the sons of bitches who did it.

I got a call from an ex-NYC detective who had become head of security for the New York metropolitan area A&Ps. He knew I caught the case of the robbery-homicide at the Ralph Avenue store and wanted to offer me money that I could use on the street to buy information. Back then the city's fiscal policy was tighter than an amoeba's asshole so we resorted to paying our informants with small amounts of heroin siphoned off from drug busts. The rumor was that each borough commander was given $1000 a month to be used in his precincts for this purpose. A borough commander was responsible for eight to ten precincts. Around $100 a month for each precinct doesn't seem like much today but in 1970 it was a considerable sum. We had long before learned the futility of trying to get some of that money. The other rumor floating around was that the borough commanders were pocketing $1000 a month.

I got nothing from the witnesses and employees so I went to the well for information. This is where hanging out in the local bars paid off. I spread some of the A&P money around and got it from one of my informants that a guy named "T" had pulled the A&P job. I checked the alias and nickname card files and came up with nothing. Either my informant was wrong or this "T" wasn't local. Most of the time my informants were right on, but this time it didn't look good.

Then the case hit the papers and it became a political hot potato. I was told I would be getting some help from Joe Joy, a detective who had worked a lot of homicides. After seventy-two hours your chances of solving a homicide dropped drastically and all of today's technical advances haven't changed that. The clock was ticking, our CIs were in overdrive and we followed up every lead with no success. After weeks of dead ends we had nothing else left but to look for similar crimes where an arrest had been made and try to get the offender to play "let's make a deal"; information for reduction of sentence. Being that criminals are creatures of habit, someone arrested for a similar offense might have secondhand or even firsthand information about the crime you were investigating.

Another month passed, and just when the brass was beginning to think "cold case," we got a break. Bobby Wing was a detective in the 73rd like me, but on a different team. He had recently transferred in from the 5th Precinct in Chinatown and knew about my committed involvement in the A&P homicide. He approached me and said, "Jim, I got something you might be interested in."

"What do you have?"

"I just nailed a guy for a jewelry store heist over on Pitkin Avenue. This putz just got out of Sing Sing eighteen days ago. Another successful rehabilitation by the Department of Corrections."

"I'm interested, Bobby. Where is he now?"

"He's in the Brooklyn House of D. His name is Lawrence MacIntyre."

Within the hour Joe Joy and I were at the Brooklyn House of Detention. We had sent up a permission slip and were waiting for Lawrence MacIntyre to sign it, which would give us authorization to interview him. If he refused, we wouldn't be able to talk to him, but that was unlikely. He figured we were looking for something from him and it might be let's make a deal time, so he signed. The word came down that our guy was waiting in an interrogation cell and five minutes later we were sitting across the table from an orange jumpsuited Lawerence MacIntyre..

"Lawrence, I'm Detective O'Neil and this is my partner Detective Joy."

"What's this about, Detectives?"

I looked him in the eye, "It's about keeping a dumb fuck out of going back to Sing Sing."

He got my drift and asked, "How can I help you?"

"Do you know anybody doing supermarket stickups?"

"Oh shit, umm . . . I do but uh . . . I really hate to tell you. When I got out my cousin took me in, fed me, gave me some of his clothes, and a few dollars. I feel bad about fingering him but I did five years in Sing Sing and I had to fight for my life every day. I can't go back there."

"If your cousin turns out to be one of the guys we're looking for I'll see to it you stay out of Sing Sing for this latest beef of yours. Okay, I'm listening."

"My cousin's name is Van MacIntyre and he's been

driving a gypsy cab since he got paroled out of Greenhaven. He told me he waited outside this supermarket with the cab running while the two guys with him went inside and stuck up the place. He heard a couple of shots and they came running out, jumped in the cab, and said something about having shot the manager."

"When did this happen?"

"While I was still in jail."

"Be more specific."

"About two months ago, I think."

Now I was getting excited but I didn't show it. "Where did this happen?"

"It was a Key Food on Ralph Avenue."

"A Key Food, are you sure?"

"I think, maybe."

"Could it have been an A&P?"

"Yes it was, it was, I'm sure, A&P—yes, Detective."

My asshole puckered. "Lawrence, if this helps us we'll be in touch."

Lawrence was escorted back to his cell and Joe and I headed over to a special unit of the state parole on Forty-first Street in Manhattan that worked exclusively with law enforcement personnel. They were a hardworking, dedicated group of professionals who would bend over backward to help you with a case. I had dealt with them on many occasions and had never been disappointed. When we got there we met with Gloria Solomon, whom I had worked with before. She pulled Van MacIntyre's file and contacted his parole officer, who told her that our guy was due to check in the next afternoon. She gave him my number and he assured her that when Van MacIntyre reported in he would be detained and I would be notified. Joe and I thanked her and called it a day.

I got in the squad early the next day and I was just getting to my desk when the phone rang. I picked up on the third ring and answered, "This is Detective O'Neil, 73rd Squad."

"Detective this is P.O. Walsh. Gloria Solomon said you wanted to talk to one Van MacIntyre."

"Yes I do."

"He's here now and I'm holding him for you. By the way I searched him and found a set of car keys on his person and a ticket stub from a parking garage two blocks away."

That was good news because a parolee isn't allowed to drive without the express permission of his P.O. Walsh wouldn't have told me about it unless I could use it to make a deal. Most likely he had MacIntyre in his office cuffed to a chair and wanted him to hear that he might get violated.

"I'm thinking of violating his parole but I'll wait until you get here, Detective."

"Good, I'll be there in half an hour—and thanks."

I figured right about now MacIntyre was hoping for let's make a deal. He had no idea we made him for the A&P job. Probably thought he could give up somebody on another case and not get violated. I picked up the scumbag and brought him back to the squad. Joe Joy had just gotten in and we took MacIntyre into the interrogation room, Joe listened and I talked. Sometimes good cop, silent cop worked better than good cop, bad cop.

"Van, you're looking at some real heavy time."

"For what? Driving without my P.O.'s permission?"

"That's the least of you're problems. We know you were involved in the A&P homicide a couple of months back on June 24. We got you nailed as the driver of the getaway car."

"Getaway car? Oh no, you got it wrong, I was driving a gypsy cab and these two guys waved me down. I picked them up and they asked me to stop at this supermarket ..."

"What supermarket and where?"

"The A&P on Ralph Avenue. So I waited about five minutes and I heard three shots and out came these two guys. They jumped into my cab and told me to step on it. When I asked them about the shots they told me to mind my own fucking business unless I wanted to get shot like the manager."

"Damn, I never saw anyone as anxious as you, Van, to do long hard time."

"Not me, I don't . . . I can't. What do you want from me?"

"I want you to stop pulling my chain," I told him. "You expect me to believe that you picked up two strangers, drove them to the A&P, waited outside while they robbed the place, and then after hearing shots waited for them to get back into your cab. Do I have "Fucking Idiot" tattooed on my forehead?"

"No. Um . . . okay, maybe they weren't exactly strangers. They were doing time at Greenhaven last year when I was there and I would see them, but I didn't hang out with them."

"Names, Van, give me names."

"Sherman Grant who goes by the street name of 'Tank' and the other guy is Ernie. I don't know his last name. I swear that's all I know."

I glanced at Joe, who remained silent but managed a smile as he stared unblinkingly at MacIntyre. My partner stayed with him while I called Gloria Solomon. She answered, "P.O. Solomon here."

"Gloria, it's Jim. I need an address on a Sherman Grant, an alumni of Greenhaven."

"I'll look right now. You want to hold on?"

"Yeah, thanks."

It took her all of five minutes to find Tank's address, "Got it," she said. "I show him staying with his girlfriend at 1502 Schenectady Street, apartment 3C."

"Can you meet me and Joe at the corner of Schenectady and Atlantic, say in an hour?"

"What, Jim?" she asked. "No time for a warrant?"

I asked Gloria to go with us because she could, without a warrant, search a parolee's person or residence at any time, for any reason, as a condition of parole. "Gloria, I want this guy bad and fast. It's personal."

"Okay, see you in an hour. By the way, I looked through his file and this guy's a nasty piece of work. Mind if I bring Bill Kramer with me?"

"Not at all, Bill's a good man. Oh, there's one other thing. I'm looking for a parolee with a first name of Ernie who was at Greenhaven the same time as Sherman Grant."

"That's going to take time, maybe a couple of days. There's over three thousand guys currently out on parole from Greenhaven. I'll get on it first thing tomorrow morning."

We left MacIntyre cuffed to the table and told him if his information was good we would try to get him a reduced sentence. Joe grabbed a carbine with a thirty-round banana clip and I reached for my friend and constant companion, the Garcia Rossi Coachman, a short double-barrel twelve-gauge magnum shotgun. With its no nonsense wood stock it felt more at home in the hands of a stagecoach driver than a 1960s New York City detective. An evil looking gun, all business with a double-trigger pull and two large medieval style hammers.

We met Gloria and Bill around the corner from Tank's place and went up to apartment 3C. Gloria knocked on the door and Tank's girlfriend let us in, and we immediately observed a big, well-muscled, light skinned male sitting on the couch. Gloria verified it was Sherman Grant, told him he was being violated and that he was under arrest. He got up and menacingly started toward her until we raised our weapons. That seemed to turn him docile. Joe Mirandized him, back-cuffed him, and threw him in our car.

Gloria and Bill headed back to their office and we brought Tank into the station house. While I was processing him in the one twenty-four room Joe went up to the squad and arranged for the witnesses to come down for a lineup. He also closed the door to the interrogation room. We didn't want Tank to know who gave him up, at least not yet.

All three witnesses had picked him as the shooter.

That was good, but if all you had was the testimony of a co-conspirator and three eyewitnesses the case could still go south, and I wanted to sew this fuck up tighter than a crab's ass. What I was looking for was a spontaneous statement. My partner opened the door to the interrogation room where we had stashed MacIntyre. I had back-cuffed Tank and was informing him that he was picked out of the lineup. I had him by the arm and as I brought him past the interrogation room I felt the muscle in his arm tighten. Now he knew it was Van MacIntyre who had dropped the dime on him.

I brought him into an office, sat him down, and informed him he was under arrest for the recent A&P homicide of June 24. He started running off at the mouth, "If that fuck Van said he had nothing to do with the robbery and that he was only driving the cab he's full of shit. He was in on it from the beginning."

"Will you testify to that?"

"Hell yes."

"What about this Ernie, you willing to testify against him too?"

"Look, Detective, Van gave me up and you got me and I'll do everything to see that he goes down, but I'm no rat and you get nothing more from me."

I pushed a pad and pen over to him and said, "Okay, write down whatever you know about Van's part in the robbery and your involvement as well."

When he finished I read his statement and I noticed there was nothing in it about him shooting the manager. Either he wasn't going to cop to the murder or his buddy Ernie was the one who killed Jimmy Dunlop. I had one more question. "Sherman, did you ever go by the street name of 'T'?"

"Mostly Tank cause I'm big and in the Army there's a Sherman Tank, get it?"

"Never mind the history lesson. What about T?"

"Yeah sometimes, but like I said, mostly Tank."

My informant was right after all and Tank sometimes known as T was going away for a long time. Now I had three eyeball witnesses, a spontaneous statement, and a confession. Two assholes down, and one to go.

It was three days before Gloria was able to go through all the files. She found seven Ernies on parole from Greenhaven but only one, Ernie Hyacinth, was local. I was sure he was our guy. Joe and I went with Gloria and Bill and gathered up Ernie. The witnesses identified him and we had our third guy.

This was a homicide that should never have been solved. If it wasn't personal—well, who knows. Rest in peace, Jimmy Dunlop.

I was looking forward to testifying but I knew it would be some time before the start of the trial so I went back on the chart and began catching cases again. Every sixth day in our rotation we would do a fifteen-hour night duty from five PM to eight AM. If things were quiet, which was rare, we were allowed to put the bedding on the bunk beds and catch a few hours sleep.

Halfway through my first of these tours since coming back on the chart, things got ominously calm, so we headed for the bunk beds. A ringing phone stopped us. I picked it up and it was a detective from the 105th Squad in Queens. His words shattered the calm. "We have a dead cop here," he told me. "He was on his way in to work when he stopped in a candy store for a pack of cigarettes and walked into the middle of an armed robbery. A gunfight ensued, resulting in his death. The officer was able to kill one of the stickup men, but according to witnesses two perps escaped. The dead perp has been identified as Marcus Benson with Hopkinson Avenue in Brownsville as his last known address. So we figure chances are the other two are from the same area. If we come over can you guys give us a hand with the investigation?"

"Of course," I answered. "We'll start putting out feelers immediately. Get here as soon as you can. . . . By the way, what was the cop's name?"

His answer hit me like a punch in the gut. "Kenneth Nugent."

Son of a bitch, Ken was a friend of mine. I had been to his house in Amityville many times and knew his family. He lived only a few doors away from the house that would be made famous in the movie *The Amityville Horror.*

By the time the detectives from the 105th arrived we had already visited several after-hours clubs and bars in the area. We worked through the night and the entire next day was spent delivering the same message to all the numbers people, everyone engaged in illegal sales of liquor, and every after-hours social club in the precinct: "We have a dead cop and there are two perps on the run. If we don't have both of them in custody within forty-eight hours all business in the area comes to a screeching halt."

Information started coming and a phone call to Fred Lambert put us on to the basement of a tenement on Bergen Street, where the gun used to kill Nugent was recovered. More calls, and we had the names of the two escaped stickup men. The word went out on the street via the Brownsville grapevine: "Turn yourself in or die." One of them surrendered and we got word that the remaining one was holed up in an apartment somewhere on Bergen Street. Fred Lambert walked up and down the middle of Bergen Street shouting, "Come down and give yourself up in front of witnesses and you're safe. If we have to come up and get you, you're a dead motherfucker."

It worked and the perp, surrounded by family members, walked out of one of the buildings and gave himself up. We turned both scumbags over to the detectives from Queens to be processed and then after forty straight hours of work we headed over to the Highway Inn for a well-deserved taste.

A few months later there was a picture in the New York *Daily News* of the detectives from the 105th Squad at a testimonial dinner. The Queens County Chamber of Commerce was presenting them with plaques commemorating their brilliant work in apprehending the killers of Kenneth Nugent.

Neither my partners nor I were looking for any recognition for catching the killers of a brother officer, but the chutzpah of those detectives from Queens accepting accolades that were rightfully ours really pissed us off.

Things got back to their normal pace and what seemed like an eternity passed before I got a call about the A&P homicide case. It was an invitation to go to the office of Assistant District Attorney Kline, a short, soft-spoken, butterball of a man.   Looks can be deceiving but, unfortunately, this time they weren't. I knew the case was in trouble when this fucking idiot said he wouldn't put in the spontaneous statement and the confession I had lawfully obtained from Sherman Grant. I really got worried when Kline told me the defense attorney was Al Brackley and he was representing all three perps as co-defendants. I had been on the witness stand before when Al Brackley was the defense attorney and he was the best I'd ever seen. Hell, the first murder case I testified in, he was the attorney for the defense and during cross-examination he tore me a new asshole. I liked him ever since then and we had become friendly adversaries.

Two more months passed before the trial started. I kept up with the proceedings and made it my business to be there for the verdict. Hung jury, ten to two for acquittal; un-fucking-believable. During the second trial Kline had me on the witness stand, he asked, "Detective O'Neil, did there come a time when you came to the residence of one Sherman Grant?"

"Yes."

"What day was that?"

"I believe it was a Tuesday?'

"You believe?"

"It was a Tuesday."

"Who was with you?"

I wondered what this idiot was doing. None of the

defendants had testified in their own defense and unless they did he couldn't mention their prior criminal record. If I said I had two parole officers with me that would indicate to the jury that the defendant had a criminal record.

"Detective Joe Joy."

"Who else?"

I hesitated.

"Did you hear the question, Detective?"

"Yes, I heard the question. Okay . . . okay, P.O.s Gloria Solomon and Bill Kramer."

Al Brackley jumped out of his chair like he had springs on his ass, calling for a mistrial. The judge granted it in a New York second. I was livid. I went right up to the D.A.'s office on the third floor and demanded to see him. Thirty seconds later I was in his office screaming about what a fucking idiot Kline was.

"Detective, take it easy."

"Take it easy . . . take it easy, me and my partner spent three months busting our asses, not a single day off. This should have been an easy win. I don't care if you lock me up, I refuse to go to trial a third time with Kline."

"I understand your frustration, Detective. Forget about Kline, I'll put Benny Schmeer on it. He's my best ADA and he's got a very impressive conviction rate."

I thanked him and then apologized for screaming at him. Two months later all three were convicted. I went back for the sentencing and was pleased to hear that Sherman Grant and Ernie Hyacinth each got twenty-five years to life. Because of his cooperation Van MacIntyre was given fifteen years and promised he wouldn't do time in the same prison as his co-defendants.

Because of my deep personal involvement in this case the court officers honored my request and allowed me the privilege of locking each of the convicts in a holding cell to await transport to an upstate prison. Sherman Grant went quietly but when I escorted Ernie Hyacinth in the cell he turned to me and said, "You fucking dog, I swear when I get out I'll find you wherever you are. I'll find you and kill you. I don't care how long it takes, I swear I'll get you."

"I just got two things to say to you. First, you're going away for twenty-five years and I'm going home and have a nice steak dinner and a big glass of twelve-year-old scotch. Second, I hope you do find me because the next time I see you I'll turn your fucking lights out and do the job right."

Ernie Hyacinth went away to Greenhaven and because of a bureaucratic fuck-up Van MacIntyre caught a bad break and also ended up in Greenhaven. The two of them met in the exercise yard where Hyacinth promptly proceeded to plant a pipe down the middle of MacIntyre's head—one less scumbag on the planet.

During the 2004 hunting season, I was in a bar called Trinca's in upstate Roscoe, New York. I saw two familiar faces and went up to George Pappas and his wife, Sharon. George was an upstate correction officer and the conversation got around to how Ernie had threatened me. I said to George, "Let me throw a name at you and see if you ever heard of him."

"Go ahead throw it out there."

"Ernie Hyacinth."

George laughed. "You don't have to worry about him anymore," he said. "He died in prison last year, of natural causes. A vicious son of a bitch to the end." Hyacinth had served thirty-three years.

We drank to his death. I have no idea what happened to Sherman Grant.

As an extension of the initial investigation we uncovered thirteen more criminals acting as interchangeable players on a team of supermarket stickup men. Every one of their trials went without a hitch and all thirteen of them were judiciously dispatched to Greenhaven. Case closed.

CHAPTER THIRTEEN

A Kinder, Gentler Police Force

While crime was soaring and homicides were increasing at an alarming rate Police Commissioner Patrick Murphy was crowned Pope of New York's finest. Instead of being a shot in the arm to a beleaguered police force, in my opinion he turned out to be a kick in the ass to the men and women in blue. I had never heard of him before he became police commissioner, appearing on the scene from out of nowhere. In actuality, Mayor John Lindsay appointed him to clean up the department on the coattails of a newly formed five-member civilian panel looking into police corruption called the Knapp Commission, aka the "Reign of Terror."

Murphy's asinine actions seemed to be geared toward projecting us as a kinder and gentler police department. I never knew his background but based on his desire to change us from an enforcement mode to a service mode I can't believe he ever worked as a street cop in a busy precinct. Under his watch the "police force" became the "police service." Divisions, usually made up of several precincts, were renamed "districts." Divisions sounded too military for the new "police service," I guess. The color of the RMP cars went from dark green and white to powder blue and white. The navy blue uniform shirt became the same powder blue as the RMPs. I heard the same comment over and over from uniformed cops: "Great, now I wear a pussy-colored shirt and ride in a pussy-colored car. I suppose that's going to make the next dirtbag I lock up get a warm fuzzy feeling about me."

Detective squads were renamed "Precinct Investigative Units" (PIUs) and another military sounding term bit the dust. It was rumored that Murphy disliked detectives, which branded him in my eyes as an overstuffed bag of shit. Similar idiotic changes went on ad nauseam. His suggestion that cops not take any police action unless directed to do so over the police radio or by a supervisor was a prime example of how little he understood about what the guys and gals in blue were up against. They were in the neighborhood, both uniformed and plainclothes, working like hell to control some of the meanest streets in the Big Apple. While this constant battle raged the commissioner sat clueless in an office at the top of police headquarters.

He wanted to make us appear softer, and turn us into a beloved police service. But the softer we looked the harder the job became and under Murphy's watch crime flourished. I didn't want any of the badasses to love me. These animals savaged their fellow citizens and all I wanted from them was fear. A lot of well-placed fear saved the lives of both good citizens and cops. At no time was the installation of fear more important than when a crime was committed against a cop. If the bad guys think they can harm a police officer and merely be arrested and afforded all the civility of our judicial system then it will be open season on cops. And in the final analysis that means open season on the good citizens.

Murphy was able to change the color of our shirts and RMPs but not the color of our resolve. Nothing illustrates this better than an incident involving a black uniformed cop from the 73rd Precinct. His name was Bobby Johnson and at two AM he was off duty in civilian clothes when he got jumped by three black males who had just exited a social club on Sutter Avenue. He identified himself as a cop from the 73rd but they still kicked the shit out of him and managed to get his off-duty gun.

He made his way to the squad to report the incident. When Bobby told us the social club was a free standing building on Sutter Avenue we knew it was the one owned by Willie "Lump Lump" Charles, a real badass who had given us trouble in the past. Bobby's description pegged one of his assailants as Lump Lump. We knew he lived on Saratoga Avenue but didn't have the exact address, so while Bobby gave his statement to Eddie Schneider, Fred Lambert and I went and talked to our contacts. Brownsville never slept and at three in the morning many of our contacts were out and about. In less than fifteen minutes we were on our way back to the squad with Lump Lump's address. Eddie Schneider brought Bobby Johnson along to ID the perps, Fred joined Eddie, I grabbed my shotgun, and we took off in one car with four uniformed cops following in a second car as backup.

We hit the apartment and found five people there; three of them were our perps. While my partners were cuffing the three perps I spotted a guy I knew and took him into another room to question him. After a few minutes I had finished and went back into the other room, only to discover that everyone had left. My partners thought I had gone back with the uniforms and the uniforms figured I was with my partners.

In 1970 walkie-talkies were being introduced, but only on a limited basis. The one for our squad was probably back at the office, and you had a better chance of being struck by lightning in a cave than you did of finding a working pay phone in Brownsville. It was 4 AM by this time and I was the only white face around, but with no ride and no way to communicate with my partners I began walking the ten blocks back to the squad. Thank God I had my double-barrel friend with me. I concealed it as best as I could so that on the off chance a gypsy cab came by he wouldn't be afraid of picking me up.

I started walking up Saratoga Avenue and had gone about three hundred feet before these two black guys standing on a stoop spotted me. Even though they were across the street

I could see the look of surprise on their face. They did a double take and said something to each other, probably expressing delight at their newly-found good fortune. I had just become a mugging looking for a place to happen. They began walking parallel to me for about a hundred feet, then split up heading in my direction with one coming up in front of me and one behind me. I waited until they were about thirty feet away, then swung the shotgun up, resting the barrel across my raised left arm, and pulled back the hammers. "Come, on," I dared them. "Which one of you motherfuckers wants to die first?"

Their eyes got as big as saucers and it was feet-don't-fail-me-now time, as they took off running down Livonia Avenue. I made it two more blocks before Fred pulled up in a squad car. He had finally figured out that I was left behind. When I told him what happened he laughed all the way back to the squad.

By the time we got back Lump Lump and his two friends had been severely lumped up and bloodied. If they had been alone when we arrested them the beatings would have been dispensed then and there, but with witnesses present it is always better to show a little restraint and wait to get them back to the squad. When I walked into our squad room my partners had made the three scumbags crawl through their own blood to where Bobby Johnson was sitting on a desk. We made them kiss Bobby's feet and then we forced them to clean up their blood.

After throwing them in the cage we headed to Lump Lump's social club, which turned out to be closed. The word was out already and the members were expecting trouble, so they had left the premises. We kicked the door down and looked around for anything flammable. We found a bunch of newspapers, which we rolled up and ignited. Walking around we set several small fires and then went outside and waited to be sure the place went up. About ten minutes passed before the firemen arrived. I explained the situation to them and asked if they could hold off fighting the fire for five or ten minutes to maximize the damage. There was a lot of camaraderie between cops and firemen back then and I had known many of these guys since my TPF days, so I wasn't surprised when they agreed to wait. When they finally extinguished the fire there wasn't much left of the building, and what little there was the firemen intentionally destroyed. The point was made: If you fucked with the bull you got the horns—and swift and ruthless retribution was the order of the day anytime a cop was attacked.

A verbal assault on a cop seldom required a physical response but one night deep into October, with the temperature somewhere between fall and winter, Fred Lambert and I were at one of our favorite eating establishments on Sutter Avenue. The Chicken and Rib Castle was only two blocks from the precinct house and served the best rib sandwiches in the world. We ate there on the arm, but for only two dollars a paying customer would get a small rack of ribs, bones and all, between two slices of bread. The sauce was a little spicy and had the consistency of molasses. Good stuff.

This particular night an obnoxious couple who felt the need to cast aspersions on my racial background interrupted our meal, "Hey you honky motherfucker this is our restaurant. What's a lily-white motherfucker like you doing here? This is soul food and whitey don't belong here."

I was doing a good job of ignoring their remarks but Fred wasn't. He walked up to them and got nose to nose with the guy. "Look, we're detectives in this precinct," he said, "and if I were you I'd shut the fuck up."

"Well you ain't me or you wouldn't be with whitey. It's a free country and I can say whatever I want and there ain't shit you can do about it."

I knew that wouldn't sit well with Fred and I was right. He bent down and took off one of his shoes. Then he smacked the guy over the head with the heel—WHAP.

The woman screamed, "Hey you can't do that. We're going to file a complaint against you."

WHAP, and the woman grabbed her head.

Both of them started screaming about putting in a complaint and Fred said, "So you want to file a complaint? Okay, I'll go with you. Start walking."

Fred handed me the keys to the car and asked me to drive alongside as he walked them to the precinct house. Every fifteen or twenty seconds Fred would smack the both of them in the head—WHAP, WHAP. The offending couple stopped complaining as they picked up the pace, now very much in a hurry to reach the safety of the precinct house. I was laughing my ass off, tears were running down my cheeks, and my stomach was hurting, but I couldn't stop laughing. I parked the car by the precinct-house steps and followed the three of them inside. The couple headed for the desk, where they promptly asked to speak to the officer in charge. Lieutenant Dolsey, a big, red-faced Irishman, was summoned and after introducing himself he asked, "What seems to be the problem?"

The couple both started complaining about police brutality—Fred used his shoe again, WHAP, WHAP. They shut up.

Fred turned to the lieutenant and said, "I'm arresting these two for disorderly conduct."

"Good job, Detective."

"Thank you, Lieutenant."

Fred and I walked out into the mild October night smiling like two Cheshire cats.

A month later winter finally gripped its frigid, gloomy fingers around the 73rd. I had just begun an afternoon tour and was at my desk cuddled up to a hot cup of coffee when the squad's police radio spit out a report of shots fired, possible shotgun involved. I was not about to run on this one with my five-shot, snub-nose, .38-caliber peashooter. This was a job for the Coachman. Not wanting to let the neighborhood know how I was armed I broke it down into three pieces. Then I stuck the tip of the barrels in my belt, hidden under the left side of my suitcoat jacket. The wooden stock and firing mechanism were similarly concealed on my right side and the wooden handgrip was tucked into the small of my back. A little uncomfortable while riding in the car but I didn't want to give away, to any possible adversaries, the firepower I was packing. Once inside the targeted location I could have it assembled, loaded, and ready for use in seven seconds. I had successfully employed this tactic on numerous occasions, much to the surprise of many potentially violent suspects. The fight always seemed to drain out of them when they found themselves staring down the twin barrels of the meanest looking gun they had ever seen.

Two minutes later Fred Lambert and I were pulling up to a six-story tenement close to the intersection of Rockaway and Livonia. Waiting for us inside on the first floor landing was a woman in her thirties.

"I'm Detective O'Neil and this is my partner Detective Lambert. We got a report of some shots being fired."

She totally ignored me, probably because I was white, and said directly to Fred, "My boyfriend shot out my bedroom window with his goddamn shotgun."

"Anybody get hurt?"

"No."

"Where is he now?'

"He's on the couch watching the TV."

"Which apartment is yours?"

"2B."

"Stay behind us, ma'am."

Fred took out his .38 and I assembled and loaded my shotgun. The door was ajar and we could see into the living room. We entered the apartment and there was the biggest black guy I had ever seen, sitting on a couch watching TV. The first thought I had was that this was the black Mr. Clean. I pressed both barrels of the Coachman against his temple but he never took his eyes off the TV until he heard the sound of a hammer being pulled back. Now that I had his attention I asked him, "What's your name?"

"Tommy."

"Tommy what?"

"Conlon."

"Tommy, you're under arrest and you're going with us."

"I ain't going nowhere with you, motherfucker."

"Here's how this is gonna play out," I informed him. "You're coming with us one way or another. You can walk out of here like a gentleman and I'll treat you like one or you can be carried out feet first. Your choice, Tommy."

I pulled back the other hammer and he chose, "I'll go, but I want my coat."

I pointed to the coat on a chair next to the couch, "Okay," I said. "Put it on and let's go."

"Not that coat. I want my lucky coat. It's on the bed."

I got suspicious and I started backing into the bedroom, all the time keeping him covered. "You make a move and I'll splatter your brains all over this apartment."

Fred never took his eyes off him either. I picked up the coat and underneath it laying on the bed was a loaded sawed-off shotgun. I removed the shells, put them in my pocket, back-cuffed Mr. Clean, and brought him and his shotgun into the squad room. We threw his gun into the evidence locker and him into the cage. I did all the paperwork and when it came time to fingerprint him I figured he might give us a hard time so I had seven of us ready and armed with baseball bats. At first he refused to cooperate but after we lumped him up a little he let us print him. The girlfriend pressed charges at his arraignment and later refused to come to any of his hearings. Two adjournments later and the charges were dropped. Since I couldn't put him and the shotgun together in the same room, the weapons possession charge wouldn't stick and Tommy was out on the street a month after we arrested him.

Two weeks after Tommy Conlon was released I got a call from Bernie Warren, a Housing Authority cop who was white, short, and wiry, with the disposition of a junkyard dog. Bernie was a very active, good, hard-working cop. He brought a lot of bad guys for us to fingerprint and we always tried to get them processed quickly for him. Back then all fingerprinting was done by detectives. Nobody liked doing it since half the time the people you were fingerprinting smelled like they had been dipped in shit. Sometimes we'd spend three hours at a time fingerprinting. We kept a bucket of ice, a pitcher of water, and a bottle of scotch on the fingerprint board.

After we dispensed with pleasantries, Bernie said, "I called because the word on the street is that Tommy Conlon is saying he's going to kill you. Just thought you might want to know."

This had to be dealt with immediately. I got my three partners, they got their weapons of choice, and I grabbed my shotgun. We drove past the tenement where I had first arrested Tommy and there he was standing in the doorway. We drove around the corner and snuck in the rear entrance of his building. He was still standing in the doorway with his back to us as we snuck up on him and I placed both barrels against the back of his head. He froze when he heard the now familiar sound of two hammers being pulled back. His whole body tensed up and I cautioned him, "Don't move or I'll blow your fucking head off."

This was different than the last time I held a gun on him. No witnesses this time—just him and us—and he had every right to think I might pull the triggers.

"You know who this is, Conlon?"

"Detective O'Neil?"

"Good guess. I heard you're telling people that you're going to kill me. If I hear that again I'll be back and I'll splatter your fucking brains all over the street. You got that?"

"Yeah."

"Listen, Tommy, we don't have to be enemies, we could be friends. Take a ride with us to the office and we can talk about it over a bottle of scotch."

He agreed and we ended up sipping scotch at my desk and talking. "Here's the deal," I told him. "I'm always looking for someone to give me information. You become my informant and in return I'll help you make a good living. You can start writing the digit and I'll make sure nobody bothers you."

"I would like that."

"Good, now you can start making plenty of money, just don't get involved with anything else illegal."

"You mean like don't do no stickups and stuff?"

"Yup, exactly. I guarantee because of your size, you could do a stickup with fifteen other guys and the only one the witnesses would remember is you. No way you don't get picked out of a lineup."

I didn't get as much information from Tommy as I had hoped but he did help me with several cases. Whenever he had something he would just walk into the station house. He didn't care who saw him. He'd sit at my desk, I would break out the scotch, we'd have a taste and he would pass on whatever information he had. This lasted for about six months until I got a call from a detective at the 79th Precinct in Bedford Stuyvesant.

"Detective O'Neil, this is Detective Rydell. The victim in a liquor store stickup picked Tommy Conlon out of the photo files and when I checked his record I noticed you had arrested him once. I was wondering if you could bring him in and I'll come over to you and pick him up."

"Sure, I'll call you when I have him in custody." I remember thinking to myself that this guy doesn't realize what he's asking me to do. But the way I looked at it Tommy was my CI and therefore my responsibility.

My partners were out of the squad so I grabbed Artie Simioli and Pete "The Greek" Panos. Artie was five-eight and slim but he had balls the size of a pregnant Mack Truck and Pete was a wiry five-ten. I filled them in on what we were going up against on the ride over to the six-story tenement Tommy called home. When we got there he was sitting on the top step of the stoop. As soon as Tommy saw us he stood up and I knew this was not going to be easy.

"Tommy I got a beef on you—you gotta come in with us so we can straighten it out."

Tommy gave us the arm. "Straighten this out motherfuckers. I ain't going nowhere."

Artie turned to me and said, "You got a jack on you?"

"Yes I do."

"Let me borrow it."

I gave it to him without thinking. Personally I never would have thought of using a blackjack on Mr. Clean. Artie walked up the steps and standing next to Tommy looked up—way up—and said, "You don't tell us you ain't going with us."

Artie jumped up and hit him over the head so hard that the leather split and the lead inside broke into three pieces. Tommy shook it off, rubbed his forehead, and screwed his face into a grimace. I thought I saw steam come out of his ears.

"Oh shit, now you did it Artie," I yelled up at him. "You really fucking pissed him off."

He started throwing us around as we tried to cuff him. Some citizen must have dropped a dime because, within minutes, fifteen more cops showed up. He fought us up six flights of stairs and onto the roof before we were finally able to cuff him. Every one of us looked like we had been in a fight. Two uniform cops grabbed Tommy by the ankles and dragged him down the stairs; six flights and his head bounced off every single step. Most men would have died but he never even lost consciousness. He had earned the pain and we had saved face. Tommy was sentenced to fifteen years at Attica and I never saw him again. I crossed swords with a lot of badasses on this job but Tommy Conlon was the toughest piece of work I ever ran into.

CHAPTER FOURTEEN

Surprised at the 73rd

Still feeling the effects of the Tommy Conlon encounter I was looking forward to a nice quiet Sunday morning tour with my partners. I was the first one up, catching cases that came in between eight and ten; hardly anything happened that early on a Sunday morning, even in Brownsville. I knew the 73rd could mess with you but I never expected to catch three homicides in two hours on an early Sunday morning.

At 8:30 I caught a white male who met his demise in an Italian social club on Rockaway Parkway. He had been run through the chest with a Civil War saber buried up to its hilt with the blade protruding about two feet out of his back.

Around 9:15 a report came in of a black female DOA over on Herzl Street with multiple gunshot wounds to the torso, followed twenty minutes later by the discovery of a large black male around the corner on Amboy Street with three gunshot wounds to the body. At this point I was trying to decide which case to concentrate on first. I remember thinking, "It's times like these I should have listened to my father and become a fireman." Eddie Schneider stayed at the social club while my other two partners and I headed to the two new homicides.

By the end of our tour we had solved all three cases. Turned out that the white victim was a gambler named Ginsberg, who made the fatal error of holding out some money on a member of the social club. By early afternoon the guy who skewered Ginsberg was in custody.

The other two homicides were ground balls. That's cop lingo for any case that's solved with little or no investigation. A guy named Odom was the shooter. Word had reached him that the female victim, his main squeeze, was screwing the male victim. Apparently this pissed off Odom to the point where felt the need to kill the both of them. Hell of a price to pay for a piece of ass.

Two perps in custody and still enough time left for a quick visit to the Highway Inn before having to take the scumbags to night court.

Throughout my time at the 73rd, my partners and I kicked down a lot of doors together and put a ton of bad guys away. We were real ghetto cops and amazing as it was during our time at the 73rd not one of us ever got shot. Oh, we were shot at plenty of times, but never hit.

Good thing, since we never wore our bulletproof vests. They were so cumbersome, with numerous steel plates encased in a heavy canvas-like material. Shit, they covered you from your shoulders to a few inches above your crotch and tipped the scales at over sixty pounds. Each vest came with a four-sided, eight-pound, helmet-like hat that completely encased your head. There were two slits in the vicinity of your eyes that you could look through. The damn thing looked like something right out of the Middle Ages. The standing joke was that if we wore them we wouldn't need to shoot any perps—they would be laughing so hard they wouldn't be able to resist arrest.

The one time we almost used them was on an FBI operation that my partners and I rolled into when we answered a "shots fired" call. The feds had established a perimeter around a suspected bank robber's apartment and then announced, "This is the FBI, you are surrounded, come out with your hands up."

The robber was able to barricade himself in the bedroom and when the feds finally did break in one of their agents walked to the back of the house, where the suspect trapped him in an adjoining room. Shots had been exchanged between the two and when we got there the FBI was in a holding pattern waiting for their bulletproof vests. The agent in charge approached me as we got to the scene and said, "I'm Agent Carson, this is an FBI operation."

"I'm Detective O'Neil. What's the situation?"

"We have an agent inside and the situation is well in hand."

"What about the "shots fired" call we came on?"

"Our agent traded several shots with the suspect."

"Agent Carson, is your man trapped in that apartment?"

"Technically I'd have to say no."

"I'll take that as a yes."

"We're waiting for bulletproof vests from our Manhattan office. As soon as they arrive we'll apprehend the suspect."

"If you want you can borrow ours. I can have them here in a few minutes."

"No thanks, Detective, we'll wait for our vests."

"What about getting your man out of danger? I can have emergency service come and help extricate him."

"No, the FBI takes care of its own and this is our operation."

The truth of the matter was Agent Carson wouldn't make a move without clearing it with his superiors and he didn't want them to think he needed anything from the NYPD. He wasn't about to call his office and I knew how this was going to go down. As soon as their vests arrived they would storm the suspect and kill him.

"You can wait here for your vests but we're going to try and get the suspect to surrender."

"Look, Detective, we're running this show and I'm telling you to back off."

"I can't do that. We got a "shots fired" call and that's NYPD business."

I had just turned to go back to my partners when I heard a voice off to my left, saying, "Detective O'Neil, it's me Ziggy."

A short, skinny black man in his late twenties was motioning to me. I had known him for about two months, ever since he got out of Attica after doing a nickel for armed robbery. Five years is a long time in any prison but in Attica it can seem much longer.

"You know anything about this?" I asked.

"That's my cousin in there."

"Will he listen to you, Ziggy?"

"Maybe."

"Wanna try and talk him out?"

"Yeah."

We joined my partners, and I apprised them of the situation. Ziggy would get a shot at talking his cousin out. I turned back to Ziggy and said, "Try and get your cousin to surrender because if he doesn't the FBI is gonna to kill him."

"I'll try."

"What's your cousin's name?"

"Victor."

As my partners explained to the agent in charge what we were going to attempt, I walked Ziggy into the house. When we got right outside the bedroom I shouted, "Victor, it's the police. I have your cousin with me and he wants to talk to you."

"I got lots of cousins."

"It's me, Ziggy. You're in a hell of a mess."

"Tell me something I don't know."

"If you don't surrender right away the FBI is gonna kill you."

"I said tell me something I don't know."

"They want you for bank robbery, that's federal so you won't be going to Attica. You'll probably do an easy six in some federal pen somewhere. Shit them federal pens are like country clubs. Did you know they even give you menus? It's your choice—fed or dead."

"Okay, but I ain't surrendering to no fucking FBI. I'll surrender to the cops."

I piped up, "All right Victor, I'll take you in. No one's going to hurt you, just come out with your hands over your head nice and slow."

We turned him over to the FBI as an FOA, an arrest for other authority. Basically that meant we got credit for the arrest and the feds would process the suspect. A hell of a lot less paperwork for us.

Things remained very busy over the next two months and then the normalcy we had settled into was shattered.

Soft-spoken Jack Abrahms was thirty-two and his partner Bobby Walsh, a real nice guy, was twenty-eight. Just two more uniforms on patrol that hot August night. They had just turned onto Sutter Avenue when Bobby reached for what turned out to be an empty pack of cigarettes, "Damn it. Jack, stop at that Bodega up ahead, I need cigarettes."

"You and them damn cigarettes, they'll be the death of you."

"Nobody lives forever. You want anything?"

"Pick me up a soda."

Bobby got cigarettes, got soda—got killed. He was walking back to the car when this lunatic came up behind him with a bowie knife and slit his throat clean to the bone, almost decapitating him.

His partner came to his aid but Bobby was gone. Bobby, Janet's husband, was gone. Bobby, little Kathleen's father, was gone.

Jack, in a voice calmed by hysterical shock put out the call, "Ten-thirteen officer down 1420 Sutter Avenue send an ambulance."

Fifteen minutes later the lunatic was in cuffs and on his way to the station house to be turned over to us. Homicides were always handled by the detectives—that was proper procedure. The arrest was also proper and this mutt was brought in alive without so much as a fucking scratch. A cop killer should've been beaten while resisting arrest but he wasn't; he should have fallen down a flight of stairs while being pursued but he didn't. I guess the arresting officers never heard the old riddle, "How many cops did it take to throw a six foot, three hundred pound perp down a flight of stairs? None, he slipped."

By all rights he should've been beaten into bad health before he was brought in. Can't remember his name but I remember what he looked like. Black, early twenties, five-ten, 185 pounds. He was very calm as we escorted him to the cage and seemed oblivious to his surroundings. His demeanor never changed, even when we began shoring up the solid wooden door to the squad room with our desks. He remained calm as some of the street cops came running up the stairs screaming, "Let's kill that motherfucker."

And as an angry mob of blue put shoulders to door, his face held that blank expression. Then I heard a familiar voice ordering, "Gentlemen, cease and desist now." It got very quiet on the other side of the door. Chief Michael J. Codd, the newly-appointed borough commander, had just made his presence known. "I just came from the scene and I'm as outraged as you are, but this is going to be done by the book. Anyone not back on the street and on the job in two minutes will be suspended. This is beneath you, go back to work."

Thank God they listened. I was spared having to make the choice of ignoring the law or shooting a fellow officer. No way I would ever have shot a cop over that piece of shit. As more bosses arrived we removed our makeshift barricade and a semblance of normality returned to the squad.

Within an hour it was business as usual and Ed Bailey, Fred Lambert, and I were responding to one of the most gruesome homicides I would ever encounter. A sixty-year-old day laborer had arrived home from work to find his wife partying with several male and female friends. After throwing his wife's friends out he proceeded to beat the shit out of her. Tired from a day's work and from beating his wife, he took a long bath, a very long bath. While he sat in the tub his wife was mixing up a batch of lye in a large pot. She walked into the bathroom and dumped the pot over his head. He never got out of the tub.

When we arrived he was sitting up, the water was bubbling and the skin was peeling off his head, his face, and the top of his shoulders. Meanwhile the widow was sitting in the living room with a glass of wine, quite drunk. She seemed surprisingly content as we arrested her and she remarked, "That's the last time that motherfucker is going to beat on me."

Couldn't argue with that.

Business got usual again when we got back to the squad and a call came in from Brookdale Hospital notifying us that they had a victim with a gunshot wound to the head. Ed Bailey and I fielded the job and five minutes later we were at Brookdale's ER. I went up to the first nurse I saw and asked her, "Where's the guy with a gunshot to the head."

"He's in exam room six, sitting on a gurney."

"Sitting?"

"Yeah, at least he was last time I looked."

My partner and I went in and found him conscious and alert. He had an entrance wound in the middle of his forehead and an exit wound in the back of his head.

Ed looked at me and asked, "How the hell is this guy still alive and so alert with a bullet through his brain?"

"I haven't the foggiest idea. This guy should be dead."

"This has to be something for *Ripley's Believe It or Not.*"

The X rays came back and with further examination by the doctor it was determined the victim was shot with a small-caliber bullet that hit him at an angle. The projectile hadn't penetrated the skull but instead whipped around the head under the skin and exited out the back of his head. The guy didn't even get a headache. Just a couple of stitches front and back and he would be released.

We approached him. "I'm Detective O'Neil and this is Detective Bailey. We'd like to ask you a couple of questions."

"I've got nothing to say. I don't need the cops to take care of my business."

I figured the next time we saw this clown we'd be arresting him for murder, unless we got lucky and he caught up with the shooter in another precinct.

Ed and I decided it was time for a taste at The Highway Inn. Earl Bellow and the patrons there loved our stories about unusual happenings and were going to get a kick out of this one.

From time to time we would get a request for assistance from other precincts. The 67th was in the Flatbush area of Brooklyn and for years had been a quiet bedroom community of mostly middle-class, working families. Peggy grew up there, and it was where she lived in 1965 when I married her. Since then Flatbush was in a slow downward spiral, being transformed from a relatively crime-free area to a dangerous place to live.

It was 3 PM on September 8, 1971, when I received a call from Detective Paddy McCambridge with the 67th Detective Squad. Paddy was investigating a homicide that had occurred at a Bohack Supermarket during the commission of an armed robbery. The regular manager was off and the manager from another store had been covering for him. He had the combination to the safe but, once the robbery was in progress, he had trouble getting it open. The thief got impatient and shot the manager in the head, killing him instantly. The four-man stickup team then fled the premises.

During his ensuing investigation Paddy had lifted nine prints off a cake box found in the cart used by one of the stickup men, who had pretended to be a customer while casing the place. Paddy got a match on the prints and that's what had prompted his call to me. "Jim," he said, "the prints belonged to a Robert 'Snuffy' Smith and after the witnesses picked him out of a photo array I pulled his record. I noticed that you had locked him up for drug possession only two months ago. Do you have any idea where to find him?"

"I'm almost positive he's still living with his girlfriend only three blocks from here. Tell you what, be in my office tomorrow morning at five and we'll hit his crib together."

Paddy showed up with two of his partners and his boss, Lieutenant Paul Short. Eddie Schneider and I grabbed our weapons and after introductions the six of us proceeded to 944 Herkimer Street. Paddy, Eddie, and I went into the vestibule, while Lieutenant Short and two of his men covered the sides and rear of the building. We had kicked the front door down so many times, taking drug busts out of the building, that the local residents had secured two large steel U-brackets to the inside of the reinforced door frame. When a large wooden board was placed in the brackets, the door couldn't be kicked in. We banged on the door for about a minute before we heard a male voice on the other side articulate one word, "Who?"

The door was almost impenetrable but it did have an Achilles' heel, a large mail slot about three feet from the floor. I slid the barrel of my shotgun through the mail slot and informed the smooth-talking son of a bitch on the other side, "Look at the mail slot motherfucker. Try to move away from the door and your balls are going to be part of the rear wall."

"Okay, I'm not moving. Now what?"

"Open the door now or lose your balls."

We heard the board being removed and the door opened. I looked at the gatekeeper and ordered him, "Go back to your apartment and stay there."

We went upstairs and found the door to 2A unlocked. There were several rooms with what appeared to be separate tenants in each room. The front room was home to three children, little more than infants, sleeping on the floor on filthy mattresses with no sheets or blankets. The parents were asleep on another mattress in the far corner of the room. There were roaches everywhere. We found Snuffy and his girlfriend in the back room asleep on a filthy mattress. He was naked and she was only wearing panties. We nudged them with our shotguns and Snuffy froze but his girlfriend made a run for it. As she headed for the door Eddie attempted to tackle her but came up short and ended up only pulling her panties down around her ankles. She still tried to run but got tripped up by her panties and took a hard flop on the unforgiving wood floor. We let them get dressed before we back-cuffed them. We picked up their drug paraphernalia off a small table and took them into the squad.

We threw Snuffy the let's-make-a-deal pitch, low and inside, but he went for it anyway. By 6:30 that morning we were kicking down a door on Atlantic Avenue and perp number two was nabbed trying to get out a second floor window. The third member of the stickup team had been arrested the day before on a minor infraction and was still in the system when two 67th Squad detectives picked him up. The fourth guy, identified as Eugene "The Bird" Twitty, was in the wind and was subsequently tracked to Texas where he was arrested and extradited to New York. Long sentences were handed down to everyone except Snuffy, who only got fifteen years.

The next time we did a drug bust at 944 Herkimer Street I was introduced to something I had never felt before: sheer terror. We got in through the Achilles' heel again and made our way up to a second floor shooting gallery where I encountered the worst addicts I had ever seen. Two heavyset males and an enormously obese female were flying high in apartment 2C. They had open sores with flowing puss on the inside of their arms from their elbows to their wrists, undoubtedly due to the numerous times they had hit themselves with dirty, contaminated needles. Their arms were so swollen, twice the normal size, that we couldn't get cuffs on them. As we led them out of the room I scooped up a set of works that was stashed in a topless Marlboro box on a dresser. I jammed the cigarette box into my left trench coat pocket and I felt a stab of pain in the palm of my hand. I immediately pulled my hand out and there was a dirty hypodermic needle sticking out of it. I almost barfed on my shoes when I realized what possible transmittable diseases might be entering my system. Bullets and bad guys didn't scare me as much as hepatitis; now I was truly frightened.

I dropped off the prisoners at the squad room then made it over to Brookdale Hospital. I told the doctor what had happened and described the condition of the addicts who had used the needle before I stuck myself with it. His eyes widened and his tongue made several slow clicking noises as he shook his head saying, "The only thing I can do for you is give you a massive dose of gamma globulin; one million units. Check your eyes every morning when you shave. Do that for thirty days and if your eyes start to turn yellow get back here right away."

Thirty-one days later, white-eyed and bushy-tailed, I rejoiced in my continued good health and looked forward to the opportunity to experience whatever surprises the 73rd would throw at me. Oh, what a great feeling, to be healthy and a cop in the 73rd .

CHAPTER FIFTEEN

Good-bye 73rd Squad, Hello Dog Day Afternoon

The NYPD's average clearance rate for homicides in 1971 was 70 percent. My partners and I had racked up a 100 percent clearance rate on homicides; we didn't leave a single one unsolved. Several were solved while the bodies were still warm, due in each case to someone dropping a dime on the perp within fifteen minutes of commission of the crime. Time we spent in the neighborhood bars continued to pay off as more and more decent people trusted us enough to volunteer information.

During the five years I was there, the 73rd had changed dramatically. The transformation started in April of 1968 when Martin Luther King was assassinated. During the days between the assassination and the funeral there were three hundred fires in the one square mile that was the 73rd Precinct. Fires everywhere, and for the first time in the history of the FDNY fire trucks were sent out on patrol. When they saw a fire they would stop and fight it. They did that for five days nonstop. The Black Panthers were asking businesses to close on the day of the funeral as a sign of respect. Most complied, but not old man Feldman of Feldman's Lumber over on Hopkinson Avenue. He said he couldn't afford to lose a day's business. He was told close down or get burned down. Martin Luther King was buried and four hours later Feldman's Lumber went to eight alarms. Feldman wasn't a stupid man but that was a stupid thing to do, unless he was heavily insured and wanted to get out of the lumber business in Brownsville.

You could stand on East New York Avenue and see nothing where the once thriving Prospect market had been. You could turn in any direction and within a ten-block radius see only burned out piles of rubble where buildings once stood. Brownsville had come down around my feet and all the king's horses and all the king's men couldn't put Brownsville back together again.

In January of 1972 Commissioner Murphy had precinct detective squads abolished and the 73rd Squad ceased to exist. He instituted specialized squads that covered districts comprised of eight to ten precincts. Detectives all over the city saw this as a possible chance to work in a squad that would interest them.

Eddie Schneider had made sergeant and was back in the bag as a patrol supervisor in Bedford Stuyvesant at the 79th Precinct.

Ed Bailey was transferred to the 13th District Homicide Squad, and Fred Lambert and I were assigned to the 13th District Robbery Squad.

The 13th District, designated Brooklyn North, took in eight precincts covering Brownsville, Bedford-Stuyvesant, and Bushwick. Our offices were the second floor of the old 79th Precinct station house over on Gates and Throop. Carved in the late 1800s, the stone seal resting above the door hinted at the age of the building, announcing to all who entered that this was the 79th Precinct, City of Brooklyn. It was smack in the middle of Bed-Sty, a crime-ridden area to be sure, but thought of as a less malignant extension of Brownsville. Teams were now made up of six detectives, unlike the four-man teams we were accustomed to in the 73rd.

Fred and I were partnered with a former 73rd Squad detective, Cleve Bethea. Cleve was six-two, 270 pounds, part black, part American Indian, and all balls. Both Fred and I had done a lot of work with him in the 73rd and we liked him and respected him. Cleve was nicknamed "Deer Foot," for the animal appendage he had ferreted away in his locker and his inventive way of using it to solicit information from a reluctant suspect. The three of us couldn't have been closer if we had been brothers, and we still keep in touch to this day.

The fourth man in our team was a second-grade detective named Bill Herrmann, a big strapping guy of German descent who had plenty of experience and street smarts. He was a welcome addition, adding muscle and savvy to the group.

The fifth member was an average-sized black man with a quiet demeanor named Ralph Anderson. He melded quickly with the team and became a pleasure to work with.

The sixth member, who we incorrectly thought would complete the team, was another 73rd alumnus: first-grade Detective Don Shea, a lucky Irishman, whose main claim to fame was that he was one of two rookie cops who in 1952 had captured Willie Sutton, the notorious bank robber. We were designated "Team C." Dave Greenberg was added, bringing our six-man team up to seven. While in uniform, Greenberg, along with his partner Bobby Hantz, had gained some notoriety for a lot of spectacular drug arrests in Bed-Stuy. Both were rewarded with promotions to third-grade detectives. A book called *The Super Cops* and a subsequent Hollywood movie of the same name featured this very flamboyant pair. They were known on the street as "Batman and Robin." Greenberg was Batman, which prompted me to nickname him "Batberg." Both he and Bobby were nice guys but I think all they were interested in, at the time, was generating some publicity to help promote their upcoming book and movie. Not that I blame them.

I suspect that the squad commander, Lieutenant Bolz, was wary of their flashy methods and he refused to let them remain partners. The lieutenant was a sharp cookie and within two years he would make captain and travel the world studying hostage situations and their outcomes. He would return to the NYPD and, working with a team of psychiatrists, design a hostage negotiation course that is still in use today.

First order of business was to get out into the new precincts, make friends, and develop some CIs. And so we began frequenting neighborhood bars and establishing contacts.

We were kept busy the next seven months, handling robberies in the newly created Brooklyn North district. Mostly mom-and-pop stuff and some small commercial heists. Every once in a while a bank robbery got thrown in for good measure along with a lot of routine street muggings, some involving weapons.

Then on August 22, 1972, a hot humid New York day, devoid of even the slightest breeze, Dave Greenberg and I had just left a meeting with two detectives in a Brooklyn South precinct house and had our radio set to the citywide band. If we had been tuned, like usual, to the Brooklyn North band we never would have heard the call of a bank robbery in progress at a Chase Manhattan Bank in Flatbush. That was in Brooklyn South but we decided to respond since we were close to the location. We arrived at the bank about the same time as the precinct cops and discovered that the thieves were still inside. They were heavily armed and had taken hostages. A stand-off order was given and as high-ranking bosses arrived communications were put in place by the hostage negotiation team. The negotiator was able to make contact with the suspects by calling one of the phones in the bank. The first step had been taken and the next eight hours of tense give-and-take bargaining began to evolve.

The bizarre story behind the robbery, the quirky personality of the thieves immortalized as "Sonny and Sal," and the tragic turn of events spawned a media circus and eventually a book, then a movie, both titled *Dog Day Afternoon*. Sonny was married and also had a homosexual lover. The proceeds of the robbery were earmarked to pay for a sex change operation for Sonny's male lover. Sal was little more than an accomplice. The robbery went bad and both of them were trapped inside with the seven bank employees they took as hostages.

Negotiations were proceeding slowly when a three-star chief of detectives named Louis Cottel showed up. I had served under him when he was a captain in the TPF. He looked a little older now but still stood ramrod straight and proud. He ordered the negotiator to inform the suspects that he would meet one of them face to face outside the bank, to talk things over. Sonny had agreed to meet with Chief Cottel and arrangements were being made. Meanwhile reporters and camera crews from all over New York were setting up their equipment. A large crowd of spectators had formed and crowd control was becoming a major problem. Greenberg and I reported to Chief Cottel to offer our services. He recognized both of us and asked us to hang around in case he needed us.

A few minutes later he stepped into the middle of the street, in plain view of those in the bank, removed his jacket, and took out his gun. He handed them to an aide and sauntered to the sidewalk in front of the bank. He sat on the front fender of a stylish red coupe and waited for about two minutes until a mousy looking guy, in his thirties, emerged from the bank with a pistol in his waistband and a rifle slung over his shoulder. The chief and the thief were two feet apart when the FBI arrived and I remember thinking, "I hope they don't try to intervene and get Cottel hurt."

I should have given the chief more credit. It seems he anticipated the FBI's arrival and had consulted with the agent in charge. An agreement was reached to let Chief Cottel run the show. After fifteen minutes Sonny went back inside the bank and the chief came back across the street. He told his aide to order four pizzas and a case of sodas, saying, "They're hungry in there. When the food arrives put it on the sidewalk a few feet from the entrance to the bank."

As soon as the food was placed at the entrance Sonny came out and brought the pizzas and sodas inside the bank.

Ten minutes later he reappeared still armed and

carrying a shoebox. When he reached into the shoebox you could feel every cop tense, until he pulled out a fistful of money and threw it into the air announcing, "Dinner is on me." I remember glancing at the flag over the bank's entrance to see if the wind was blowing in my direction. The flag wasn't moving at all and the money fluttered to the ground no more than three feet from where Sonny stood. He continued until there was no money left, then he went back inside. A couple of guys picked up the money and placed it into an evidence envelope. Too bad, a good steak dinner on Chase Manhattan would've gone down nice and easy.

Negotiations resumed with Chief Cottel making several more trips across the street. Each time he came back I noticed Greenberg was buzzing in his ear. I was getting curious. Then I noticed Greenberg was joined by a lieutenant friend of his who I recognized as a scumbag whistle-blower in the 1970 Knapp Commission hearings on police corruption. I got closer to them to see if I could overhear what they were telling the chief. They were trying to convince Cottel to set up an exchange for the hostages. I almost shit when I heard Greenberg say, "Why not ask if they'll switch the two of us and Detective O'Neil for the hostages."

I couldn't believe my ears. The first chance I got I grabbed Greenberg and took him aside, telling him, "Listen, asshole, I overheard that. If you and that rat bastard, piece of shit, lieutenant friend of yours want to swap yourselves for the hostages, be my guest but nobody, and I mean nobody, volunteers me for anything. You're thinking about promoting your book. Me, I'm thinking about my wife and kids."

The chief shot down the swap anyway. My guess is that he figured it for what it was, just a stunt for Greenberg to grab some publicity to bolster the sales of his upcoming book.

It was very late in the afternoon when negotiations seemed to stall. Sonny and Sal were refusing to budge on their last demands. They wanted to be taken to Kennedy Airport and flown out of the country. Once they were safe on the plane they would release the bank hostages and hold the plane's crew as hostages, until safely on foreign soil. Imagine my surprise when Chief Cottell announced to the media that the demands were going to be met.

Right after the announcement I saw him confer with the FBI. Twenty minutes later two white vans pulled up in front of the bank. The drivers were wearing slacks and white dress shirts—these guys were FBI agents. They got out and walked around the vans to where they couldn't be seen by anyone in the bank or anyone from the media. From my vantage point I was the only one who could see them strap on pistols in ankle holsters. The FBI was streetwise enough to know they'd be searched and the guns would be discovered, so I figured something was going to happen soon. I didn't have long to wait. The agents walked back around the vans into plain view of the bank, and waited until Sonny came out. A few minutes later he walked through the doors, onto the street, and proceeded to search one of the agents. I figured when he got to his ankle it would be all over. I watched as his hands went over the agent's ankles . . . nothing. Then the same thing happened with the other agent. I thought, there is no way he could have missed those guns. Then it dawned on me: it was all a setup. Sal's fate had already been sealed. The way I figured it to go down was that Sal would get whacked by the agent driving his van and Sonny would surrender to his driver. I was even more convinced of the outcome when I saw Sonny come out of the bank and get into the first van by himself. That poor bastard Sal came out surrounded by all the hostages, figuring that a sniper wouldn't be able to get a clear shot at him. Sal and the hostages entered the second van—dead man riding. This guy really thought he was going to live through this. I wasn't privy to the negotiations but my cop's nose told me I was right about the setup.

Later that night I heard on the news that the tense

hostage situation came to a swift and tragic end when one of the thieves was shot to death by the driver of the van transporting him and his hostages. The other thief—the one who had been negotiating with the police during the entire incident—had surrendered once he realized the hopelessness of his plight. Neither in that broadcast nor any other of the numerous reports following it was there ever a mention of Sonny's part in the demise of his friend Sal.

I couldn't help thinking how devious the FBI had been. But hey, you don't play fair when innocent lives are at stake.

CHAPTER SIXTEEN

War with the BLA

In late September of 1972, a commercial robbery I caught took a strange turn that would put us on a collision course with one of the most vicious groups ever encountered by the NYPD. Many cops would die and many of the bad guys would be killed. It would be like a modern day *Gunfight at the OK Corral*.

My involvement started with a payroll heist on Putnam Avenue in the 79th Precinct. A white business-owner had just withdrawn money from a local bank in order to make up his payroll. He was held up at gunpoint by two black males who then attempted to make their getaway on foot. They had only gotten about one hundred feet when a dark-colored sedan with three well-dressed black men inside pulled up next to the victim. The driver asked, "Did those guys just rob you?"

"Yes, they did," he answered.

"Okay, you wait right here. We'll take care of this."

The car took off in pursuit of the thieves, catching up with them in a matter of seconds. The three, whom the victim assumed were detectives, jumped out of their car with guns drawn and apprehended the two crooks. Then a funny thing happened. The car never came back. The victim, thinking this was a bit strange, came into the station house and ended up at my desk. The complainant described the incident in detail, to which I replied, "What we have here is a case of the stickup men being stuck up."

"Son of a bitch, I knew it was too good to be true that there would be a cop there when I needed one," the victim complained.

"Do you think you could ID any of the men who were involved in the robbery?"

"I don't know," he said. "It happened so fast and I was so scared."

"Well, we can cross that bridge when we get to it."

See, a lot of business robbery victims report the crime for insurance or tax purposes but don't want to make an ID. Sometimes they fear retaliation but mostly they don't want to get involved with multiple court appearances. Just when I felt the case going south he handed me a crumpled piece of paper and said, "Maybe this will help. I don't know why I did it, you know, thinking they were detectives and all, but I wrote down their license plate number."

I remember thinking, "I can't believe I'm getting this lucky."

I ran the plate and it came back as belonging to a car rental agency on Prospect Park South. Padraic Nugent (a detective from another team), and I paid a visit to the rental agency's manager. At first he was totally uncooperative but after leaning on him a bit he pulled the original rental agreement that had a copy of our guy's current driver's license. The redheaded black male pictured there was listed as residing at 3347 Prospect Park West, Apartment 3C, and went by the name of Timothy Hundley.

We went to his apartment and spoke to his wife, who informed us he was out and wouldn't be home until later that night. I left her my card and told her, "Have him contact me as soon as he can. I'll be in my office at eight tomorrow morning. Tell him it's in his best interest."

There was a change in the wind coming and the brass could feel it, so we began exercising a little more caution when apprehending suspects. That's why the next morning around

8:30 I called an ADA to see if he felt we had enough for an arrest. He didn't and said, "Jim, try to develop the case a little further, at this point with the victim saying he can't make a positive ID I can't okay an arrest."

The case was weak but we still had to go through the motions of an investigation. Five minutes after I got off the phone with the ADA, a redheaded black male and a short, rotund, balding, white guy came walking into the squad room. I recognized the white guy—it was Solly Greenstein, an attorney I had dealt with before and had found to be more interested in his fee than his client. This was a good thing for me. The black guy I had figured to be Timothy Hundley and I was right. Solly waved to me and said, "Jim O'Neil, we have to talk."

"Sure, but first introduce me to your client."

"Detective O'Neil, this is Timothy Hundley."

I acknowledged him and said, "Have a seat at my desk while I talk to your attorney in private."

I took Solly into a vacant office and explained the situation to him. "I can still cause your client some trouble but I'd rather get him to work for me as a CI. If you advise him to do that, he won't get locked up, you'll get paid, and I'll break some cases."

"Sounds good, I'll talk to him."

Fifteen minutes later Solly was gone and I was talking to my newest CI. It took about an hour to brief Timothy on the type of crimes I wanted information on. He seemed eager to start, especially when I informed him that many commercial robbery victims, such as supermarkets and banks, offered reward money. "I think I have something you'd be interested in, Detective," he said. "Let me talk to somebody and get back to you tomorrow."

The next afternoon Timmy came in with a tall, slim, black male and said, "Detective O'Neil, this is Roy Benjamin. I think you might want to hear what he has to say."

"I do, but not at my desk. I have a vacant office we

can use." Once inside I closed the door. "What is it you got, Roy?"

"I have some information on a bank robbery but I got this problem."

"What kind of problem?"

"I need a little help getting out from under a drug bust."

"Well, if your information is good I'll talk to the DA and try to get the bust tossed."

"Okay," Benjamin began. "I was in Brownsville the other day and this guy started telling me about a bank heist he did with eight other people in the Bronx where they pistol-whipped the manager before making their getaway. They had stolen two cars to use for their escape but after crashing one of them they all piled into the remaining car and got away clean."

"This guy got a name?"

"All I know, Detective, is his first name, it's Johnny, and he lives on East New York Avenue in Brownsville. He also told me that he had been busted for a murder in Brooklyn two or three years ago but had beaten the rap."

"Did he happen to tell you the name and location of the bank?"

"I think he said it was a Manufacturer's Hanover but I'm not positive. He never told me the address but I remember him saying it was in the Bronx."

"All right, wait here. I'm going to get one of my partners and I want you to tell him what you just told me."

I got Bill Herrmann, and I listened as Roy Benjamin repeated the information to Bill. I was satisfied Roy had no more information to give us and I told him if it turned out to be good I would talk to the DA like I promised. Timothy Hundley and Roy Benjamin left while Bill and I went back to our desks. None of us had realized it, at the time, but that meeting was the beginning of the end of the Black Liberation Army, commonly known as the BLA. They were an extreme militant group of blacks that was holding up banks and shooting cops all over the country. I don't think there was a cop in America who wasn't aware of them. But until the events put in motion by Roy Benjamin's information unfolded, no one in law enforcement was aware that the BLA was based primarily in New York City, more specifically, in Brooklyn.

Since robbing an FDIC bank is a federal offense, Bill called his friend Tom Sher, the special agent in charge of the New York office of the FBI, and gave him everything we had just learned about the bank heist. Tom got very excited and told Bill, "That's excellent information, the pistol whipping of the manager and the crashed getaway vehicle were never in the papers. Bill, I'm going to send over a couple of agents to work with you."

"That's fine as long as they don't get in our way."

Bill hung up the phone and smiled. "The information is good," he told me. "Now all we got to do is find out who this Johnny is and how to get our hands on him."

I had an idea. "We know the information is good so let's check the Brooklyn homicide book for a Johnny from East New York Avenue who beat a murder rap. Let's go back three years and see what we come up with."

All homicides in Brooklyn were listed in a large book at a central location. There were over eight hundred homicides committed during the three-year period and we checked every one of them. No Johnny on East New York Avenue. We eyed each other with that "oh shit" look on our faces. I was the first one to speak. "Look, the other information was good, right? We had to miss something. I say we go through the book again."

Bill concurred and we started over again. Still no Johnny on East New York Avenue but we did find a Johnny Rivers acquitted of a murder charge, listed as residing at 2341 Hopkinson Avenue. That was in my old precinct, the 73rd, and I was familiar with how the street numbers ran. I was sure that 2341 was only a few houses off East New York Avenue.

In addition to his address we found his B-number, a number assigned on a first arrest anywhere in New York that remains with the perp for life. I told Bill I was sure we had our guy, and his "oh shit" look was replaced with his "Got you, motherfucker" look. We called the photo unit in Manhattan and using Johnny's B-number we ordered half a dozen wet prints, so named because when you needed to pick up mugshots in a hurry they would usually still be damp from the developing process. Next Bill called his friend at the FBI, who assigned two of his agents to work with us. We told one of them, Danny Coulson that we thought we had a hit on one of the bank robbers and asked him to meet us at the photo unit. When we got there Danny and his partner were waiting for us. We gave them some wet prints so they could set up a photo array for the witnesses at the bank. They headed to the Manufacturers Hanover at 1355 Oak Point Boulevard in the Bronx and we headed back to our office.

I had just walked into my office when my phone rang. It was Danny, excited. "We got the son of a bitch. Every witness has positively ID'd Johnny Rivers as one of the bank robbers. You and Bill did a hell of a job."

"Thanks, well we're off to a good start, now let's get the mutt."

"I'm still at the bank. My partner and I are going to head over to our office and write up our report. Keep me posted."

I brought my partners up to speed and it was decided that Cleve Bethea and I should see some of our old contacts in the 73rd. We started at Pacey's bar, which was right around the corner from Johnny Rivers' last known address. As soon as we walked in we saw Buddy, who immediately stopped writing the digit and gave us a respectful nod. I went up to him and whispered, "Buddy, I got to talk to you in the kitchen."

We had a drink first, then I walked back like I was going to the bathroom but went into the kitchen instead. A minute later Buddy appeared.

I handed him the mugshot and asked, "Do you know

this guy?"

"Shit, that's Johnny Rivers. I've known him since he was a little kid. What did he do?"

"Robbed a bank."

"That's heavy stuff."

"Do you know if he's still living at 2341 Hopkinson?"

"Yeah, on the first floor. His apartment is the one at the end of the hall facing the entrance of the building."

"Good."

"If I see him he's yours, Jim. Give me a while to check the street and I'll be back."

I waited until Buddy left and I joined Cleve at the back of the bar. We were bullshitting with the bartender when Buddy walked back in and nodded his head toward the kitchen. I waited a minute, then sauntered back and met him in the kitchen, "Damn that was fast, Buddy," I told him.

"I got lucky, as soon as I turned the corner I saw Rivers going into his house, but he's not alone. He has some guy with him whose walking with a limp. I don't know the other guy but he looks like a real badass."

"I knew I could count on you, Buddy."

Buddy went back to the bar and I made a pit stop in the men's room. I got Cleve and filled him in. He smiled and said, "Let's go kick the fucking door down."

At first I thought it was a good idea but some inner sense made me cautious. "Cleve," I told him. "These guys in the bank were carrying nine millimeters that hold sixteen rounds. Our snub-nosed .38s only have five rounds. Partner we're outgunned. What say I call Bill and have him bring over some shotguns and bandoleers with ammo?"

"I like that idea. Yeah, go call Bill."

I'm probably alive today because I made that call. Fifteen minutes later Bill drove up outside of Pacey's bar. Cleve and I jumped in and loaded our shotguns as Bill drove around the corner. We parked on Hopkinson Avenue across from 2341 and headed off to round up Johnny Rivers and company. Bill and I stood on each side of the door to the apartment while Cleve came running down the hallway and drop kicked the door. Shit, he took out the door, the frame, and the hinges. Then we all charged in, shotguns at the ready and yelled, "Police." We found Rivers' wife, Priscilla, alone in the apartment. We had scared the shit out of her and she wet her pants. We questioned her about her husband and his friend with the limp. She said she didn't know where her husband was and she had never met the guy with the limp before. All she knew was that her husband called him Butch, and that Butch had asked her for an aspirin because his leg hurt.

With the element of surprise lost we knew Rivers wouldn't be coming back to his apartment and we'd have to find him another way. We put Roy Benjamin on the case and told him if he found Johnny Rivers for us, I could practically guarantee he'd beat his pending drug rap. The next afternoon I got a call from Roy telling me that our guy was at the pool hall over on East New York Avenue with two other guys. Fred and I were the only ones in the squad so I grabbed my Coachman and we headed over to Brownsville. With weapons drawn we entered the pool hall and surprised the occupants, who in turn surprised us. The few we anticipated turned out to be fourteen. As I leveled my shotgun at the crowd a hush fell over the pool room and when I cocked the hammers I heard a collective gasp.

Fred announced, "Everybody stay cool, we're here looking for somebody." He turned to me and said, "Jim, we're going to need some backup. Can you hold them for a minute while I get on the car radio and get some help here?"

"I'll handle it."

Fred ran out the door and I started waving my shotgun back and forth yelling, "Everybody freeze, the first one of you motherfuckers that moves dies and a few more of you might go with him." I had a reputation in the neighborhood and these guys knew I wasn't fooling, so nobody moved. They also knew they were staring down the barrels of one mean fucking weapon. As Fred came back in I could already hear the sirens. Within a minute, half a dozen cops were there checking the crowd for Johnny Rivers. He was nowhere to be found but after patting down the crowd the cops turned up five illegal handguns. We threw the cops the five collars and headed back to the squad.

The next day I got another call from Roy Benjamin, who told me, "Your guy will be on the corner of Pitkin Avenue and Atkins Street tomorrow morning at nine."

"Are you sure this time?"

"Yeah, because I spoke to him, and he's on the run, and desperate. When I offered him money to help me with a drug deal I had going down, he agreed to meet me there."

"Okay, Roy you did good. If this information is accurate I'll be talking to the DA for you soon."

"Oh it's accurate all right."

It was 8:30 in the morning and Bill Herrmann, Cleve Bethea, Danny Coulson, and I were in the back of a surveillance step van at the corner of Pitkin and Atkins. I'll give Rivers credit for one thing—he was punctual. He showed up at 9:00 on the dot and stopped not more than five feet away from the back of our van. We threw open the back doors and leveled the shotguns at him. He knew he was fucked and you could see the fight drain out of him. He offered no resistance as we back-cuffed him and removed two loaded pistols from his waistband. He looked bored as Cleve read him his rights, a look that disappeared when I threw him into the back seat of a waiting unmarked car. I sat next to him and he turned toward me and asked, "Did that fuck Roy Benjamin set me up?"

"I ask the questions here, not you. Now shut the fuck up."

He didn't say another word until we had him in interrogation back at the squad. We sat him down and I said, "Johnny I want to introduce you to Special Agent Danny

Coulson of the FBI, he has something he wants to say to you."

"Johnny Rivers, you are under arrest for the robbery of the Manufacturer's Hanover Trust at 1355 Oak Point Boulevard in the Bronx. Now you're going to get a fair trial and after you're found guilty you'll get twenty-five years. I will personally see to it that you do every fucking day of the twenty-five unless you cooperate with us immediately."

Rivers looked at me and asked, "What do you want me to do?"

"I want you to tell us everything you know about the robbery, and who else was involved. The more information you give us the less time you do."

He filled us in on all the details of the robbery and then started giving us names: Joanne Chesimard, Freddie Hilton, Woode Green, Avon White, and Twyman Ford Meyers. There was one other guy but he didn't know his name.

I continued with the interrogation. "Any of them ever been arrested before?"

"As far as I know every one of them," Rivers answered. They been doing bank robberies all over the country and killing cops in New York and throughout other states."

"Are we talking about a militant group?"

"Yeah, the Black Liberation Army."

"Why are they shooting cops?"

"I just want you to know I never shot a cop."

I leaned over and yelled, "Just answer the fucking question."

"They figured the shootings would piss off cops all across the country and the cops would react violently against all blacks. That would start a race war."

We were stunned at what we were hearing. What we thought was just an isolated bank robbery had led us to one of the biggest cases in New York's history.

"Who was that guy with you the other day when we kicked your door down?"

"Shit, that was you guys? You destroyed the door and it cost me two hundred dollars to get it fixed. Not to mention you scared the piss out of my wife."

"I asked you for his name."

"Twyman Ford Meyers but everybody calls him Butch."

"Why was he limping?"

"He's carrying around a bullet in his leg he got from a shootout with cops in St. Louis, Missouri. It hasn't slowed him down and I gotta tell you, whichever three of you it was that busted up my door, you're lucky to be alive."

"Oh yeah, how's that Johnny?" I inquired.

"Butch and me had just left my apartment and were standing in a doorway about thirty feet from where you had parked. When Butch saw the three of you getting out of your car he pulled out his nine millimeter and said, 'It's the fucking pigs. I'm gonna waste all three of them.' Then he saw your shotguns and decided not to chance it. We stayed in the shadows until the three of you got back into your car and left."

We knew who the animals were, and now the hunt would begin. We had to nail these shitheads, and shithead number one was Joanne Chesimard, also referred to as "Lovin' Mama," the leader of the BLA.

We ran the names Johnny Rivers had given us and every one of them had criminal records. Using their B-numbers we were able to locate their files and get wet prints.

From here the investigation intensified. The bosses decided to form a nine-man team headed up by Sergeant Andy Alongi and eight detectives. The team would be off the chart working exclusively on this case. Among the eight were Jack Flynn, Phil Hogan, me, and five of my six partners; Greenberg had been excluded probably due to his penchant for publicity. Jack and I had been friends and neighbors for years and this would be the first time we worked together on the job. He was big, and heavy, and tough, and a damn good detective. Phil

Hogan was a fearsome-looking large, muscular, black man with a shaved head, who could scare the shit out of perps just by scowling at them. The entire team was made up of seasoned ghetto cops. There was no black or white, only blue. We all wanted these scumbags who were killing our brother officers. We knew the BLA's days were going to end violently and we knew there would be casualties on both sides. Up until now no BLA members had been killed, but that was about to change.

Halloween was a week away and I had just finished researching some records over at the 73rd Precinct. It was one of those rare times I didn't have a partner with me. No partner, but I did have my very good friend. On the seat next to me was my trusty Garcia Rossi Coachman, loaded and ready to go. It was unseasonably warm and I remember driving on Sutter Avenue with my window down when a call came over the radio, "In the Seven-Three Precinct . . . report of shots fired . . . one person shot . . . Saratoga and Sutter . . . in a real estate office."

I was two blocks away so I picked up the mike and said, "This is thirteenth robbery central, I will respond."

As I neared the real estate office I barely took notice of a man and a woman entering a Ryder rental van. I pulled up in front of the real estate office and jumped out of the car. My trusty friend and me. Inside was a bald, elderly man slumped forward and lifeless at his desk, with a large hole in the top of his head. His two co-workers, a man and a woman, were at their desks,. All three were Jewish and in their fifties. The woman was sobbing and the man was visibly shaken. I introduced myself. "I'm Detective O'Neil. Can anyone tell me what happened?"

The man was on the edge of tears and his voice trembled as he answered me, "This is crazy, Detective. The bitch walked in here and said, 'This is how the Black Liberation Army takes care of whities who exploit blacks,' then she walked up to Saul and shot him."

Now I made the connection. Using Ryder vans was an

old trick of the BLA and that woman I had just seen getting in one had to be Joanne Chesimard. I excused myself and ran to where I had seen the van but it was gone. I ran back to my car and put the message out over the air, "Be on the lookout for a Ryder van with one black male and one black female. If seen call for backup and use caution, it's the BLA."

I was too late and they got away. If only the original radio dispatch had been just thirty seconds sooner I might have nailed the bastards. If only I had made the connection about the Ryder van sooner. Yeah, and if only my grandmother had wheels, she'd a been a bicycle. To this day I regret having let Lovin' Mama get away. I had a chance to nail that murdering piece of shit and I blew it. I went back and waited at the real estate office for the homicide squad to show up. I gave them all the information and then I took off.

I was pumped and my adrenalin was flowing, so I decided to head over to the Highway Inn for a taste, to calm me down. Two minutes later I was belly up at the bar, sipping on a scotch and unloading on the bartender, Earl Bellow, about how I let the leader of the BLA get away.

Earl poured another one for me. "Now Jim, you be careful," he said. "I'd hate to lose a good fishing partner."

Thousands of fliers featuring pictures of these BLA scumbags were distributed to every police officer in New York and New Jersey. Now that we had their names and their faces in the field, the hunt would gain momentum. Everyone had their CIs working overtime and information started to come in. Our investigation revealed that the BLA was probably responsible for the murder of two 32nd Precinct uniformed cops in Harlem, Piagentini and Jones. Piagentini was white and Jones was black. They were gunned down in a housing project that stood on the old Polo Grounds, former home of the New York Giants. Shot in the back by these cowardly BLA scummers.

We also developed information that linked the BLA to the assassination of two uniformed cops downtown in Greenwich Village, Gregory Foster and Rocco Laurie, another black and white team. These BLA bastards were equal opportunity killers.

There were strong indications, based on what we knew about the BLA that they were responsible for machine-gunning two cops in an RMP car. While they were guarding the Manhattan DA's home after he had prosecuted some Black Panthers, Officers Curry and Benitti observed two black men driving the wrong way down a one-way street. The officers caught up with them and made them stop, at which point the driver of the stopped car ducked down and the passenger opened fire with a machine gun. Both officers survived but were severely wounded.

The atmosphere on the job was tense and as a precaution the brass assigned detectives in unmarked cars to follow uniformed officers in RMPs.

Our focus shifted, temporarily, from Joanne Chesimard to Woode Green. We received information that he had been involved in the killing of Foster and Laurie in Greenwich Village. We wanted this bastard real bad. The problem was that our information was like deer tracks in the snow. You knew where the deer had walked but not where it was now. We were always days, sometimes even weeks, behind our quarry.

Monday, January 15, 1973, would be the start of one of the busiest weeks of my career. A couple of us had gone to Brownsville and were contacting some of our CIs when I ran into two black housing detectives, Roy Ruffin and Phil Stubbs, whom I had known for several years. Phil was the son of a night bartender at the Highway Inn and we would often get together for a drink and talk shop. We were all on four-to-twelve tours that night and Roy asked, "Jim, why don't you meet Phil and me for a taste at the Highway Inn after your tour?

"Sounds like a good idea. See you later."

My partners and I finished contacting informants and headed back to our office. Danny Coulson was there and we spent several hours going over the latest developments of the case and sharing new information. Mostly I talked and Danny listened. No surprise there, since all the informants were ours. When we finished up it was after 1:30 AM and I was exhausted. I hopped in my car and drove down Atlantic Avenue. I caught a light at Saratoga Avenue where I had to make a right to go to the Highway Inn. It was close to 2 AM and I remembered I had to take my son to the dentist at 10:30 the next morning. The light turned green and I continued down Atlantic Avenue heading toward Long Island and home. Besides, I could see Roy and Phil another time.

For years after, I would wonder how events might have been altered had I made that right turn. About the same time I was stopped at the light on Saratoga Avenue two black males had entered the Highway Inn. They noticed two guys at the end of the bar wearing jackets and ties and made them as detectives. Roy and Phil were about to meet Woode Green and another BLA member. Using a ruse they lured the two detectives outside. Once out of the bar Woode and his associate spun around with nine millimeters drawn and opened fire, hitting both Roy and Phil. They went down before they could even get off a shot. Phil recovered completely from his wounds but Roy lost his spleen.

Tuesday flew into Wednesday and it was late in the afternoon when a bunch of us were sitting around the squad's conference table kicking ideas and information around while knocking back a few beers. We tended to think better at these sessions with a Bud in our hands. After his second Bud one of the detectives said, "I just thought of something. Isn't Woode Green's first wedding anniversary coming up soon?"

We checked the file and found that he had been married on January 22, 1972. His anniversary was in five days. We decided to put a tap on his wife Brenda's phone. Two of our guys went to the DA's office and got a judge's signature on a wiretap order. The next morning we were in business. The phone company had placed a tap on her phone and we had set up our recording equipment in a day-care center two blocks from her apartment. We had two-man teams working four-hour shifts monitoring the phone.

An uneventful Thursday dragged into Friday. Jack Flynn and I had been catching up on record keeping, a necessary but evil part of the job. It was late afternoon when the phone rang. A uniformed cop named Dennedy was telling me that I better get over to John and Al's Sporting Goods on Broadway because there was a lot of gunfire and a cop had been shot and most likely was dead. Jack and I grabbed shotguns, donned our bandoleers, and ran down the stairs and out the door to our car. I could have sworn I heard someone say, "Who were those masked men?"

We made it there in five minutes. We found out that John and Al's had been in the process of being stuck up by four black males in army fatigues and combat boots, when the owner hit the silent alarm. The uniformed cops who responded had come under fire and were pinned down. An emergency service cop named Gilroy lay dead on the ground. He had taken cover behind an el pillar, one of the steel structures supporting the elevated train tracks that ran above Broadway, and was unaware that the suspects had commandeered rifles with scopes. When he looked out from behind the el pillar, he was shot in the head. He would lay there for hours until the Department got an armored personnel carrier down from the Rodmans Neck range to extricate the slain officer's body. The four perps were holed up inside with fourteen hostages and we had a good old-fashioned standoff. I was thinking BLA because of the level of violence involved but it turned out I was wrong.

Friday became Saturday and the hostage negotiators had set up in a store basement four blocks away. They called John and Al's number and one of the suspects answered the phone—negotiations had begun. I was a qualified hostage negotiator, but I didn't want to deal with these guys on the phone. If there was going to be any action it was going to be on the street and that's where I preferred to be. Besides, when was the last time a bad guy was shot by a hostage negotiator over the phone?

Negotiations had stalled, followed by a brief round of gunshots that shattered what little glass was left in the store's picture windows. Saturday melded into Sunday and we got a lucky break. The hostages were locked, unattended, in a windowless room on the second floor. One of them, a longtime employee of the store, remembered that years ago paneling had been installed over a doorway that opened into a staircase leading to the roof. The hostages were able to remove the paneling and make their way up to the roof. Emergency service cops on an adjoining building got the hostages to safety. This time when one of the suspects answered the phone he heard a different tone in the negotiator's voice. "Your hostages escaped. Surrender or die, assholes. We'll bomb the fucking place if we have to."

Like most of the scumbags who do stuff like this they chose the easy way out and became advocates of nonviolence, surrendering like the cowards they were. Fifteen minutes later I took cover behind an el pillar twenty feet from the front door of the sporting goods store. I trained my shotgun on the entrance and shouted to the first guy, "Advance to the window. Don't come outside until I tell you." He did what I told him. "Now, hands on your head, step out of the window and advance to the curb." As soon as he stopped at the curb an unmarked car pulled up and two detectives emerged. They gave coward number one a quick pat down, back-cuffed him, threw him in the back seat, and took off. This procedure was repeated three more times and the siege of John and Al's sporting goods ended. I was pissed off that a good cop died, and I never got the chance to kill at least one of his murderers.

I went back to my office and traded my shotgun for a Polaroid camera and proceeded to Central booking, located in the 90th Precinct house in Williamsburgh. That's where the suspects had been taken and I wanted pictures of each of them. The first three mutts cooperated but when I went to take a picture of mutt number four he hesitated saying, "Allah will not permit me to have my picture taken."

"You motherfucker, Allah won't permit you to have your picture taken but he will permit you to kill cops."

With that three other detectives yanked him to his feet and slammed him into the wall—twice. I got my fourth picture and headed off to the ICU at Brookdale Hospital to see if Roy or Phil could identify any of them. They couldn't and Sunday ended on that sour note. Tomorrow was Woode Green's anniversary and I was hoping he would try to contact his wife.

Ralph Anderson, a detective from our team, had volunteered to man the wire. He was listening that Monday evening around 8:30 when a call came in and Brenda answered, "Hello."

"Hello baby. Know who this is? Remember what day this is? It's Woode. Buttercup, know where the Big T bar in Brooklyn over on Broadway is?"

"Yes, baby."

"Why don't you come down here and we'll celebrate with some champagne?"

"I'll see you there. Give me one hour. I want to look good for my man."

"I'm here waiting."

Ralph notified the squad and everyone headed for the heavy artillery. It was decided that Cleve Bethea and Phil Hogan should go into the bar because if one of the white guys went, it would be an instant combat zone. Besides, Cleve and Phil said they wouldn't mind a taste before going into battle. As soon as they entered the bar they spotted Woode and Brenda at a table in the back. They sat about twenty feet away, at the end of the bar, and ordered drinks while observing the couple.

Another black male, who they didn't recognize, joined Woode and Brenda at the table. He turned out to be Anthony White, who had shot two cops uptown but had not yet been tied to the BLA.

Cleve and Phil decided to make their move. They stepped back from the bar pulling out their guns and badges and Cleve said, "Police, put up your hands."

As Cleve was ending his sentence Woode Green and Anthony White drew their nine millimeters and opened fire. As the patrons hit the floor and scrambled for cover, Cleve took one in the chest, and one in the leg that shattered his bone, making him a cripple. Phil caught one in the chest but managed to empty his gun at them. He looked down at Cleve, who was lying on the floor, mouth open, eyes shut, and covered in blood. Phil thought Cleve was dead as he reached down, grabbed Cleve's gun, and emptied it in the general direction of Woode. Phil dove out the door yelling, "Cleve's shot. I think he's dead."

Everybody outside opened up with carbines and shotguns to keep Woode and Anthony's heads down while one of our guys crawled in after Cleve and dragged him out. He was unconscious but alive. It wasn't until Cleve was safe that Phil realized he was also wounded. Both of them were rushed to the hospital while one of our guys was screaming into the radio for Central to notify the hospital that two seriously wounded detectives were on the way in and to have a trauma team waiting. We kept firing and soon the windows were all gone and the door was confetti. Jack Flynn worked his way to the corner of the building armed with a custom-made twelve-gauge, double-barrel, magnum shotgun with pistol grips. It was loaded with two rounds of twelve gauge, magnum, double-O buckshot, that's nine .30-caliber balls per round. You could bring down a B29 with that gun. Jack peeked through one of the shot-out windows as Anthony White popped his head up from the far end of the bar and let go a round in Jack's direction.

Jack managed to dodge the bullet but he was pissed. He decided to count to fifteen, turn, aim at the far end of the bar, and let go with both barrels. Thirteen, fourteen, fifteen—Jack turned and fired both barrels at once as Anthony White popped his head up. Jack caught him with all eighteen balls in the face and splattered his head all over the Big T bar. The kick from the shotgun knocked all 270 pounds of Jack right on his ass.

In the middle of all this, a uniformed housing police sergeant pulled up, got out of his car, emptied his gun over the heads of the detectives, got back in his car, and drove away. Everybody wanted a piece of these cop-killing scumbags.

The shooting tapered off and when we entered what was left of the Big T bar, we found the remains of Anthony White. Most of him was lying on the floor behind the bar and the rest was splattered all over the rear wall. Brenda was screaming while Woode Green lay motionless on the floor, blood running out of a bullet hole in his head. He was on his back and his eyes were following everyone's movement. One of the detectives walked over and put his foot on Woode's neck trying to snap it. Sergeant Alongi walked in and seeing what was going on said, "What are you doing, you're standing on his neck?"

"Oh shit, Sarge, I didn't notice." The detective smiled, gave a wink and regrettably removed his foot. No matter, the scumbag died in the hospital two hours later and the world became a little better place. Being a member of the BLA was starting to get more dangerous.

Being a wounded cop in a Brooklyn hospital wasn't as safe as it use to be either. If the BLA knew where to find Cleve and Phil they would try to kill them. That's why Phil was secreted away to a hospital in Queens and Cleve was taken to Hempstead Hospital on Long Island. The Hempstead police had thrown up a protective ring around the hospital and put two cops outside Cleve's room. I showed them my identification and informed them I was his partner but they wouldn't let me in until Cleve told them it was okay.

It had been three days since he was wounded and he was still in some pain but his spirits were high. He said he was dry and asked me to get a bucket of ice and a pitcher of water from the nurse's station. I was about to put some ice in his glass when he asked me to open the bottom drawer of the table next to his bed. Inside was a bottle of scotch and some cups. We spent the next three hours sipping scotch and talking about all manner of things unrelated to the job, with one exception—Jack Flynn lived on a canal close to me and had an above-ground swimming pool at the back end of his property only a few feet from the canal. For years somebody had been randomly throwing all kinds of marine life—from blue claw crabs to eels to flounders to five-foot sand sharks—into his pool. It got to the point where Jack began staking out his pool at night with a shotgun ready to blast a hole in the boat of "them sons-a-bitches" that were doing the dumping. He was always complaining to the guys in the squad about it and I always felt Jack suspected some of us were involved but never could prove it. Of course everyone in the squad knew it was Eddie Schneider, Vinnie Mollo, Ed Bailey, and I who were them sons-a-bitches—everyone except Jack. My confession didn't surprise Cleve but that didn't stop him from laughing so hard he almost split his stitches. I loved him like a brother and it was great to see him this upbeat only three days after catching two bullets. The several operations to repair the shattered bone in his thigh had been successful but the metal leg brace he wears to this day serves as a reminder of his close brush with death and his forced retirement from the job he loved more than life itself.

Phil Hogan recovered as well, and like Cleve had to go out on a disability pension. Phil passed away in 1994. Cleve no longer lives in New York State, but we keep in touch by phone like brothers should.

Right after the shoot-out at the Big T bar I was notified of my promotion to sergeant. That meant I wouldn't be able to stay with my team and I would be pulled off the

BLA investigation. I went to my boss, Deputy Inspector Tom Gleason, and tried to decline the promotion. He understood my frustration but told me that it was mandatory and I was scheduled to attend a pre-promotion course in three days. I was off the investigation and all I could do was say good-bye to the finest group of detectives I had ever worked with. Unofficially, I was able to keep my fingers in the investigation with the help of my now ex-partners. There were subsequent shoot-outs where Sergeant Andy Alongi ended up catching a nine-millimeter in the chest and a detective named Bob Jakes took one in the stomach.

Now the team turned their attention back to Joanne Chesimard. They were unable to locate her and then, three months after the Big T shootout, she was arrested for killing a New Jersey State Trooper. She was subsequently convicted and sent to jail, where I figured she'd be until she died. Life in prison was too good for her. True justice would have been death by cop. As it turned out she spent very little time in jail. Four BLA members broke her out, got her to Mexico, and eventually to Cuba where she lives to this day.

They finally caught up with Twyman Ford Meyers in the Bronx on his way to a meeting that had been arranged by one of our informants. Heavily armed detectives and FBI agents had blanketed the location where the meeting was set to take place. When Meyers arrived Agent Danny Coulson revealed himself and shouted, "FBI, put your hands up."

Without hesitation Meyers pulled out his nine millimeter and opened fire. Two more detectives got hit that night. Jack "The Stick" Clark, a tall, very thin 13th Robbery Squad detective from Brooklyn, took one in the leg and a Bronx detective named Colonel Holland got shot in the ankle. Meyers continued to fire until he slumped lifeless to the ground. There he lay in a pool of his own blood riddled with forty-one bullet holes, many of them delivered post mortem. This fuck would never kill another cop. Bye-bye, Twyman.

There were several more arrests subsequent to this but none as spectacular. A year later and the BLA was little more than a bad memory. Most of them had been locked up or killed.

CHAPTER SEVENTEEN

Internal Affairs Division

After finishing my pre-promotion course I was assigned to the almost crime-free 69th Precinct in Canarsie, Brooklyn. It was adjacent to the 73rd and included an industrial area that acted as a buffer between the crime-infested streets of Brownsville and the quiet Italian and Jewish residential neighborhoods of Canarsie.

I wasn't ready for the lack of excitement the 69th offered. The rush I got from working high crime areas was almost narcotic and since coming to the 69th I'd been going through withdrawal. Almost ten months of relatively crime-free tours and I was climbing the walls. The boredom pushed me into a direction, that as a good cop, I never imagined I'd go.

It was mid-December when my old partner, Eddie Schneider, called and said he wanted to meet me at the Highway Inn to discuss a proposition. Eddie was already sucking on some suds when I got there. As I walked to the end of the bar I motioned to Earl Bellow to set me up with a beer and parked myself on a barstool next to my old partner.

"Okay, here's the deal," Eddie began. "I was approached by Internal Affairs about transferring into their outfit. Seems they don't have any bosses with investigative backgrounds. Not one ex-detective in the entire division."

"Yeah, well I'm not surprised," I told him. "You're not going to join up with that bunch of scummers are you?"

"That depends on you."

"Me? What do I have to do with it?"

"I know you, Jim. You miss the excitement."

"True, and that's the only reason I'm still listening. Go ahead."

"There's this cop named Clifford Dumont, who works in the Bushwick section of Brooklyn. They know he's dealing drugs. But they've been after this guy for three years and can't get the goods on him."

"There aren't many saints on this job but I draw the line on stuff like that," I told him. "A cop dealing drugs needs to be taken down, like any other dirtbag. I love this job too much to let my hatred for IAD stand in the way of getting a scum-sucking pig like this Bushwick cop off the streets."

"I was counting on you to feel that way," Eddie responded, "because I told IAD I'd take the transfer if you came with me."

I finished my beer, shook Eddie's hand, smiled and said, "Let's get that son of a bitch."

Two weeks later 1974 was just starting as Eddie and I reported to our new assignment. Without letting anyone in IAD know what we were doing we began putting a team together that would be capable of getting enough on Dumont to send him to slam city for a long time.

We set up a temporary office in the basement of an old, unused precinct house in Brooklyn. I grabbed three undercovers out of narcotics and had them assigned to my team. There was nothing on paper to indicate where they went and nobody in their units knew what happened to them—they just weren't there anymore.

Eddie and I knew a lot of good uniformed cops whom we trusted and we decided to pick four of them to work with us. On paper it looked like a routine transfer to narcotics on a thirty-day renewable tour. Of course none of these guys actually went to narcotics and now we had our backup team.

I wanted to bring one more boss into the team so I called a friend of mine, Joe Defina, whom I had known when he was a second-grade detective in the now defunct Police Commissioner's Confidential Investigations Unit (PCCIU). Joe had made sergeant and was in uniform at the 90th Precinct in the Williamsburg section of Brooklyn. A week later he joined us and we now had all the minds and muscle we needed.

The most experienced undercover on our team, "Angel," was going to pose as a drug dealer and attempt to buy drugs from Dumont. Angel needed a flash car, something a successful drug dealer wouldn't be ashamed to be seen in. So while the guys were settling into their new digs I called the chief of the borough, who was aware of our assignment, and asked if he could help us out. He placed a call to the captain in charge of the Police Department Motor Transport division's impound yard and told him to give me any car I wanted. An hour later I was being given a tour of the impound yard by an inquisitive Captain Johnston. After all it isn't every day that the chief of the borough tells a captain to give a sergeant anything he wants. I told the captain nothing. The cars I saw were unimpressive and no self-respecting drug dealer would want to be seen driving any of them. I noticed that Captain Johnston was steering me away from one corner of the yard. I pointed to the unseen corner and said, "Captain, let's take a look over there."

"Oh there's nothing there that you'd be interested in," he answered.

"Well, let me take a look anyway."

"You're wasting your time."

And there it was, a brand-new white Lincoln, "Captain," I proclaimed. "That's exactly what I'm looking for, I'll take it."

"I'm sorry," he told me. "That's been promised to another investigative team. Any other car is yours but I can't give you that one."

Even with my decreased sense of olfactory sharpness I could smell a contract and I was willing to bet that he had taken one on that car. I thanked him and started walking for the gate.

"O'Neil, where are you going?" he asked.

"I'm going back and tell the Chief that you won't give me the car I want."

Half an hour later I was driving down the Long Island Expressway behind the wheel of a new white Lincoln. I was on my way to an obscure office on the seventh floor of police headquarters. There was no sign hinting at what took place in the small office behind the door designated only as room 703. Very few people on the job knew of its existence. This was where you went when you needed a fictitious identity for an undercover. This is where Angel the cop would become Angel Robles the drug dealer and all that was needed for the transformation was his physical description and some general information.

Three days later I picked up a package containing all the ID needed to substantiate the existence of a drug dealer named Angel Robles. The Lincoln had been registered in his name, he had a clean driver's license, several credit cards, backdated bank accounts, an impressive rap sheet, even a voter's registration card, and a variety of membership cards. The entire team's private cars were also set up with fictitious registrations in case anyone ran their plates.

Next thing to do was find an office somewhere away from Brooklyn. It had to be where we could come and go without the possibility of any suspicious activity getting back to Dumont. Manhattan seemed like a good choice. This was a job for Tricky Dick, whose birth certificate read Richard Lannon. Tricky was a buddy of mine who had been wounded so many times in the line of duty that the Department forced him off the street and into the quartermaster division; their way of keeping him alive.

Tricky Dick agreed to meet me at the Rockfront, a local watering hole in Valley Stream out on Long Island. When I arrived, Tricky was buying drinks for the bar. He must have had a good day at the track.

I knew I could trust him so I filled him in on the entire operation and told him I had to get my team out of Brooklyn and into a safe place to operate from. He told me to meet him the next afternoon in the old police headquarters on Centre Market Street in Manhattan. He was in charge of the entire building and was using it to store surplus equipment.

The next day Tricky ushered me into the old chief inspector's office, really three offices with a private bathroom. He bragged, "Nothing but the best for my friend. You even have your own private shithouse."

"I knew I could count on you, Tricky."

He had a fourteen-man cleaning crew working to get the offices ready.

"By tomorrow this place will be shining like a new silver dollar. Have your guys come over here and pick out whatever furniture and equipment you need and we'll have it moved in by the next day. Now I have a surprise for you."

"There's more?"

"I took the liberty of picking out your desk. I figured you'd get a charge out of having the desk Teddy Roosevelt used when he was the police commissioner."

By the next afternoon everything was in place. We even had bunk beds we could stretch out on after a nighttime operation. By the following day we had four phones installed. Two were in a separate room to be used exclusively by the undercovers. Their phones were listed to a Brooklyn exchange, but when dialed would ring here in our Manhattan offices.

The ridiculously large budget we were given indicated to me how eager they were to nail this rogue cop.

The office of the special state prosecutor provided us with all the electronic surveillance equipment we required. We got a battery-operated transmitter, called a "body wire," that would be taped to the undercover. The microphone was very small and so sensitive that any movement of the body against clothing caused such loud static that it drowned out the conversation. Wrapping it in cotton eliminated the problem. The conversations would be captured on two portable, battery-powered, reel-to-reel tape recorders, housed in fiberglass attache cases. The body wire was our ears, and a night owl scope, with an attached thirty-five millimeter camera, became our nighttime eyes.

When Angel was in his car we needed to be able to follow him with no chance of being spotted. That's where the Wackenhut bumper beeper proved to be invaluable. It was a black box, smaller than a pack of cigarettes, that we attached to the under carriage of the flash car. Its tiny antenna transmitted a signal to a receiver, which indicated its location. We were able to follow that car all over town without ever seeing it. The equipment we used back then was state of the art but by today's standards they were little more than toys.

In addition to Angel's car we had two valid medallion Checker taxis and a van. The cabs were equipped with receivers for the bumper beeper and the portable tape recorders. A nondescript van with tinted windows hid the backup team from prying eyes and was equipped with a tripod for the night owl scope. We had walkie-talkie communications, on a confidential band, so the cabs and the van could communicate with each other in secrecy.

Angel would be the only one doing the actual drug buys. The other two undercovers would be used as ghosts, staying very close to Angel but not revealing themselves unless his life was in immediate danger.

Now we were ready to rock and roll and I thought, "Watch out, Dumont, we're coming to get you and you don't even know it."

We began tailing him when he was off duty and found out that his favorite watering hole was the Cozy Corner, at the intersection of Pennsylvania Avenue and Fulton Street in the heart of the always-dangerous East New York section of Brooklyn. A large circular bar in the middle of the floor dominated the room, which meant we could use two ghosts without attracting any attention. This was where we would have Angel make first contact with the target.

A streetwise female CI we trusted had already been approached about buying drugs from Dumont and had agreed to try. We decided to let her have a go at him before using Angel. We concealed a mini tape recorder in her pocketbook and on her first meeting she was able to get Dumont on tape selling her a bundle of heroin. A bundle was twenty-five stamp size glassine envelopes, with each one referred to on the street as a "bag." He suggested she charge $10 for each bag and gave her instructions on how to contact him for a reorder. He told her that if she wanted to increase her profit she could take a little from each envelope and make up two or three extra bags. Now we had our first drug purchase, referred to as an "A" buy. When we listened to the tape I shook my head and thought it was hard to believe this piece of shit was a cop.

We were off to a good start and were optimistic as we went to the fifty-seventh floor in Tower Two of the World Trade Center and reported the initiation of our investigation to the office of the special state prosecutor, Maurice Nadjari. We were assigned a prosecutor who would work with us during the investigation. When we let him listen to the tape the asshole told us, "Forget about this tape. I won't use a civilian as an undercover or as a witness. Get a cop to make a buy."

Some of these jerks weren't happy unless you handed them a slam-dunk—God forbid they take a chance that might hurt their conviction rate.

Back to square one. Angel would have to start with an "A" buy and use subsequent buys to prove that the first one wasn't just a casual thing between friends. The second or "B" buy would establish Dumont as a drug dealer. We wanted an ironclad case and had planned on going a little higher up the alphabet.

Angel turned out to be a dynamite undercover. Each night before we would go out he would pound his fist into the palm of his hand while repeating, "I'm going to make a buy tonight."

It helped him get into the skin of his character and it psyched him up. With Angel wired for sound it was time for him to head out to the Cozy Corner. By the time Angel arrived there our team was in place. Both cabs were parked on either side of the bar less than two blocks apart, Eddie Schneider and I in one and Joe Defina and one of the uniform cops in the other. The backup team, in the van, was parked in the twenty-four hour gas station across the street, rear doors facing the bar. The last members of our team were the ghosts. They were to enter the bar shortly after Angel and blend in with the crowd. Originally we were going to use both undercovers as ghosts but because one of them looked too young to be in a bar, we had to switch him with a cop from the van.

Both cabs were receiving Angel loud and clear and we switched on the tape recorders as soon as he entered the Cozy Corner. Angel went in and noticed Dumont standing at the far end of the bar. He stood right next to him and ordered a drink. Eddie and I started nursing two Heinekens as we settled in and began listening to Angel work his magic.

After a couple of sips he turned to Dumont and said, "Hey Cliff, how're you doing?"

"Do I know you?" Dumont answered.

"Yeah, we met at a party two months ago. Maybe you don't remember me 'cause you was flying high. I remember though 'cause that was some great snort you had that night. Best I ever had, and I'm in the business."

"What's your name again?"

"Angel."

"Mmm, I think I do remember you."

Before long they were conversing like old friends.

"Hey Angel, how would you like some of that good snort?"

Eddie and I were listening to this and couldn't believe how good it was going and how talented Angel was. By the end of the night we had Dumont on tape selling Angel a bundle of cocaine. This "A" buy would stick.

When they finally parted company they had exchanged phone numbers and agreed to meet again. The phone number Angel gave would be answered only by him; not even the other undercovers would touch that phone.

A call came in three days later. Angel answered it on the second ring.

"I'm looking for Angel Robles," he heard.

"Well, you just found him. Is that you, Cliff?"

"Yeah buddy. I called to see if you wanted to meet at the Cozy Corner later tonight."

"What time you gonna be there?"

"Around eight."

"Sure, sounds good. By the way do you carry any other product?"

"I do."

"Great, bring it with you tonight. Okay, Cliff?"

"You got it."

When Angel got there at eight Dumont was already at the bar. They greeted each other like old friends and an hour later Angel had purchased a bundle of heroin. We had our "B" buy on tape and Dumont was one step closer to a jail cell.

The team rendezvoused at our office where everyone congratulated Angel on a job well done. I took him to the side and asked him to do me a favor, "Try and stay away from the jukebox next time," I told him.

"Why, Jim? Is it hard to hear us talking?"

"No, I can hear you fine but they keep playing the same song and it's driving me crazy."

"Which one?"

"It's the one where they sing, *Do it . . . do it . . . do it, til you're satisfied*."

Three days later on the next meet Angel got there before Dumont. We heard him order a drink and ask the bartender, "You got four quarters for a dollar?"

I heard quarters being deposited, then in a low voice Angel said, "This is for you, Jim." And of course he stood next to the jukebox and I had to listen to that goddamn song four times in a row.

Angel went back to the bar and a minute later Dumont came in and they exchanged greetings. Not long after that they went to the bathroom to do the drug deal. While in there they ended up showing each other their guns and we heard Dumont remark, "Go Angel, nice weapon, an automatic and all I got is this snub-nose thirty-eight." Now we had our "C" buy on tape.

Angel and Dumont were at the Cozy Corner doing business again and it looked like we were close to getting a "D" buy on tape, when all hell broke loose. Eddie and I were listening to Angel and Dumont when all of a sudden Phil, the young looking black undercover assigned to the van, yelled into the walkie-talkie, "Holy shit." The rest of the transmission was lost because of the erupting gunfire. We were there in a matter of seconds. There were people running all over the street shooting at each other. We opened up on anyone with a gun who wasn't part of our team. The battle lasted about a minute and a half, a long time when you consider most gunfights last no more than twenty seconds. The bullets stopped flying when all three of the bad guys lay bleeding on the ground. They had robbed the gas station and shot the owner on the wrong night and at the wrong time.

I was amazed that no one on our team had been hit and, at that instant, the words Sergeant Dylan O'Day said so many years ago echoed in my ears: "So why aren't there more dead cops? Proficiency lads, proficiency."

The operation was blown for that night. Angel knew enough to get out of there as soon as possible. When he got back to the office, I asked him, "What do you think, is the operation blown?"

"No, not at all. Everyone in the bar figured the cops had gotten a tip that the gas station was going to be hit and had staked it out."

"So we lucked out?"

Angel laughed, "The operation is okay but we can't let Phil be seen again 'cause nobody is going to forget the little black kid wearing a shield on a chain around his neck." Everyone was amazed that a kid that young could be a cop. Phil looked like he was in high school even though he was twenty-three. I kept him working at the office and out of the field. He wasn't happy but he understood.

Angel kept meeting Dumont and buying drugs. They had become good friends and would travel around from bar to bar in the Lincoln. With the "H" buy on tape we decided it was time to snatch Dumont up—the next meet would be his last. Angel would get him to leave the Cozy Corner on some pretext and we would make the arrest.

Around two in the morning they got in the Lincoln and started driving. I got on the walkie-talkie and gave the order for all units to swoop down on them. A block away and a minute later we had Dumont in handcuffs in the back seat of one of the cabs. When I informed him he was under arrest for the sale of drugs and read him his rights he just stared at me in silent disbelief. Angel was also led away in cuffs and put into the other cab in hopes of preserving his cover for as long as possible. We took Dumont to the special state prosecutor's office where I continued questioning him for another hour. When it became apparent he wasn't going to talk without a little incentive, we brought Angel into the room. When Dumont saw him with an automatic pistol tucked in his waistband and a smile on his face he knew he was in trouble. His face drained of all resolve and he looked at Angel and whimpered, "You're an undercover, I should have known it."

Angel's smile broadened and he told Dumont, "We got you every which way but free. Got you on tape making eight drug deals and that means you're going away for a long time. I don't have to tell you what it's like for a cop in the joint. Here's some friendly advice, listen to the deal Sergeant O'Neil has for you and take it."

"The prosecutor has given me permission to offer you a deal," I told him, "but it's only going to be on the table for one minute, not a second longer. If you take it you'll be allowed to resign from the job and get minimum jail time."

The brass was more interested in purging the job of cops involved with drugs than sending one cop to jail.

There's a saying in the department, "When you got them by the balls, their hearts and minds will follow." And I had Dumont by the balls, but good.

I wasn't surprised when he asked, "What do you want?"

"I want you to write down the name of every cop you know who's using or selling narcotics. Keep nothing back and I will see to it that our end of the deal is held up."

No one was more surprised than I was when, an hour later, we had a list with fifty-one names on it. We processed Dumont through the system and had him released without bail. He cooperated with us and no one would be the wiser.

We began checking out the list and noticed a pattern emerging. The fifty-one names were almost all uniformed cops from Brooklyn who were hired in 1968 and 1969. Back then the Department was having trouble finding enough recruits to fill the ranks so they lowered the standards for entry. Relaxing their stringent character investigation had allowed guys to get on the force who should never have been cops. And now it was time for the Department to reap what it had sown.

It took my team of real cops three months to nail

Dumont, something these IAD scummers couldn't do in three years. My team went on to bring down another sixteen dirty drug-dealing cops. We felt good about that. Then our satisfaction turned to shit when we found out that all sixteen of those fucks were given the opportunity to resign from the job with no jail time. They never even went to trial—fucking departmental politics.

Shortly after we flipped Dumont I got called onto the carpet by three high-ranking IAD bosses: a deputy inspector who asked the questions and two of his lackeys who observed the interrogation. It seems that some bullshit cases involving minor infractions had been compromised and they figured I was the one tipping off cops. I denied it, very confident that I had covered my tracks. In my most convincing tone I told the inspector (officially he was a deputy inspector but protocol demanded he be addressed as "Inspector,") "Me? No way, sir."

"Look, Jim, we know it has to be you. We don't want to hurt you, we just want you to admit which cases you compromised so we can reinvestigate them."

"Yeah, and the IRS has a heart. If you had anything on me I'd already be suspended or locked up." I held my arms out and said, "I don't admit to a goddamn thing, Inspector. If you think you can prove your charges slap on the bracelets. Oh, and don't hold your breath waiting for me to slip a noose around my own neck. Lock me up if you want, but be prepared for a lawsuit."

That infuriated the bastards and the leader of the pack's words slithered out, "You're out of here, O'Neil, as of this moment you're a bad IAD memory."

I spat back, "That's fine with me. I'm tired of dealing with this rat pack. Now go ahead and make me a real cop again."

And they did. They would have loved to demote me but sergeant was a civil service rank and they couldn't do it. Instead they transferred me to one of the most crime-ridden areas in the city, the 32nd Precinct in Harlem. To their way of thinking that was the worst thing they could do to me. To my way of thinking it was salvation. And it ushered me into the most violent and rewarding years I would spend on the job.

CHAPTER EIGHTEEN

Dodge City—32nd Precinct, Harlem

I figured I'd never get an investigative assignment again, even though Eddie Schneider was going to purge my IAD file of any derogatory comments as soon as was prudent. With that knowledge I closed the IAD chapter of my career. Thanks to Eddie I would once again have a clean slate and thanks to me the other guys at IAD, who had tipped off cops, would skate.

Now that I was going to the 32nd Precinct I would be able to get back to playing cops and robbers. With that realization, in January 1975, I reported to Deputy Inspector Jimmy Maher. He was a good boss, who was soon destined to lose his command due to another typical IAD fuck-up.

The 32nd Precinct ran from 127th Street to 159th Street, bounded by Saint Nicholas Avenue on the west and stopped by the Harlem River on the east. One square mile cut out of the living, throbbing, heart of Harlem only seventeen blocks from Central Park but a world apart.

Harlem was Brownsville with class. Unlike Brownsville's mostly poor inhabitants Harlem was a study in contrasts running the gamut of poor, middle-, and upper-class blacks with a smattering of white families. Thousands of hardworking people took the "A" train every day to their downtown jobs, their commute immortalized by Duke Ellington in his song "Take the 'A' Train."

Numerous high-rise housing projects with flowery

names like Esplanade Gardens and Colonial Houses hinted at a better life. This was where many of the middle-class working people lived. Not far from there was a three-block run of private residences, expensive brownstones that were home to doctors, professionals, and corporate executives. People who had beaten the odds and become successful lived there on "Strivers' Row." People whose success never steered them from the Harlem they loved. Somewhere between the middle-class working people and the wealthy were those who inhabited Lenox Towers at 135th Street and Lenox Avenue.

The poorest people were concentrated at the epicenter of the precinct, in an area overburdened with six-story tenements. Crimes, violence, and drugs were rampant there. Calls of shots fired, persons shot, gunfights, and homicides were all too common and earned the precinct the nickname "Dodge City."

Some famous bars and restaurants, as well as some not so famous ones, spawned renowned black entertainers, one of Harlem's most important contributions to the world.

Small parks with always-populated basketball courts dotted the area and one hospital with its dedicated, overworked staff of predominantly black doctors and nurses ministered to the more than 200,000 local residents. I can't recall ever being in the emergency room of Harlem Hospital when it wasn't overflowing with patients.

The station house was located on 135th Street and was just as busy as the hospital. It was ancient and smelled of felonies, homicides, muggings, and all manner of crimes.

Being a desk officer in a busy precinct was the worst job in the department. Whenever I reported to work and found that I was assigned to the desk, I cringed. The desk officer had so many responsibilities that it was almost impossible to do the job. A tour in the 32nd was worse than the chaotic ones that would be portrayed in the TV series *Hill Street Blues*.

At the start of a tour the desk officer had to review the roll call and certify it as accurate. A blotter entry had to be made attesting to it. Next the evidence room had to be inventoried and everything accounted for—another blotter entry. Any post changes had to be recorded. All prisoners had to be searched in front of the desk officer and then it was his responsibility to book them. Any evidence seized required a voucher to be made out. Sometimes there would be eight to ten prisoners on one side of the desk waiting to be searched and as many on the other side waiting to be booked. There was always a constant stream of civilians, with legitimate complaints that had to be addressed. You could always count on the stray psycho wandering in off the street ranting and raving about something. All this going on, while the phones were ringing off the hook. Every complaint brought in and prepared in the one twenty-four room had to be reviewed then signed.

I was doing a four-to-twelve tour on the desk when the cop covering the borough office called with a complaint of some guys drinking beer on 136th Street. Glester Hines, a retired postman who had managed to file 232 bullshit complaints in one year, had struck again. The radio had been busy coughing up shots-fired calls, muggings, burglaries, and assaults. I told the borough cop, "I'm up to my ass in serious calls here and you want me to assign a car on some guys drinking beer on the street. Forget it, ain't gonna happen."

"But, Sarge, you have to take it and give it a number."

"Just make an entry in your telephone message book as follows: I spoke to Sergeant O'Neil on the three two desk and he said I won't take the telephone message. We are up to our asses with work over here. And add to the entry that Sergeant O'Neil doesn't give a rat's ass about Glester Hines and he can take a flying fuck to the moon for all I care."

The next day when I came in I had a message to call the clerical man, Paddy Pesche, at the borough office. When I got him on the phone, he said, "When the Chief got to your entry he started laughing. He was laughing so hard tears were rolling down his face. He made everyone in the office read it and he said that he had at least one sergeant in Harlem with a big set of balls."

Being on the desk pushed you to your limits. I remember one day doing a four to twelve with Sergeant Jerry Morgan, a big bear of a man. He was the desk officer and I was assigned as the patrol supervisor. It was particularly busy so I stayed in for a while to give him a hand before hitting the street. At the height of the bedlam a civilian came through the door ranting about his car being vandalized. Ignoring the prisoners lined up on either side of the desk he approached Jerry and began yelling and cursing at him. Jerry told him to calm down and have a seat and that he would get to him as soon as possible, but the guy kept the tirade up and then he spit at Jerry. That was it, Jerry came out from behind the desk yelling, "Get the fuck out of my station house you crazy bastard."

The guy backed off physically but not verbally and then he spit again. That set Jerry off and he screamed, "I told you to get the fuck out of here you crazy psycho motherfucker." In an instant Jerry was on the guy choking him and screaming, "You fucking lunatic I'll kill you, I'll kill you."

By the time I vaulted over the desk and pried Jerry's hands free, the guy's eyes were bugging out. He struggled to his feet and staggered out the front door.

Jerry walked back to the desk muttering something about rather having leprosy than a desk assignment.

Even the prisoners were laughing and they shouted, "Hey Sarge, you should've killed him. We know that fucking madman from around the neighborhood."

We never saw or heard from him again.

There were plenty of psychos to go around. According to the Department under Commissioner Murphy, they weren't psychos—they were emotionally disturbed persons (EDPs). We had an EDP on 143rd Street and Lenox Avenue whose name was Cato. He was a highly-decorated war hero who had his brains scrambled while fighting for his country. He was harmless until he cashed his monthly disability check and got loaded up on Colt 45 malt liquor. Then he'd become a danger to himself and his neighbors. Cato was very large, very strong, and very dark-skinned. It generally took six to eight cops to put him down and cuff him, but because of his war record we tried to be as gentle as we could. After all it wasn't his fault that he was fucked up in the head.

One afternoon on patrol we heard over the radio, "One hundred forty-third Street and Lenox Avenue report of a man harassing passersby." I told my driver, "John, get us over there as quick as you can. I think I know what this run is about."

Sure as shit we pulled up and there was Cato going nuts. I got out of the RMP and yelled back to John, "Notify Central on what we have and get us at least three backup cars."

I heard him yell into the mike, "Three-Two Sergeant to Central, ten-eighty-five Four-Three-Two Precinct units to this location."

Central came back with, "What's the condition there, Three-Two Sergeant?"

"We have an EDP here that bears a strong resemblance to King Kong."

When I heard that I thought, "Oh shit, there goes his career and probably mine as well."

Four cars responded and fifteen minutes later Cato was in Harlem Hospital and a bunch of New York's finest were sporting various scrapes and bruises.

Luckily nobody had picked up on John's transmission or he might have retired as Patrolman John Laffy instead of Two-Star Assistant Chief Laffy. I remained friends with John his entire career and he always maintained that his description wasn't meant to be disparaging, he was just awed by Cato's size and would have given the same description had Cato been white.

The best job in the department was being a patrol supervisor in a busy precinct. I loved going from one radio run to another, never knowing what I would come across. I remember the first time my driver was Timmy Gallagher, a tall, wiry young lad with the map of Ireland on his face. On one sunny June morning, we were proceeding slowly down 141st Street when Timmy yelled out, "Hey, Sarge, look up there." He was pointing to a window on the top floor of a six-story apartment house that had flames leaping out of it.

"I see it. Timmy, call Central to send the fire department to this location and report that we are entering the building."

We ran up to the top floor and began banging on doors. In each instance startled residents responded and hastily exited the building. The last ones to leave the building, Timmy and I gulped street air through singed nasal passages. We had made it out unharmed and believed we had evacuated all the residents. Wrong—a middle-aged man with shaving cream still covering the unshaven part of his face asked, "Did anybody get the deaf-mute woman out of 6B?"

We had assumed the sixth floor apartment was vacant.

I turned to Timmy and without a word passing between us we headed back into the building. The smoke had gotten thicker and more toxic as fire claimed more of the old wooden structure. By the time we reached the sixth floor, amber-red flames leapt up the walls accompanied by a loud crackling windlike sound. The heat was so intense that it began to burn our skin under our uniforms. Tears flowed from our eyes and breathing was becoming a chore. When we kicked down the door to 6B, we found a small woman in her late fifties frozen with fear, sitting in a rocking chair. Once it registered that help had arrived, hope filled her face and she jumped out of her chair. She was able to walk without any assistance and started down the stairs on her own.

I turned to Timmy and said, "We better check the roof and make sure nobody panicked and ran up there to escape."

"Right behind you, Sarge."

We searched the roof until we were confident that no

one was up there and then we opened the door to reenter the building. But by now the sixth floor hallway was completely involved and we were met with thick, billowing, black smoke.

"Come on, Timmy, let's use the fire escape."

When we got there we found that the bolts securing the top of the fire escape to the building had let go and were pulled about a foot away from the wall.

I was afraid of heights as it was, and there was no way I was setting foot on that rickety excuse for an escape route. "Shit," was all Timmy said.

We were trapped between a roof and a hot place as our fire-fighting brothers worked feverishly to reach us. The longest twenty minutes of my life passed before they cleared a path through the fire but by then Timmy and I had taken so much smoke that we smelled like two charcoal briquettes. Our legs had turned to rubber so we had to be carried down to a waiting ambulance. Our lungs felt like they were on fire and we were spitting up blood as we wound our way through Harlem streets on the way to the hospital. My mind drifted back to all the times during my father's thirty-six-year career with the FDNY that he was rushed to a hospital with everything from burns to the time a wall collapsed on him. Back to reality and minutes later we arrived at Columbia Presbyterian Medical Center where we were treated for smoke inhalation and released.

Most people don't realize it but there are many occasions when a cop is the first one into a burning building. That was only the second time on the job I had eaten smoke, but it made me realize that my decision to fight bad guys instead of fires was the right one for me. I was proud to be a cop and especially a cop in Harlem. Almost all the cops in Harlem, men and women, were excellent. They had to be or they didn't survive; working Harlem was not for the faint of heart. I remember a newly promoted sergeant named Paulson who was transferred in from a desk job at headquarters. We referred to an easy assignment like that as "being in the woodwork." Paulson had been in the woodwork his entire career.

His first tour as a sergeant was a midnight to eight. He and his driver spent the first two hours responding to normal Harlem radio runs. Everything from shots fired jobs to gunshot victims. Around 2 AM his driver needed to go to the bathroom so they came back to the station house. Paulson looked like he was in a state of semi-shock as he stood staring at the wall opposite the desk, which was covered with pictures of members of the 32nd killed in the line of duty. Every precinct in the city had a wall like that but none had as many pictures. Under each picture was a plaque and Paulson was reading one after the other. When his driver came out of the bathroom Paulson asked him, "All these guys killed worked here?"

"Yeah, Sarge, every one of them."

"Any sergeants in this precinct ever get killed?"

"Sure, over here," and he pointed to a picture to the right of where they stood. "That's Sergeant Tusten, he got killed over on Lenox Avenue a couple of years ago. A guy got him with a shotgun blast."

Paulson stayed in the station house for the rest of his tour and in the morning he went to headquarters, turned in his gun and shield, and quit the job. That was a good thing because nobody needed a coward in their midst. Cowards usually never got hurt but they tended to get those around them injured.

The opposite of Paulson was Sergeant Louie Anemone. Louie's soft good looks fooled you into thinking he was meek, but in reality he was fearless. Whenever I turned out the men and he was patrol sergeant I would caution them, "Don't forget to wear your vests. Be careful and remember there are no routine radio runs out there. And if you get any heavy runs like shots fired watch out that Sergeant Anemone doesn't run you over trying to be the first one through the door."

In addition to being fearless Louie was very intelligent and I figured he was destined to go higher in the job. I was right. He rose to the rank of Four-Star Chief and as Chief of

Department he grabbed crime by the balls and squeezed until New York was well on its way to becoming one of the safest cities in the country. I was proud to have served with a Harlem sergeant named Louie Anemone, a man who loved what he did.

But then most of the Harlem cops loved their jobs, although none showed it as uniquely as Officer Ellio Sanchez. We got paid every two weeks on a Thursday and without fail Ellio would perform the same ritual every payday. He would hold his check up and say, "Lookie here, look at all the money they give this Puerto Rican boy. Ten jeers ago I was in Puerto Rico with no shoes and horseshit between my toes. I come to this country, wash my feet, get shoes and they make me a policeman. Look at all the money they give me for doing something I would do for free." Then falling to his knees in front of the American flag he would sing "God Bless America." Every two weeks he did it and every two weeks we laughed. That little levity was such a contrast to what we had to deal with, day in and day out, that we never tired of hearing it.

As much as I loved being a patrol officer and running on calls there was one call I hated taking, especially in the summer, and that was a ripe DOA. Sometimes extreme heat waves would kill the elderly and they would lie for days, even weeks, decomposing until a relative or a friend would get concerned and call us. Or sometimes we would get called because of a bad odor emanating from an apartment. We would run on the call and if it was a really bad case you would smell it as soon as you got out of the radio car, even if the DOA was on the fourth or fifth floor. There was no smell in the world that rivaled that of a rotting human corpse. A skunk in a dead bear's ass would smell like perfume in comparison. The stench would cling to your uniform unless you had it dry cleaned immediately.

I had made too many of those calls, and during an extreme heat wave I'd get as many as three a day. We would burn rags in a metal container to try and get the smoke to knock down the smell or spread ammonia all around or smoke cigars but nothing helped.

Besides the nauseating smell, the bodies would be falling apart. I remember one particularly bad case in Lenox Towers, and it wasn't even during a heat wave. An elderly woman's neighbors called to report that they hadn't seen her in weeks. When we arrived there and got out of the car we didn't smell anything but that could have been because all the apartments at Lenox Towers had sealed steel doors. We went up to the third floor where we found the neighbors waiting in the hall. As soon as I put my nose up against the edge of the door I knew what we were going to find inside. When we opened that door the smell was going to hit us like a wall. Trying to spare the neighbors I told them to wait down at the end of the hall.

We finally got the door open and the smell rolled over us and spread out. Some of the neighbors began vomiting. I observed the swollen decomposing body on a couch. Then I saw it, a black pulsating cloud hovering about two feet above the body. The cloud was slowly raising and lowering itself by only a matter of a few inches. I had no idea what the hell it was until I got closer. It was thousands of flies that had hatched from the maggot eggs. The body was covered with maggots. Even with my poor sense of smell I almost tossed my cookies. There were two other officers with me, Eddie Garrity, a seasoned veteran, and a rookie named Tommy Trainor. Garrity looked fine but Trainor didn't. When Garrity went to the woman's refrigerator and took a drink of orange juice Trainor vomited.

There was always something going on in Harlem and that's why I loved being on patrol. One day we were driving down Lenox Avenue when we saw a crowd gathered around two guys who were engaged in an altercation. I told my driver, Jimmy Wilson, a young freckle-faced rookie, to stop the car. As we approached the two guys I noticed the smaller one had a pipe wrench in his hands and the other guy was wielding a large hunting knife. They were circling each other, searching for an opening. I drew my service revolver and ordered both of them to drop their weapons. The guy with the pipe wrench dropped his weapon and jumped behind me. The other guy refused to drop his knife and he started walking toward me. When he was about thirty feet from me I yelled, "Drop it or I'll shoot."

He stopped but still held on to his knife and at that moment an incident that happened when I was still a rookie flashed through my mind. Back in 1963, a sergeant named Johnson and two cops had responded to a report of a knife-wielding psycho in a basement downtown on The Bowery, New York's version of skid row at that time. The psycho, slight of build but muscled up on booze, was holding a knife at his side. As he walked toward the cops they were yelling for him to drop his weapon. When he was twenty feet away he raised the knife and started running toward them. Sergeant Johnson and the two cops opened fire—eighteen rounds they fired, hitting the guy nine times. The nine hits were fatal and the guy died seconds after the knife, propelled by his forward momentum, plunged into Sergeant Johnson's heart. There were two deaths that day in that basement. One was unnecessary and that's why I had every intention of shooting this asshole unless he dropped his weapon before taking another step. I cocked my gun and aimed at his head. I yelled, "Take one more step toward me and I'll put one between your fucking eyebrows."

In a Harlem heartbeat he dropped the knife. My driver snapped it up and slapped the cuffs on both guys. I breathed a sigh of relief. They both got charged with disorderly conduct and possession of a weapon. As it turned out neither one had a criminal record so chances were they would see no jail time.

Hell, even the good people in Harlem carried a weapon for self-defense. I remember being called to Harlem Hospital on a recovered gun report. A seventy-two-year-old man had been taken there suffering a heart attack. When his clothes were removed the attending nurse found a loaded gun and we were subsequently called. Upon our arrival at the hospital, the weapon was turned over to us and it became my unpleasant duty to inform the elderly gentleman that he was under arrest for weapons possession. I didn't want to aggravate him but I had no choice. When I placed him under arrest he took it very well and offered me words of comfort. "Son," he said, "you look distressed. Don't let this bother you. Tell you what, I'd rather you officers catch me with it than a mugger catch me without it." If it was up to me I would have just confiscated the gun and left the old guy alone—case closed.

We left the hospital and within a half an hour we were back, this time covered in blood. We had just turned onto 138th Street when I saw a middle-aged man staggering into the street. When I first pointed him out to my driver I thought the guy was drunk but as we got closer I realized he was bleeding heavily from a wound in his neck. It must have just happened because he was still on his feet. It looked like someone hit him in the neck with an axe. I knew this guy was in big trouble and couldn't afford to wait for an ambulance. As I threw him in the back seat of the RMP I noticed that a severed blood vessel in his neck was pumping blood at an alarming rate. I stuck my fingers into the wound and pinched off the damaged blood vessel. I yelled to my driver, "Jimmy, notify Radio Central that we have a victim with a badly slashed throat and ask them to call the ER at Harlem Hospital and tell them to have a team waiting. Let them know we are transporting the victim by RMP with an ETA of two minutes. Turn on the light, hit the siren, and get the fuck out of here."

A medical team was waiting at the door when we pulled up, and as they loaded him on the gurney I continued to pinch off the vessel while he was wheeled into the emergency room. A doctor clamped off the vein and I was able to remove my blood-soaked hand from the wound. We went and washed up, then cleaned the blood off the back seat of the RMP.

When we were finished we checked to see how the victim was doing. One of the doctors told us he was in the operating room and that if he survived it was due to our quick thinking. I felt really good about myself. That was what being a cop was about, helping people, protecting people, and not just about locking up scumbags. Three days later I visited the hospital and he told me the doctors said he was going to make a full recovery. Then he looked at me and said, "You know I've heard a lot of bad things about white cops in black neighborhoods, but you are one white cop I'm glad was in my neighborhood."

I felt good again and on the way home I felt like rolling down the car window and yelling, "I saved a man's life." But I just smiled and when I got home I told Peggy.

That night I sat in my nice safe suburban home and reflected on my last two trips to Harlem Hospital. I thought about what it must be like living in a place where a seventy-two-year-old man felt the need to carry a gun for protection and then I thought about how I would feel sending my kids to school every day in that kind of place. And that's when my joy of having saved a life turned to sorrow with thoughts of the tens of thousands of parents in Harlem whose children would be walking to school tomorrow through harm's way.

Nothing underscored this problem more than what was happening at the intersection of West 127th Street and Eighth Avenue. All the drug dealers and addicts congregating on the sidewalks prevented the flow of pedestrian traffic. The good people living in the housing project, across the street, had to walk in the traffic lanes to get anywhere. It was a goddamn shame and I was determined to clean up that intersection. A uniformed cop named Jerry Evans approached me with a solution. He said, "Sarge, if you get me assigned to a regular foot post on that corner I'll clean it up."

I went to the roll call man and told him to make sure Jerry Evans got assigned that corner on every one of his tours. Jerry was a tall, well-muscled, dedicated black cop who wanted to make life a little better for the decent people of Harlem, even if it was one block at a time. He never carried a nightstick, opting instead for a hydrant wrench. It was metal, about sixteen inches long and had a five-sided opening on the end used to open or close fire hydrants. Jerry used it for its intended purpose, some of the time. The rest of the time, well let's just say there were a lot of drug dealers and addicts who wore a distinctive five-sided bruise upside their head. The results were dramatic as the ranks of dealers and addicts began to diminish.

One day we were driving down 127th Street and we saw Jerry with a guy at a fire hydrant. There was a trickle of water coming out and the guy had his hands cupped to catch it. He drank the water then held his cupped hands out. Jerry ripped open a bag of something and dumped the contents into the guy's hands. The guy stuffed whatever it was into his mouth and then got more water and swallowed. I turned to my driver and said, "Get me the hell out of here. I don't want to see this."

A little while later we saw the guy running north on Eighth Avenue with that telltale five sided bruise on his forehead. When I ran into Jerry at the end of his tour I asked him, "Did I see what I thought I saw when you and that guy were at the fire hydrant?"

Jerry laughed and said, "Sarge, I told that motherfucker several times before that he wasn't going to be selling drugs on my post anymore. Today I caught him with ten bags of marijuana and I told him he could eat them or go to jail. You saw the choice he made. When he was done I clocked him across the forehead with the hydrant wrench and told him to stay the fuck off my post."

Jerry's brand of instant justice precipitated many visits to the civilian complaint review board. He always had a plausible story and I always backed him up. They never nailed him.

Conditions on "Jerry's block" steadily improved and the decent people living there got back the use of their sidewalks. Cops like Jerry Evans were the rule rather than the exception in Harlem and I was so proud to serve with them.

Even good cops get lax and screw up occasionally, but

if luck is with you nobody gets hurt and you learn from your mistake. Here I was, a seasoned veteran, with hundreds of arrests under my belt and about to fuck up. It was a cool but pleasant enough day when two officers responded to a minor complaint at a tenement on 148ᵗʰ Street. As they walked down the hallway they passed an open door and noticed a pile of hypodermic syringes on a bed. Three males were present and were promptly arrested. Department regulations required the patrol supervisor be summoned on any drug arrest. We fielded the 10-85, a call to meet somebody, and responded to the location. When my driver and I entered the room we saw the three perps handcuffed wrist to wrist. I should have given the officers my handcuffs so they could back-cuff each perp but it was a bullshit collar so I just told them to search the three of them and the immediate area. A more extensive search of the apartment would require a warrant and we probably wouldn't have been granted one anyway.

When we arrived at the station house we deposited the perps upstairs in the detective squad's cage where they would wait to be processed. While they were waiting I ran into three old friends I had worked with on the BLA case squad. Once the BLA was destroyed that squad had become the Major Case Squad, which now worked citywide. They were decked out in bulletproof vests and were carrying shotguns. These guys were the crème de la crème of the detective bureau. We exchanged smiles and handshakes and I declared, "Wow, did they give you guys a crash course in being civilized and let you out of Brooklyn?"

They all made low growling noises. I got my answer. Then Tommy Buonno, the largest of the three, continued, "Yeah, and we all had our rabies shots too."

"Well, welcome to Harlem. What brings you here?"

"We had a bank robbery this morning and a security guard was shot. We identified the perp as doing several other bank jobs and found that he comes from up here. We're going to hit a few locations and wanted to check in here first to let you guys know that we were in the area. We wouldn't want some uniformed cop mistaking us for a trio of bad guys."

"Okay, I'll pass the word."

"Thanks, Jim. By the way, is Lieutenant McKenna still the detective squad boss up here?"

"Yeah, as a matter of fact I saw him upstairs a few minutes ago."

They went up to the detective squad room and never got to the lieutenant's office. They only got as far as the cage. One of the three guys we had recently arrested for the hypos was the guy they were looking for. They dragged him out of the cage and strip-searched him. His coat seemed a little heavy and when they examined it they found a hidden pocket containing a loaded revolver with one spent round. It had to be the weapon used to shoot the security guard. I almost shit. He could have pulled that gun and used it on us at any time.

We had let our guard down and become lax because we were making a bullshit low-level collar. We didn't realize we had a real badass on our hands. As patrol sergeant I should have insisted they be rear-cuffed. I never made that mistake again.

Fortunately Tommy Buonno and the other two detectives were friends of mine and they concocted a story on how they recovered the gun, and my screw-up never saw the light of day.

CHAPTER NINETEEN

May the Force Be with Us

In March of 1976 Tommy Cox, my captain at the 32nd, approached me with an offer I couldn't refuse. "Jim," he began, "the sergeant in the detective squad, Freddie Shepard, went to headquarters this morning and put in his retirement papers. His terminal leave won't be up for three or four months and I can't get a replacement until then. I have twenty-nine sergeants in this command and you're the only one with any experience as a detective. Do you want to fill in up there until the department assigns someone?"

"Captain, do you know why I was assigned here?"

"You mean that bullshit about getting kicked out of Internal Affairs Division? Hell, as far as I'm concerned they should have given you a medal for that."

"There's nothing I'd like better than to get back into doing detective work, even if it's only temporary."

"Then it's settled, starting tomorrow you're second whip on the detective squad. Lieutenant Jim McKenna is the whip and you report to him. Good luck, Jim."

It's funny how a person's fortunes can turn. I figured my career was shot after that IAD fiasco. If the concept of specialized detective squads covering multiple precincts, instituted in 1972 by Commissioner Murphy, hadn't failed I probably would've retired while still in uniform. But because the Department went back to each precinct having its own detective squad my captain had the authority to assign me as a boss within his command.

The next day I showed up in a suit and tie and, although I didn't know it then, I would never go back in the bag and would serve out my remaining years as a detective squad boss. I reported to Lieutenant McKenna, a soft-spoken man of average height and build. A real gentleman who all the detectives respected. He was a good boss and we worked well together, eventually becoming good friends. We shared the administrative duties, which left me time to get involved in the investigations. Most of the squad was made up of experienced detectives who proved to be excellent investigators. Thank God, because this was one of the busiest detective squads in the city and it was about to get a lot busier.

Just as I was settling into my new job two things occurred, one good and one bad.

The good thing: my old boss from the TPF, Michael J Codd, had taken over as commissioner and was beginning to reverse the damage done by Murphy.

The bad thing: a drug war broke out and it was shaping up to be real ugly.

I guess you could say that I was ushered into my new assignment by The Good, The Bad, and The Ugly.

Drugs were a big business and drew customers from other parts of the city and even from other states. Heroin, cocaine, and angel dust were the drugs of choice. Heroin and cocaine fostered a euphoric high while angel dust's by-product was some of the most violent behavior I had ever seen.

In 1976 the undisputed kingpin of the drug trade in New York City was Leroy "Nicky" Barnes, an ex-addict who had taken his first bust for possession in 1961. His operation grew until it reached into the Deep South and as far west as Detroit. He ran it from The Taureans Two, an illegal after-hours club he owned, located at West 152nd Street and Eighth

Avenue.

Vying with Barnes for control in the area were several smaller drug gangs whose members were extremely violent and had no regard for human life. These animals would pay twelve- or thirteen-year-old kids to carry their guns for them. This way if the cops stopped them the dealer would be unarmed and the kid would be arrested and taken to kiddie court. The kid would get a slap on the wrist and be back on the street in no time. Whenever he needed a gun all the drug dealer had to do was put out his hand. The kid would slap the gun in it, much like a nurse in an operating room would hand over a requested scalpel to a surgeon's outstretched hand. In a single thirty-day period at the intersection of West 147th Street and Eighth Avenue there were seventeen people shot, three of whom died. The place was becoming as dangerous as Vietnam. We were happy when we heard that some scumbag dealer got killed and if they were the only victims we would have gladly let them kill each other, but innocent people were getting caught in the crossfire. It was so awful that when certain bad guys walked down the street mothers would rush out and drag their kids inside. A feral atmosphere pervaded the community and the news media was beginning to pick up the scent.

We didn't really have a handle on who all the players were, in part, due to ex-Commissioner Murphy's paranoia about alleged police corruption. Under his reign, bars and restaurants had been classified as corruption-prone locations. And God forbid if you were in close proximity to a location where someone was writing the digit. Detectives stopped frequenting these information-rich places and consequently lost many good contacts, but this was about to change.

We started building organizational charts of the different drug factions and recording them on large sheets of oak tag paper. We had some information coming in but not nearly enough. I had one detective in particular, George Roberts, trying his best to stay on top of what was going on in the streets.

One day Captain Cox walked into my office and said, "Jim, the news media is kicking the shit out of us about all these shootings and homicides. They're saying drug trafficking is rampant and the Department can't seem to stop it. That area north of 145th Street has become a major embarrassment to the Police Department and the city administration. The Chief of Department has summoned the zone commander and me to his office to discuss the problem. I want you to go with us."

"Sure thing, Captain. Would it be all right if I brought George Roberts? He knows as much about the problem as anybody."

"Definitely."

The three of us left to meet the zone commander, Inspector Charles O. Henry. He was a tall, imposing man with a calm demeanor and a quick smile. At that time he was one of the highest-ranking black men in the job. Introductions were made and the four of us entered the Chief's office, where George and I brought out the oak tag organization charts. We pointed out what we knew and what we didn't know and how difficult it was obtaining information because of all the restrictions placed on us. The Chief stood up and excused himself, saying, "Gentlemen, I'm going to fill in Commissioner Codd on this and I'll be right back. I'm going to suggest we form a task force, so think of a name for it."

The Chief left and I glanced at Inspector Henry who had pursed his lips and was stroking his chin. I asked, "Well, Inspector, what do you think?"

A big smile and he answered, "Jim, I think we'll call it Star Wars."

"Star Wars, sir? Why that?"

"Because it's going to put stars on my shoulders."

I got the drift. He wore eagles now but a promotion to deputy chief would put a star on each shoulder. That would be equivalent to a brigadier general in the Army. I had only just met him but I was beginning to like him already.

The Chief returned and addressed Inspector Henry. "Charlie, an order is being cut to form a task force with you as the commander. Pull in any assets or personnel you need and use any tactics you deem necessary. Just put a stop to what's going on up there."

We went back to Inspector Henry's office and he turned to me and said, "Jim, I have carte blanche so you are now the first member of the task force. I was never a detective so you tell me what has to be done and the eagles on my shoulder will make it happen."

"Inspector, how about making George member number two?"

"George, welcome to Star Wars. Captain Cox, you'll still command the three-two but you'll be assigned as an advisor to the task force. Jim, you got anything you want to add?"

"Yes sir, I do. If we're going to be successful, George and I have to get out in the street. We have to be able to operate like detectives did pre-Murphy. I promise you nobody is going to take a hat, not even so much as a penny. We have to get to know the smart money people up there that run the Harlem rackets. They have to know that cooperating with us is in their best interest and that not cooperating with us will be bad for business. IAD might have the cameras cranking overtime on us. Give us your guarantee that you'll back us up and we'll get to work."

"You have my word, I'll back you to the wall. You do whatever you have to do. Go and take back our streets."

I was starting to get excited and I remember thinking, "This is going to be a hell of a ride."

The task force area would run ten blocks long from 145th Street to 155th Street and two blocks wide from Seventh Avenue to Bradhurst Avenue. We would handle any drug-related shootings or homicides within that area. We would also be assisted by the 6th Division Homicide Squad under the capable command of Herman "The German" Kluge. The 6th was possibly the busiest homicide squad in the world and their experience and expertise would be invaluable. They would handle any non-drug-related homicides.

Inspector Henry turned out to be a joy to work for. He was a very pragmatic man and at the same time very down to earth. A lot of people at his level were quick to give commands but slow to listen to suggestions, especially when coming from a "mere" sergeant. He was the opposite.

As Star Wars gained momentum it picked up liaisons within the Department with the Intelligence Division, Public Morals, and Narcotics. On a federal level we added a representative from the Drug Enforcement Agency (DEA) and two agents from the Treasury Department's Alcohol Tobacco and Firearms Division (ATF) whose job would be to trace back to their point of manufacture any firearms recovered, with particular attention being given to its point of sale. When the thought of bringing the FBI into Star Wars came up I felt that they would be of little help. We had our own police laboratory, which was excellent, and a ballistics squad as good as any at the FBI.

We had to start with the basics so I recruited some of the best uniformed cops in the 32nd Precinct. They would become our eyes and ears on the street. Once I had lined up all the players I called a meeting. I explained that we had to open up sources of information and the best way to do that was to get the attention of the smart money people. Once they knew we could hurt them in their wallets they would have an incentive to help us. The underground world of the numbers racket and the illegal sale of alcohol in after-hours clubs were multimillion-dollar revenue producers in Harlem. Even White Lightning was being imported from the Deep South and sold up here. This stuff was going on openly and I blame ex-Commissioner Murphy and his cohorts for their idiotic rules that took the teeth out of the police bite.

I decided to concentrate on the numbers racket because everybody played the digit and there would be a wealth of information, if I could flip the numbers banker. Playing the digit was the poor man's Atlantic City minus the bus ride. The profits to the banker were huge. They even published a "Dream Sheet" that people bought with the promise that it would divine the winning numbers by interpreting their dreams. Hell, one of the guys I worked with in Brooklyn went into the Dream Sheet business after he was forced to retire from the force due to his extensive gunshot wounds. Even old Jesse who ran the shoeshine stand in our muster room would write the digit for a lot of the cops, while giving them a shine. Numbers was a clean, easy, and quasi-legal way to make a ton of money.

I asked the uniformed guys to get me the address of every location in the task force area where someone was writing the digit and to find out who the numbers banker was. It didn't take long before I had the addresses of fourteen numbers locations, and the name of the banker controlling them, and where I could find him. I never knew his real name but he answered just fine to "Doc." When I introduced myself as Sergeant O'Neil it didn't faze him at all. His confidence was warranted, given that he had been allowed to operate with impunity for the last several years. So I wasn't surprised that he laughed at me when I told him, "I'm going to need some information about what's going on in the area and as long as you help me out I'll leave you alone to conduct business as usual."

"The cops haven't been allowed to fuck with us for years, but nice try. You can't touch me, so go take a hike."

I took his advice and hiked on over to Inspector Henry's office. After I filled the Inspector in on our friend Doc he asked me, "So what do you want to do about it, Jim?"

"I'd like Public Morals to send undercovers to all fourteen locations to play the digit. That will give me something to hold over his head."

Thirty seconds later he was on the phone with the boss

of Manhattan North Public Morals. "Captain McCabe, this is Inspector Henry," he said. I'm sending my aide, Sergeant Jim O'Neil, over with a list of locations I want given attention. He will fill you in on what we want done."

When I got to Captain McCabe and told him what we wanted he remarked, "But we don't do that anymore. Those are all corruption-prone locations."

"Look, Captain, we have an important job to do and we have clearance from the Chief of Ops office to use any tactics we deem necessary. Besides Murphy's gone now and Mike Codd is at the helm."

"Okay, Jim, I hope you know what you're doing. I'll put my men on it right away."

Two weeks later fourteen numbers locations were raided and arrests were made. The arrests were bullshit and only drew small fines. But the real hurt came from each location's loss of a day's business and the fact that all monies found were confiscated along with their betting slips. The next day anyone in the neighborhood could claim they had the winning number. It wouldn't be honored but they might get back the money they bet.

I waited two days and then went to see Doc and told him, "I didn't want to hit your places but I need some help here."

"Okay, I'm a reasonable man. Will five thousand dollars help you out?"

"Stuff it. All I want is information."

"You know we were back in business the next day. It was like a mosquito bite, annoying but not serious."

"I tried to be nice about this but you're forcing me to be a hardnose. If I have your joints hit again you won't be back in business the next day, and maybe not even the next month."

He laughed, "Yeah, sure."

I took another hike and an hour later I was in Inspector Henry's office giving him a report on what had transpired. I told him, "Doc isn't worried about a mosquito bite so let's show him what a snakebite is like," and when he heard what I wanted to do next he said, "Wow, let me call Captain McCabe." He got McCabe on the phone and told him, "I'm sending Sergeant O'Neil over again and whatever he tells you, consider it an order from me."

When I saw the Captain and told him what I wanted his jaw dropped, "You want to do what? Run that by me again."

"All fourteen places have to be dropped again. Only this time take emergency service and tell them to bring trucks and chain saws. Have them cut up and remove the counters. Cut the bulletproof partitions into pieces. Confiscate the tables and chairs and then rip the fucking paneling off the walls."

It took a couple of weeks but all fourteen locations were destroyed. It was time to see Doc again and this time I took two cops with me. Now that he knew he couldn't buy me off he might try to kill me, and I wanted to play it safe. Once I knew I'd be okay I asked the cops to wait in the car.

I wanted to talk to Doc alone. "Look, Doc," I told him, "you're either on my side or you're the enemy. If you're on my side then you're back in business and nobody will bother you. I have nothing against you making money with the numbers. But if you're not on my side you better start looking for another city to operate in. Besides, all this shooting and killing is bad for business. Help me clean up the streets and I bet you'll see your business double. Bullets are bad for business and when they start flying, your customers stay home instead of coming here to play the number."

"You got a point there, Sergeant O'Neil. Besides, I never liked the drug dealers anyway."

He was coming around and I finally convinced him to cooperate by assuring him, "I have never, ever given up a source of information. I guarantee that nobody will ever find out you helped me."

"Okay, I'll help you. So how soon can I get back in

business?"

"Tomorrow morning if you want. One more thing, Doc. If I ever find out that you bullshitted me, fucked me, or held anything back, all bets are off. And then I'll be coming for you."

"I understand."

After he gave me his private number, I told him, "Doc, this is the start of a mutually beneficial association. You get richer, we clean up the neighborhood, and the decent people who live here will be able to walk their streets again. The only losers will be those vicious drug gangs. They'll be disbanded and put in jail, or into the ground."

We used the same tactics on the owners of the illegal after-hours clubs. They all fell into line except for the owner of The Big Track located at 356 ½ West 145th Street. It was the biggest after-hours club in Harlem and the only one that was open twenty-four hours a day. It got its name from the long tracklike ramp that stretched from its street-level steel entrance door, to its large basement that spread out underneath three tenements. Inside were several fully stocked bars, a large assortment of gaming tables, a dozen or so rooms that could be rented for sex, and barely enough bathrooms.

The owner was Manny Dupree , a sixtyish black man, tall, and thin. He always wore a wide-brimmed hat and must have had fifteen long gold and jade chains around his neck. He reminded me of an aging Huggy Bear from the hit TV series *Starsky and Hutch*.

George and I gave him "the heat's on" pitch, but he wasn't buying it. We found out later that he was considered the Godfather at this end of Harlem and wasn't accustomed to taking heat from anyone. So we decided to teach him how to become a little more pliable. He would bend or break.

All of a sudden calls started coming in to 911 about trouble at The Big Track, an assault in progress, or a man with a gun, or various other criminal happenings. Each time the cops would respond they would force their way in, causing the patrons to flee and thoroughly fucking up business for the night. After a week of this people started going to other after-hours clubs. Funny thing, the other clubs, whose owners were cooperating with us, weren't plagued by any 911 calls like the ones Manny's club was getting. Imagine our surprise when we learned that all those emergency calls to The Big Track turned out to be bogus.

One of the radio runs resulted in fifteen tickets being issued for gambling, but only the one issued to the operator of the game was valid. That meant fourteen tickets issued to players had to be voided, but Manny didn't know that. About three hours later one of my uniformed cops, Jimmy Cullen, came in holding a well-dressed guy by the collar and announced, "Hey Sarge, we just answered a radio call on The Big Track about a man with a gun." Jimmy sneaked me a smile and a wink. "We didn't find anybody with a gun but we did snag this dumb bastard trying to ditch a foil of cocaine. I guess he got nervous when he saw us randomly searching people."

A low-level amount of drugs back then didn't call for an arrest, only the issuance of a desk appearance ticket (DAT). The guy figured he was going to get arrested so I didn't inform him to the contrary. I told Jimmy Cullen to take him up to the arrest processing room and hold him there until he got a call from me.

I called George Roberts into my office. "George," I said, "I think it's time to blow some smoke up Manny Dupree's ass. Grab a set of keys and let's head out to The Big Track. I'll fill you in on the way up there."

We banged on The Big Track's door and after spying us through the peephole Manny let us in. As we walked to his office I made conversation. "So, Manny, how's business been?"

"Terrible."

"Economic downturn or what?"

"Economic downturn my ass. Cops is my trouble. They

keep coming in here saying they're looking for a guy with a gun. I don't allow guns in here, that's why I have metal detectors at the door. Last night the cops showed up and gave a shitload of tickets to some of my customers who were doing a little innocent gambling."

"Manny, that's why I'm here. As a gesture of friendship I squashed almost all of those tickets. Here, take this list of names of people whose tickets I took care of and tell them to just throw the tickets away. I had to cover my ass so I didn't squash the ticket on the guy running the game, but I called a friend at the DA's office and the fix is in. Send your man downtown with a hundred dollars and tell him to plead guilty. He won't do any time and his fine will be small."

I hadn't called anybody but I didn't have to since New York's liberal judges never handed out jail time for gambling offenses. Even repeat offenders got away with fines of $50 or less.

Manny asked me, "You can do this?"

"Manny, there's a lot I can do for my friends."

"You know a couple of hours ago the cops were in here looking for a fucking gun again. They didn't find one but they arrested a good friend of mine for trying to ditch a foil of cocaine."

"What's your friend's name?"

"Willie Perkins."

"Let me see what I can do for your friend. Can I use your phone?"

"Sure."

I called the precinct and got the cop who arrested Willie Perkins. "Cullen, this is Sergeant O'Neil. I'd like you to do me a big favor. Cut Willie Perkins loose and just issue him a DAT to cover your ass. And don't put him in jail, he's a friend of a friend. Thanks, Cullen, I owe you one."

I hung up the phone and informed Manny, "I'm going to the station house to pick up your friend and I'll bring him back here within a half an hour."

"You can do that?"

"I can do a lot for my friends."

I proceeded with the same line I used on Doc, stressing how much better Manny's business would be if he cooperated

Ten minutes later we left The Big Track with Manny's private phone number and information on some perps who were involved in several local shootings and one homicide. The games were about to begin.

The leader of one of the warring drug factions, Ivan Johnson, was out on Eighth Avenue one night when he was spotted by Bobby Byrd, a vicious rival. Byrd stopped, jumped from his car, ran over to Johnson, and stitched him with six bullets. Johnson slumped to the ground and bled to death in a matter of minutes. After the body was removed, members of his gang got on their hands and knees, lapped up Johnson's blood, and swore revenge. Harlem had just become a little more dangerous.

We had built the foundation of our intelligence network just in time. It was April, springtime in Harlem, with the drug wars about to blossom. And as they did, we began receiving valuable information on those involved. We were able to put Bobby Byrd as the shooter for the Ivan Johnson homicide. Byrd had a cocaine operation on Eighth Avenue just north of West 152nd Street next to Nicky Barnes's after-hours club, The Taureans Two. Byrd was in the wind now but his partner, one Eddy Cooper, was still operating the business. We called our Star Wars guy from narcotics and asked him to get undercovers in there to make some low-level buys. Big enough to nail Cooper but not so big that we couldn't get him out from under the charges if he flipped on his partner for the homicide. The undercovers did their job and a week later we picked up Eddy Cooper and had him in interrogation.

There's a technique to questioning people, especially hostile prisoners, that usually works. Keep the table clear of all objects that could distract from the exchange between him and you. Ease into what you want to talk about. Ask easy innocuous questions at first, questions that are nonthreatening, even friendly, like "What's your name?" or "Do you have any brothers or sisters?" You're conditioning the person to give you answers. After you have a dialogue going you can start with the serious questions and reveal how much you know in hopes of scaring him into cooperating.

George Roberts and I had Eddy Cooper to the point where we thought we could play "let's make a deal" and get him out from under the drug charge in exchange for information on the whereabouts of Bobby Byrd. We realized how wrong we were when he said, "You know I did ten years in Attica where I had to fight for my life every day. But you're the enemy and I'll do another fifty before I give you any fucking information."

I stood up, walked around the table, and said, "Eddy, let me shake you're hand, you're one of the few standup guys I've met while doing this job." He was still a piece of shit but it was so rare to meet someone who wouldn't flip to save his own ass, and I admired him for that.

Bobby Byrd went on to kill five more people and miraculously survived two attempts on his life. During the first attempt he was hit fourteen times and two months later he took three to the head. When we eventually nailed him and I sat across my desk from him, we had a civil fifteen-minute conversation. I couldn't help remarking, "I can't believe you killed six people—you seem like such a nice guy."

He replied, "I am a nice guy and I never killed anyone who didn't deserve to die." Even though the mindset of this guy and his complete indifference to human life amazed me I understood his fucking mentality and I couldn't help thinking, "Here's a guy who killed six drug dealers, and I'm glad we got him off the street but part of me wishes we hadn't caught up with him until he had racked up five or six more." His arrest sent shock waves through the drug dealing community. Here was a guy being hunted by rival drug gangs and it was the task force that finally took him down.

The number of shootings and homicides in the task force area was growing but thanks to our informants we were making arrests and clearing cases. With every arrest our reputation grew and the bad guys were beginning to squirm. Everybody arrested was interviewed and most of these lowlifes would give up their own family to cut a deal. One arrest would usually lead to others.

A few weeks after gaining Manny Dupree's cooperation a guy got shot in the head right in front of The Big Track. He was dead before he hit the ground and the shooter disappeared into Colonial Park. Someone must have called 911 immediately and the run went out over the radio. Two cops in an RMP responded and saw a black male fitting the description of the killer running out of the park at 148th Street. George and I got to the crime scene in a matter of minutes, established a perimeter, and looked for witnesses. I got a bunch of cops to search the suspects escape route for the murder weapon but they came up empty and so did George and I. We probably had the shooter but with no murder weapon or any witnesses we might have to cut him loose.

I called Manny and said, "I'm sure you're aware of the shooting in front of your place."

"Hell yeah."

"This is going to bring some heat down, especially if I have to cut this guy loose. I need some witnesses and fast."

Half an hour later, Manny Dupree was sent up to my office with two men and a woman. Manny said, "Here's your witnesses. I told them to cooperate with you and identify the shooter. If you need anything else from them just ask them and they'll do it."

The Godfather had spoken.

The first thing we did was separate them and then we started looking for fill-ins for a lineup. One witness at a time would view the lineup so as not to influence each other's identification. It was fair for the suspect and necessary if you wanted the identifications to hold up in court. All three witnesses identified the shooter and within hours we had cleared the homicide. A job well done, thanks to the actions of two sharp uniformed cops and Manny Dupree.

At least three times a week we would brief Inspector Henry on the progress of Star Wars and update the organization charts on his wall. Newly identified members were added and murdered ones were removed. In addition we added any new shootings or homicides to a growing list. The press was still all over the Department and we wanted the inspector to be up to speed on our progress.

At the end of one of the briefings, Inspector Henry told George and me to be in his office at one the next afternoon. When we showed up at the appointed time, he picked up the phone and called downstairs to the desk, "Tell my driver to bring the car around and wait for me in front." He stood up and said, "Let's go, guys."

We were driven to the corner of Fifty-seventh Street and Fifth Avenue. When we got out I turned to Inspector Henry and said, "What are we doing here sir?"

"Jim, you and George have been busting your asses and getting some great results. And I know you've been working through a lot of lunch hours, but not today. You're both going to be my guest for lunch at The Playboy Club." We spent the next two hours eating a great lunch and getting our cheeks dusted by bunny tails. There weren't many bosses in the job who would do something like that, but Inspector Henry wasn't like most bosses.

When we got back to the office we contacted our representative at the Drug Enforcement Agency (DEA), Larry Gerhold, and he put us in touch with a team they had working the Harlem area. In the ensuing months we exchanged a lot of information that proved beneficial to both the DEA and our

task force. We were given unrestricted access to their computer
data bank and used it frequently. Buried deep in the bowels of
their offices on West Fifty-seventh Street and Eleventh Avenue
was a war room containing organization charts, complete with
photographs and names of the members of every known drug
gang in the country. As information flowed into our task force
it was given to the DEA and they were able to add it to their
charts and their data bank. The information was instrumental
in bringing down one of Harlem's biggest drug czars—Frank
Lucas.

The DEA even had surveillance films of numerous
social events attended by members of drug gangs. When
Leroy "Nicky" Barnes threw himself a $25,000 birthday bash
at an exclusive downtown nightclub it was well attended, and
captured on film. The DEA was unable to identify many of
the guests and asked if we could help them out. I brought in
ten of the uniformed members of Star Wars to their war room
to view the film and they were able to ID many of the guests
as well as pass on information as to where they operated their
drug locations and who their associates were. We were asked
back many times to view films and always were able to provide
additional information.

In the spirit of cooperation the DEA team covering
our area would stop in my office on a regular basis to exchange
information. Between us we had developed so many sources
that information was flowing in at a steady rate. We had gotten
more and more of the bad guys identified, which led to our
ability to set them up with low-level drug buys. Once they
were arrested we used that as leverage for turning them. Some
of our street-level informers proved invaluable. We were even
able to recruit a member from the inner circle of the Barnes
organization named Carl "Jukebox" Jones, a short, heavyset
parolee from Attica who would do anything to keep from
going back inside. With his help we gained a glimpse into the
internal workings and pecking order of the Barnes gang.

On one visit to my office the DEA team brought a mug shot of a guy they had been after for over a year. They had made a sizeable drug buy from him but before they could arrest him he had disappeared. The guy's name was Thesolonious Cutler, known on the street as "Trick Man." I told them to leave his picture with me and I would see what I could do. Later that afternoon one of our informers, Marcus Dixon, came in and I showed it to him. He squinted through thick glasses at the picture and announced, "Hey, that's Trick Man, I know where he hangs out. I'll give you a call when I find him." An hour later Marcus called and said, "He's in a social club on 126th Street and Eighth Avenue but I don't know for how long."

George Roberts, his regular partner Jimmy Donovan, and I headed over to the social club. Within five minutes we were at 126th and Eighth. The social club was dark inside but we spotted one guy who resembled the picture. We approached him and I asked his name, to which he responded "Thesolonious."

To which I responded, "Turn around and put your hands behind your back, Trick Man."

He had no idea this was about a drug deal that went down over a year ago and he offered no resistance. When we turned him over to the DEA he looked like he was going to have a stroke. They couldn't believe how lucky we had gotten to find Trick Man in just hours. Lucky, yeah we were lucky, but my position was that the harder you worked the luckier you got.

There was an increased uniformed police presence, the precinct narcotics squad was doing buy and bust operations, Public Morals got into the act, as well as precinct anti-crime units, and we acted as the investigative arm. Drug transactions were being driven out of the task force area by all this heat. They were shifting to 143rd Street between Lenox Avenue and Seventh Avenue, only two blocks away. Unofficially the task force area had grown. Whenever we were spotted entering

143rd Street in an unmarked car a lookout would yell, "Raise up." That was a signal that "The Man" was present and "Raise up" would be passed from stoop to stoop and door to door. All drug sales would cease and people would melt into doorways and cellars until we were gone.

Some of the drug dealers were as young as twelve years old. Wayne Banion was thirteen and because he was such a pain in the ass he was known on the street as "Hemorrhoids." He must have had a cash flow problem and couldn't afford to buy the real product because he began selling "beat bags" (glassine envelopes filled with talcum powder instead of narcotics). The danger to the seller was that the people who were beaten out of their money got really pissed off and went looking for revenge. Hemorrhoids had allowed for that and wasn't worried.

Some DOA's from overdoses began showing up. Not an unusual occurrence, but when results from toxicology started coming back it showed something unusual. The victims were OD'ing on rat poison. If the word got out on the street it could drive business away and hurt the entire drug trade. That would not be tolerated, and it wasn't. Before we could arrest Hemorrhoids someone put a bullet in his head and he ceased to be a pain in the ass.

We encountered another juvenile killer whose murders were handled by the non-drug-related homicide arm of the task force led by Herman "The German" Kluge's 6th Division Homicide Squad. His name was Willie Bosket, a vicious little shit who was a stone cold killer and only thirteen years old.

One cool Sunday in March, around 5 PM, Willie left his apartment, walked about seventy-five feet, and boarded a northbound subway train at the 145th Street station. In the same car was a kindly Hispanic gentleman named Noel Perez. Willie got off at 155th Street with Mr. Perez's wallet. Noel Perez never got off that train, dying before he hit the floor from an unannounced shot to the head delivered by Willie Bosket as the train was entering the 155th Street station. Total proceeds from the robbery/murder–eight dollars and two subway tokens.

A successful crime usually leads to a repeat performance, so nobody was surprised when Willie struck a week later. Again he entered the subway train at 145th Street, again he approached his victim as the train entered the 155th Street station, and without warning shot him in the head. The victim this time was Moises Perez who, like Noel, died before hitting the floor. As the train came to a stop Willie took his victim's wallet and disappeared into the crowd.

Both victims shared the same last name, took the same train, but had never met each other. The only thing that tied them together was that they were both senselessly murdered by a thirteen-year-old named Willie Bosket.

Detective Marty Davin, an excellent investigator, caught both cases. Witnesses to both homicides were questioned and said they would be able to ID the shooter. Luckily for Marty the suspect had been bragging to his friends about his exploits. His friends told their friends and eventually that information reached the ears of one of my many informants. Marty had Willie in custody four days after the Moises Perez homicide. There's no doubt that he would have killed again if Marty Davin hadn't picked him up so quickly.

Because of his young age he couldn't be tried as an adult and was sent to a juvenile detention facility. At least he was off the streets but I had the feeling we hadn't heard the last of Willie Bosket.

The public and the Legislature were so incensed at these savage killings that subsequently the Juvenile Offender Act of 1978 was enacted in New York State. It allowed juveniles to be prosecuted as adults for certain crimes and would be the only good thing that ever came from Willie Bosket.

The number of killings and shootings continued to grow. Toward the end of May on 155th Street a white male shot a black male in the neck over a drug deal gone bad. The victim lived and when questioned told us he had no idea who the shooter was. There was one witness to the attack, and as luck would have it, he was an informer of ours who recognized the shooter. He didn't know the guy's name but remembered seeing him doing graffiti on the subway a few years earlier. The shooter's "tag" was unusual and had stuck in our informer's mind. A tag is the way a graffiti artist signed his work and our guy used "Earth" to identify his subway art.

Graffiti had been such a problem for years that the transit police had formed a graffiti squad, but it had recently been disbanded. We got in touch with the sergeant who had been in charge of that squad and he told us they had kept a record of all graffiti artists on a file card system. He said if we gave him a few hours he'd try to identify our guy and get back to us. By that afternoon we had the B-number for Earth, a white guy named John Corey.

We called the photo unit in Manhattan and ordered wet prints, one of which we included in a photo array. Our informant picked out the heavyset, ruddy-complected John Corey immediately. We went to his last known address and grabbed him as he was leaving his apartment. When he was searched we found a loaded gun in his waistband. Ballistics tests revealed that it was the same gun used in the shooting. Another bad guy was off the streets but the drug trade still flourished and the violence escalated so we decided to take it up a notch.

There were six bars along Eighth Avenue where drugs were being sold, and where there were drugs there would be guns. We began a campaign of harassment by driving four or five RMP cars single file up Eighth Avenue. We would pick one bar as a target and pull our cars up onto the sidewalk in front, turn on our revolving lights, exit the cars, and run into the bar. Everybody inside would see us coming and try to off the drugs and the guns. They didn't have time to hide anything so they just threw their shit onto the floor and tried to look innocent. We would randomly search a few customers and never find anything on them but we always left the bar with a bagful of drugs and a shitload of illegal weapons recovered from the floor. We might hit the same bar the next night or pick one of the other six target bars. We put a serious dent in the drug trade in those six bars and significantly reduced the number of illegal firearms carried by their patrons. Many of their customers began frequenting other establishments outside the task force area.

With so much money at stake, the shootings and killings continued as drug gangs fought to expand their turf. The area was still unsafe and the life expectancy of a drug dealer began to shrink. Law-abiding citizens were afraid to venture outside as eighteen- and nineteen-year-olds prowled the streets in new Mercedes, Cadillacs, and Lincolns. Something was very wrong with this picture.

CHAPTER TWENTY

The End of Star Wars

Not only did crime have a tenacious grip on the streets but its hold had seeped into subterranean Harlem as well. If you were familiar with the network of tunnels that ran beneath the Harlem streets you could traverse the task force area without venturing above ground. These underground passages allowed drug gangs to appear, disappear, and reappear undetected.

One warm June afternoon some members of a drug gang opposing Nicky Barnes emerged from a cellar. They were high on angel dust and when they spilled out onto 152nd Street they were facing the front of The Taureans Two. Raising their machine guns they opened fire and literally blew Nicky's club to pieces. People were jumping out second-story back windows to escape the barrage of bullets.

As quickly as the shooters had appeared they were gone, swallowed up by the tunnels until they reappeared on 147th Street where two of Barnes's lieutenants were sitting in a brand-new, powder blue, 1976 Thunderbird. Not yet down from their angel dust high the gang lit up the T-Bird with over eighty bullets. Miraculously only eleven bullets struck the occupants and even more miraculously both of them lived.

Again the gang disappeared. They must have stashed the machine guns because when they reappeared on Seventh Avenue, fifteen minutes later, they were armed with handguns and with the viciousness angel dust inspires. All dusted up they opened fire on a young man whose father was a black detective in the 6th Homicide Squad. The high school honor student would never attend the Ivy League college he had been accepted to.

Barnes was fighting a war with several smaller drug factions and had managed to hold onto all his turf and even reopen The Taureans Two. He might have kept it open long after the drug wars were history but he made a terrible mistake. Word was coming back to us that he was bragging how he had the cops in his hip pocket and was paying them so he could openly run his illegal club.

George Roberts and I went to Inspector Henry and told him, "Our informants are telling us that Barnes is bragging how he owns the cops."

"Oh really. Let's put that accusation to rest, fast, before people start believing that drivel. How do you want to proceed?"

I told the inspector, "We need to get undercovers into Barnes's club and observe the illegal sale of liquor. Then we can raid the place and dismantle it, all nice and legal."

Two weeks later the raid happened and emergency service cops with chainsaws tore the place apart. Whatever goods were not destroyed were confiscated and loaded onto trucks. A large crowd had gathered and the question was put to them, "Anybody here still think cops are being paid so Nicky Barnes can operate an illegal club?"

The Taureans Two never reopened.

The press was still on our case, so when a freelance writer indicated that he wanted to do an article for *New York* magazine about the Star Wars task force he was given permission, and the promise of our full cooperation. His name was Randy Young and he spent ten days with us asking questions, taking notes, and gathering material for his article. One of the nights he was with us the phone rang and when I picked it up the uniformed cop on the other end said, "Sarge, you've got another homicide on Eighth Avenue just north of 146th Street."

"On our way." I hung up the phone and asked, "Randy, you ever been at the scene of a homicide?"

"No, never. But I would like the opportunity to see one, so I can get a flavor for what it's like."

I gave him a walkie-talkie and said, "Here, take this. I can't guarantee that I'll be able to stay by your side all the time but if people see the walkie-talkie they'll assume you're a cop and you won't get mugged or kidnapped. Let's go we have a fresh homicide uptown in the task force area."

When we got there the victim was lying on his back in a doorway; his unfired automatic pistol lay close by. From the numerous times he'd been hit I guessed there was more than one shooter. It looked like an all too familiar drug hit. We began to tape off the crime scene when gunfire erupted. About 150 feet north of us six guys, three on each side of Eighth Avenue, were firing at each other from behind parked cars. I couldn't believe that with so many cops in the area they had the balls to do that. A young cop caught up in the moment shouted, "Holy shit, Sarge, let's go get them."

I told him, "Don't move, just watch me and I'll show you how to become an old cop. We could wait and let them shoot the shit out of each other and then take on the winners or we could try this." I cocked the hammers on my shotgun, pointed it up in the air and fired both barrels. The shooters froze for a second, then bolted for the cellars and disappeared.

Sixty to seventy shots had been fired but nobody had taken a hit, so we went back to our homicide. I turned to see how Randy was enjoying his first visit to a homicide crime scene and he seemed to be frozen, eyes wide open and jaw agape. I guess he noticed me staring at him and he said, "Sergeant O'Neil you staged that for me, didn't you?"

"Follow me."

We walked up to where the gunfight had taken place and when he saw the bullet-ridden cars he said, "You mean that was real?"

"Absolutely, shit like this happens up here all the time. Welcome to Dodge City."

The color drained from his face and the death grip he had on the walkie-talkie tightened. "Can you get someone to take me back to my car?" he asked.

I had one of the uniformed cops drive Randy back to his car. He stayed with us a few more days but declined all further offers to soak up more flavor. I didn't blame him at all but I think his actions defined the difference between civilians and cops—we're the ones running toward the gunfire.

Months later, on August 28, 1976, his article was published in *New York* magazine. The title was, "Dodge City—The Deadliest Precinct in Town."

We had decided early on that for Star Wars to be completely successful we had to address the proliferation of guns in the area. It was to this end we had brought the ATF in with us. They sent two of their agents, Bill Fredricks and Bill De Armand. Bill F. was short and had a Nordic look about him while Bill D. was darker and wore a constantly pensive facial expression. Nobody could have anticipated the amount of intelligence we would develop on gun trafficking and where it would lead us.

The first thing we did was design a form to be filled out by the arresting officer on all gun arrests made in the precinct. There were questions about the weapon as well as the location and circumstances of the arrest. The two Bills would pour over the forms as they came in and look for any patterns that might lead to the weapons point of sale or place of manufacture.

I had worked with ATF agents before and always found them to be dedicated professionals. The two Bills were no exception and during the first year they investigated 983 firearms that had been taken out of the one square mile comprising the 32nd Precinct. None of those guns was voluntarily surrendered but all were taken during the arrest of a bad guy or during the commission of a crime.

Some patterns began to emerge. Most of the guns were brought to Harlem from the Deep South and were bought by the same few people. They would go to Southern states where you didn't need a gun permit to purchase a handgun and the only ID required was a driver's license. They'd spread their purchases out over many gun shops, buying two or three weapons at each shop. These were large-caliber revolvers and automatics of very good quality made by well-known manufacturers. Most could be purchased for $200-$300 and then sold on the streets of Harlem for as much as $1500. We had stumbled onto a very lucrative gun-running operation. Bill F. and Bill D. solicited aid from their counterparts in the Southern states involved and after several arrests the flow of guns into Harlem slowed down to a trickle. The Southern gun shop owners seeing all the heat this brought realized there was a chance their Federal Firearms Licenses (FFLs) could be revoked and they voluntarily tightened up their act.

The city and the seasons were in flux in 1977 as the summer of the Son of Sam and the Great Blackout tiptoed into fall. The turning of the leaves heralded the turning of the tide in our battle with the drug gangs. The number of violent crimes started to decrease as we made more and more arrests. We had built up such an extensive network of informants that the shootings and homicides were being solved at a steady rate now, sometimes within hours of commission of the crimes. Not every crime solved resulted in an arrest. Many times we identified a perp but before an arrest could be made he'd be killed in retaliation by a rival drug gang. We would close the case out with what we called "exceptional clearance," meaning we knew who the perpetrator was but an arrest was impossible.

Our progress didn't go unnoticed and in November, Commissioner Michael J. Codd summoned the members of Star Wars to headquarters for an "ataboy." One by one we were introduced as he expressed his appreciation for our individual efforts that had contributed to the success of the operation. After a group photo he thanked us again and asked us to keep the pressure on the drug gangs.

Two months later Star Wars paid off and Inspector Henry got his stars, one on each shoulder. Deputy Chief Henry threw a promotion party on the fourth floor of 24th Precinct. Everything was top shelf, the best food and the best liquor. Almost every high-ranking boss on the job attended. About an hour into the celebration the new chief called for everyone's attention and then asked George and me to stand on either side of him. He put his arms over our shoulders and addressed the attendees. "Everybody is congratulating me and telling me what a great job I did with the task force. I just want all of you to know that Detective George Roberts and Sergeant Jim O'Neil are my task force and it's because of them I'm wearing stars on my shoulders."

From that moment George and I became fireproof. Nobody on the job would fuck with us because our rabbi was Deputy Chief Charlie Henry. I thought what he did was wonderful and my admiration for him was on the same level as the admiration I held for Commissioner Michael J. Codd. I would have walked through fire for either one of them and I counted myself lucky at having been afforded the privilege to work for them.

Chief Henry became second in command of Patrol Borough Manhattan North, which was made up of ten precincts. Geographically he was responsible for everything from 59th Street to the northern tip of Manhattan.

The new boss of the task force was a big, well-built Irishman named Francis X. Smith. He was a streetwise boss who recognized the success we had achieved and wisely chose to let us handle things as we saw fit. Over the next six months we chipped away at the dwindling violence.

By July of 1978 things in the task force area had slowed down dramatically. We had solved every case that came in and the bad guys knew if they wanted to kill anybody they had better take them outside the task force area or they would get caught.

Besides keeping Inspector Smith up to date I filled in Chief Henry, who would then advise the borough commander on what was transpiring.

There was seldom a shot heard anymore in "Dodge City" and people freely moved about in the streets, even at night. Business was booming in the after-hours clubs and the numbers locations had long lines in front of them.

Manny Dupree asked to meet with George and me. It seems The Big Track was doing so well that he was going to take his family on vacation for two weeks and he wanted to let us know if any violence erupted while he was gone we should contact his second in charge. Manny had left strict orders with him to cooperate with us completely. Didn't want to disturb the newfound prosperity now, did he?

Everybody was making money except George and me. We had been offered money on many occasions—not as a bribe either, but as a gratuity. We expressed our gratitude each time but always declined, feeling that taking anything no matter how small would have destroyed our credibility.

Star Wars had truly made a difference in the quality of life for the citizens in this section of Harlem and had proven to be an economic shot in the arm for the area as well.

It had been a long time since I had a vacation day and I needed some rest. The Great South Bay beckoned. The fluke were in and the bay was full of striped bass and bluefish. Blue claw crabs were practically dancing on the surface just begging to be caught. I told Captain Cox and Inspector Smith that I was going to take ten days off but if anything happened to call me at home and I would come in. When I told Chief Henry he asked me if I was going away at all and I told him, "Nope, I'll be on my boat drowning a few worms and killing some Budweisers."

"Enjoy your vacation, Jim, but don't forget who your

friends are and how much they love seafood."

I was home for three days when Chief Henry called and I anticipated the worst until he said, "Jim, the task force is being disbanded. We haven't had so much as one shooting in the last six weeks. We totaled up the number of cases you and George handled. In the two years since the task force began you had thirty homicides and fifty-six shootings and you solved every single one. Why, you turned that place into the garden spot of Harlem. You should be proud, very proud."

"I am. Chief, what can I do to help you wind down the operation?"

"Nothing, this call is about what can I do for you. When the task force ends you're slated to go back in the bag at the 32nd Precinct but I think you belong in the investigative end of the job. We have an opening for a boss in the Manhattan North Senior Citizens Robbery Unit (MNSCRU) and I have fourteen resumes on my desk for the assignment. I have to interview all fourteen candidates but say the word and the job is yours."

"I'll take the job, Chief."

"Okay, finish your vacation and when you get back I'll see the borough commander and get you assigned."

I thanked Chief Henry and asked about the current boss of the MNSCRU, "What happened to Harry Doyle?"

He laughed a little before answering, "Sergeant Doyle and one of his detectives took an unmarked car the other night to a restaurant in Manhattan South and tied a load on. Coming back they wound up running over this poor guy on a bicycle. Doyle will be taking the spot you were slated for in the 32nd."

CHAPTER TWENTY-ONE

Senior Citizen Robbery Unit--I Get SCRU'd

I couldn't wait for my vacation to end. Being the boss of a SCRU, especially the one in Manhattan North, was a very prestigious assignment. I knew I would have some of the best detectives on the job in that unit.

When I returned to work I sent my resume along with an application over to Chief Henry's office. The next day he called me and said, "Jim, we got a problem."

"What's wrong, Chief?"

"I brought your resume into the borough commander and told him you're the guy I want for the job. When he saw it was you he said it was an excellent choice. He was familiar with the job you've done on Star Wars and remembered how you broke the case on the Black Liberation Army. He commented on the number of medals and commendations you had received as he continued to read your resume. Then he stopped and looked up at me and said, 'Wait a minute, Charlie, why did Jim O'Neil get transferred back to uniform in Harlem after only one year in Internal Affairs? This might be a problem.' I told him I was sure there was a good explanation and he agreed but wants to hear it anyway. He wants to see you in his office today."

I told Captain Cox what had transpired and that I would be at the borough office, in case he needed to reach me. I grabbed an unmarked car and drove to my meeting. At the same time, unbeknownst to me, Captain Cox was on the phone with the borough commander telling him, "What difference does it make why he left Internal Affairs? He just spent the last two years putting out the fire up here for you. He got the press off the Department's ass and he did an all-around good job."

When I got to Chief Henry's office he ushered me into the borough commander. Harold Schryver was a two-star chief, a well-built bull of a man whom I had known since he was a deputy inspector in the Brooklyn Detective Bureau. He was a nice enough guy but a no-nonsense boss. He shook my hand and thanked me for my work on the task force and then he said, "What happened at Internal Affairs that got you transferred back into uniform in Harlem?"

"Do you have about fifteen minutes to listen to my explanation?"

"For you, Jim, I have as much time as it takes. Pull up a chair."

I told him about the drug-dealing cops we went after and the unfounded accusations leveled at me about tipping cops off on some low-level cases. I concluded by saying, "I was glad I got out of that prick outfit and happy for the opportunity to be a real cop again. Those guys from IAD, who couldn't find hair on a bear, were on a fishing expedition. I admitted to nothing and denied everything. If they had any proof I would have gotten Department charges or been locked up."

After a pensive pause, he told me, "Jim, the job is yours effective tomorrow."

From the look on his face I knew his acquiescence was a courtesy. I hadn't fooled this man and he had just paid me back for my two years hard work on the task force.

The next day I reported as the boss of the MNSCRU. Geographically we were responsible for the ten precincts that encompassed all of Manhattan, north of 59th Street, and were referred to by the Department as Patrol Borough Manhattan North. It included Central Park, as well as the affluent West Side from Central Park West to the Hudson River, and the super-rich East Side from Fifth Avenue to the East River. Further north was Harlem, Spanish Harlem, and the northernmost precinct, the 34th, which would become the busiest in the city. The diversity was astounding and ran the gamut from the poorest of the poor, where people were consigned to shelters and soup kitchens, to the fabulously wealthy, where the residents lived in opulence and luxury.

The wealthiest precincts were relatively crime free, compared to the 34th, which took in Washington Heights and Inwood, where the crime figures were so staggering that it became a major embarrassment to the Department and the city administration. So embarrassing that it was broken into two precincts, in order to bring the crime figures down. The upper half would remain the 34th Precinct and the lower half became the newly formed 33rd Precinct.

The MNSCRU had sixteen detectives who were responsible for almost a hundred thousand senior citizens. What seemed like an impossible task was made doable because we were very selective when staffing the unit. All applicants were handed an eight-page biographical resume to fill out. We figured that anyone who took the time to complete it really wanted to work in the unit. About 70 percent of the applicants never made it past the first step but those who did finish the eight pages were granted an interview. Only the best of the uniformed force would make it through the interview. They had to be very dedicated and very compassionate and willing to go that extra mile. Out of the numerous applicants, we took only sixteen.

And because we were very specialized our caseload was lighter than other precinct detective squads. We only handled robberies committed against victims sixty or older, and only when the robberies occurred indoors.

As a result we could spend more time investigating each case, which was reflected in our clearance rate. The average citywide rate of robberies solved was under 14 percent while ours was consistently between 40 and to 50 percent. With a 90 percent conviction rate, we were one of the most successful investigative units in the country. There were six other Senior Citizen Robbery Units that covered the rest of the NYPD and their clearance rates averaged around 30 percent.

We were constantly being called by police departments from all over the U.S. asking us for advice and questioning us on our operation. They were interested in how we selected personnel, conducted investigations, and how we handled the problems inherent in dealing with the elderly. Many times they would send some of their people to observe us in person and we were always glad to help.

I never heard any one of the guys in the unit say, "That's not my job" when it came to helping seniors. It wasn't hard to get motivated when you saw how savagely some of the seniors were victimized. The animals that preyed on them weren't always satisfied to make their score and get away. Too many times they took delight in beating and torturing their victims, some of whom were in their eighties and nineties.

The detectives in the MNSCRU were unique in that they doubled as social workers. We would provide transportation both ways when a complainant had a grand jury or court appearance or if they needed to come to our office to view a lineup. We had contacts in the New York City Victims Services Agency who would provide numerous social services. We worked closely with other city agencies and senior citizen advocate groups. We would go to senior citizen centers and give talks on how to stay safe in the street and at home. We could supply almost anything a senior crime victim needed. We could have doors or windows that were broken during the commission of a crime repaired free of charge. Visiting nurse service could be arranged and Meals on Wheels could be provided whenever necessary. Stolen pension checks, social security checks, or even cash could be replaced.

Some of the seniors suffered from various degrees of frailty, disabilities, and senility. We were told that senility was caused by arteriosclerosis causing depletion in the amount of oxygen reaching the brain. If a victim wasn't too senile and had a court appearance or had to view a lineup we found that fifteen or twenty minutes on oxygen at a local hospital would help him or her to be more lucid.

Dealing with elderly crime victims was an ongoing experience and the SCRU units had to write the book on it. Squads dealing exclusively with this type of crime had never existed before.

Many of the seniors on the West Side were forced to live in single-room occupancy hotels (SROs) in terrible neighborhoods. An SRO resident had his or her own room, but had to share a single bathroom located on each floor. The bathrooms were very often filthy and poorly maintained. To exacerbate the problem, many of the old timers had no family or were abandoned by the ones they had. They were forced to live on limited incomes as shut-ins under terrible conditions and in constant fear for their lives. Many lived on the same floor as drug addicts, pimps, prostitutes, and thieves. We would often find that these seniors had been victimized nine or ten times before we became aware of their plight.

Not all of the SROs were hellholes; some were clean, well maintained, and had excellent security. When encountering a person who had been victimized repeatedly we would contact Victims' Services and arrange for a room in a decent SRO. Then four or five of us would get shopping bags and boxes and pack up all the victim's belongings, load everything into two unmarked cars and make the move. All SRO rooms were furnished so we didn't have to move any beds or dressers.

There was this one Jewish man in his eighties who had been beaten and robbed so often that he couldn't remember exactly how many times he'd been victimized. He was living in one of the worst SROs in the city, so we moved him into a clean, secure building in Brooklyn. When we arrived at his new SRO and when he saw his room, clean and freshly painted, he started to cry and tried to kiss my hand. I was so embarrassed that this old gentleman had been overlooked by the system, which I was a part of, that I vowed to help as many seniors as was possible. Every detective in the MNSCRU felt the same way I did. I can't even express the satisfaction I felt when I was able to help an elderly person who had no one else to turn to. The difference we made in the quality of life for hundreds and hundreds of seniors was by far the most satisfying experience of my career. Every time I put a bad guy away it became a little safer for the seniors of Manhattan North and that's why I loved, so very much, what I did.

Of the many SRO hellholes in Manhattan perhaps none was worse than the Arvia House on West 112th Street just off Broadway. Its elderly residents were subjected to the most deplorable conditions and day and night lived in fear of being preyed upon at will. The crimes were seldom reported for fear of retribution. One such victim was Alisa Deischer, who had moved into the Arvia House with her mother in 1948. After her mother died she stayed on by herself. Alisa was descended from Hungarian nobility and was a very proud and independent woman. Even though the building changed from a decent residence to one described as a "horror house" she refused to move and became a frequent victim.

We convinced her to move and got her a room at the Saint George Hotel in Brooklyn but when we offered to contact the Special Victims Service Agency or Social Services for her she asked us not to. She felt it was welfare and would have none of it. All we could do was check on her periodically to see if she needed any further assistance. She was finally safe and seemed to be doing well, but the Arvia House had taken its toll, and what little money she had left was dwindling. Upon taking stock of her finances she realized there was only enough money left either to survive for one more year or to cover the cost of a funeral. She was confined to a wheelchair so getting a job was not a viable option. Despondent and alone on the day after Thanksgiving in 1981, Alisa rolled her wheelchair to her twelfth floor window, rose up, and fell forward, plummeting to her death. She had been too proud to accept public assistance in life and she made damn sure that it wouldn't be forced upon her in death.

Too late for Alisa, but because of her, we gave the Arvia House a lot of attention and got other city agencies involved. Conditions there were appalling, with filthy communal bathrooms, falling plaster, leaking water pipes, rat and roach infestations, and a steady procession of low-life, human predators. On one of our regular unannounced visits, two of my detectives, Sy Cohen and Vinnie Cea, heard low moaning coming from a room on the second floor. After knocking repeatedly and getting no response, Sy got a sledgehammer from a construction crew working nearby and, over the building owner's objections, knocked the door off its hinges. As the landlord continued to object Sy responded with, "Sue me." The apartment had been thoroughly ransacked and a woman in her eighties lay on the floor in a semiconscious state. She had been there for several days and was near death. Vinnie and Sy rushed her to the hospital and she survived. When she was discharged we moved her to one of the better SROs in the city.

The elderly would continue to be victimized all over the city, mostly in buildings similar to the Arvia House, but they were targets even in nice areas. Arnold Weiner was eighty-nine and his wife Anne was two years younger. They were married for fifty years and lived in a comfortable apartment in a well-kept building at 155 Riverside Drive. They were getting on in age, so they hired a live-in maid, twenty-three-year-old Denise Godbee. She had only been in their employ for a week when she left to go shopping. A few minutes later her thirty-four-year-old, two hundred pound, ex-con boyfriend, Frank Cable, entered the apartment to rob the Weiners. He punched Arnold in the mouth and kneeled on his back while tying him up. Frank's weight was too much for the frail old gentleman and several of Arnold's ribs cracked, causing him to die a short time later at home.

We got involved because the original classification of the crime was a robbery. Al Genova, one of the best detectives I ever worked with, caught the case. He recovered a distinctive ring that the perp dropped at the scene. Al questioned Denise Godbee about her movements and was told that she returned during the commission of the crime and had been threatened with death by the "unknown man." Al feigned belief to throw her off guard but decided she was a prime suspect. Some discreet inquiries around her neighborhood revealed that she had a boyfriend named Frank Cable who was known to wear a ring matching the one found at the scene. Al got Frank Cable's mug shots and did a photo array for Mrs. Weiner. Despite her age she proved to be an excellent witness and without hesitation picked out Cable as the perpetrator. We hit both his and Denise Godbee's last known addresses, just missing them.

We turned to the New York Post, which ran a Most Wanted column. It featured pictures of criminals wanted for heinous crimes and a story depicting why they were wanted. Two days later our two suspects were on the pages of one of the city's most popular newspapers and the phones began ringing as the tips started coming in. We were steered to a rooming house in Brooklyn where we just missed the pair by only minutes. The owner said they had left hurriedly after seeing their pictures in the paper. Every lead was chased down. We put the word out on the street that if they gave up, their safety would be guaranteed but if they forced us to hunt them down there would be no guarantee as to what might befall them. The heat was on all over town and they were on the run with nowhere to hide. We kept the pressure on and in a few days, broke and worn out, they came in and surrendered.

Phil Messing, a reporter for the Post, wrote an article

on how effective the Most Wanted column was in helping capture these two violent criminals. Phil wrote a follow-up article when they were convicted of murder, noting, "The jury returned a quick verdict of guilty and they were both sentenced to fifteen years in prison."

Although the MNSCRU was very specialized we never turned away any complaint if we could be of help, even when a robbery wasn't committed. Such was the case with Frieda Cortelli, a seventy-five-year-old widow living alone in a nice apartment house at 323 West 83rd Street. The building was well maintained and had a tenants' association.

She needed someone to help her with the cleaning and to do the shopping, so she hired fifty-year-old Rudy Frank, who came highly recommended. She quickly came to regret her decision. Rudy was a thief and over an eighteen month period—through intimidation—he forced the quiet, passive woman to let him use her place to store stolen goods, filling room after room up and leaving only narrow passages to allow movement within the apartment. There were typewriters, televisions, boxes of food and candy, cases of wine and beer, cassette tapes, and all manner of items stacked ceiling high. Even the bathtub contained stolen merchandise.

The building superintendent finally became aware of the situation and threatened Frieda with eviction. She went to the tenants' association for help and they contacted us. When we got to the apartment we couldn't believe our eyes. There was enough merchandise there to stock a large store. I don't know how he accumulated so much in just eighteen months, including some items so big that we had to take the door off to get them out of the apartment. We hauled away several large truckloads to a police storage facility where as much as possible would be traced back to the owners and returned.

Rudy Frank was arrested and later sentenced to three years in jail. We contacted a local senior citizen group who arranged for volunteers to help clean up the mess and restore

Frieda's apartment to normal.

We were glad we could help her and continued to take cases that were outside our specialized area. So when my truculent friend and barkeep Jack Donohue asked me to look into the circumstances surrounding the sudden poverty of a senior friend, I agreed to check it out. It didn't sound like a robbery but I promised Jack I'd look into it anyway.

Eleanor Cosgrove, eighty-eight and widowed for many years, had been left very well off. "Enough money to live on for the rest of your life," her husband had said. But now after fifty years in the same apartment on Dyckman Street, the widow had fallen on hard times just as her neighborhood had. The once fashionable Washington Heights was now crime-ridden and a very dangerous place, and Eleanor suddenly found herself one step from needing welfare assistance.

Detective Sy Cohen and I decided to visit the widow and headed up to Dyckman Street. When we told her who we were she smiled warmly and invited us in. Her bright, lively, blue eyes hid the fact that some senility had dulled her wits. We realized the old girl wasn't as sharp as she use to be when she told us her dilemma. "My husband, he's with God now, left me enough money to live comfortably for the rest of my life but it disappeared and I don't know where." Other than the loose grip on her financial situation she seemed to be capable of functioning on her own.

We asked her if we could have a look around her apartment and she consented. We found no signs of any break-ins but were amazed by the hundreds and hundreds of stock certificates from blue-chip companies and corporate giants that littered her desks and tables. A small fortune to be sure but her two bankbooks told a different story. Up until two weeks prior to our visit, one contained $57,000 and the other $72,000. Now they had been emptied and closed. This was starting to smell.

We inventoried Mrs. Cosgrove's stocks, then brought her and them to the bank across the street. We got her a safety deposit box and arranged for the fees to be paid by a senior citizens' group. With her stocks safely locked away we brought her back to the apartment and made sure she had enough food before we left.

It was time to visit both banks where her accounts had recently been emptied and closed. Upon examining the withdrawal slips from each bank we found they had been signed by her and were countersigned by Eric Reid, attorney-at-law. He had been issued two teller checks totaling $129,000. Both bank managers told us if those checks had been cashed they would be in a check repository at 200 Park Avenue.

Sy and I headed off to find them, which turned out to be easier than finding the check repository. We must have driven up and down Park Avenue for an hour without finding 200 until we finally realized that it was the old Pan-Am Building, which straddles Park Avenue. It's a good thing for a "super sleuth" to feel like an ass once in a while. It keeps you humble.

An hour lost but none the worse for the wear we were finally talking to the suave-looking middle-aged gentleman proclaiming to be a vice president of the repository. "I'm Sergeant O'Neil and this is Detective Cohen. We need to see two checks that may have recently been cashed by Eric Reid."

"I'm sorry but our policy prohibits anyone from seeing those checks," he replied.

"I'm not anyone, pal, I'm Sergeant O'Neil. Now we can do this the easy way or the hard way. The easy way, you show us the checks so we can determine who signed them, where they were cashed or the account number they were deposited into. The hard way, I go downtown and get a subpoena for every check this Eric Reid ever cashed and I tie up half a dozen of your employees for a week. Your choice."

"Mr. Suave" was back in ten minutes with both checks. Eleanor Cosgrove had signed them and Eric Reid had countersigned as her attorney. They had been deposited in Reid's account at the Hudson Valley National Bank in Bronxville.

We got on the phone with John Moscow, a very good ADA we had worked with before, and after listening to what we found he said, "Listen, guys, jump in your car and start heading downtown to my office. I'm going to type up a subpoena for all records pertaining to the account number you found as well as any other accounts he has at that bank. By the time you get here I'll have it signed by a judge and ready for you."

We picked up the subpoena and drove to the bank in Bronxville. When Sy and I got to Reid's bank we presented the subpoena to the manager, who seemed glad to help us and quickly assigned a woman to work with us. She sat at the computer, her long slender fingers flying across the keyboard, and made a printout of all Eric Reid's transactions. The account in question turned out to be an escrow account, whose sole purpose was to hold money in a fiduciary trust for Reid's clients. On the printout there was a deposit of $129,000 right around the time Eleanor Cosgrove's accounts were closed. Nothing illegal yet. And then there was a check drawn on the account for $13,000 made out to Potamkin Cadillac and another for $10,000 that was a down payment on a Florida condo. The car and the condo were in Reid's name. Two $20,000 CDs accounted for a $40,000 withdrawal, one for Mr. Eric Reid and one for his wife. There were other withdrawals as well. That piece of shit lawyer had cleaned the old lady out.

The next morning we were in John Moscow's office. When he saw what we uncovered he was amazed at Reid's stupidity and said, "This guy is going to be arrested. I'm going to call him right now and tell him to come down here."

"What good will that do, he's an attorney," I reminded him. He's not going to come in here and talk to us."

"Jim, anyone stupid enough to do what he did will be stupid enough to think he can talk his way out of this."

John was right and within an hour Eric Reid was sitting across from him, sweating profusely as each check was produced. The only response he could muster was, "There may be some improprieties but certainly nothing illegal."

John leaned across his desk until he was eyeball to eyeball with Reid and asked, "Do you know what they call attorneys who do what you did?"

"Uh ... no."

At the top of his lungs John shouted, "Convicted felons, Mr. Reid, convicted felons."

Reid turned pale and managed a barely audible, "Ohhh."

"I could throw you into a holding cell pending arraignment at night court but I'm going to let you go home and come back with your attorney tomorrow morning," John said. Now I'm going to tell you a story about a priest and a lawyer stranded on a barren island with no food or shelter. About one hundred feet of shark-infested water separated them from the mainland and safety. The priest fell to his knees and prayed for help to no avail. The lawyer shouted, 'I'm an attorney and I must get to the mainland or I will die' and all the sharks came together and formed a bridge over which both men walked to the mainland. Both were allowed to live, the priest because he was with the lawyer and the lawyer because he was a shark. That's professional courtesy and that's why I'm letting you go home. After all, we're all sharks aren't we?"

We reached out to another shark, John Eagle, a retired NYPD sergeant turned lawyer. He was so incensed by what Mrs. Cosgrove's attorney did that he represented her pro bono and within a week had a lien on everything Eric Reid owned. In return for making complete restitution to Mrs. Cosgrove, Reid was given no jail time. He was also disbarred, never to practice law again.

CHAPTER TWENTY-TWO

Return of the Rabbi

Whenever Chief Henry would ask me to go with him to some Department function or a community group meeting I was glad to oblige. Questions would come up relating to senior citizen problems and he would turn those over to me to answer or ask me to make a note of the problem for future resolution. These problems would always be addressed and alleviated whenever humanly possible. On those rare occasions when it wasn't possible, a detailed explanation was given to the person who brought the issue to our attention.

Public relations was an important part of the job. Attending senior citizen organization meetings and city social service agencies earned us many powerful friends. When political infighting within the Department threatened the continued existence of the SCRUs our friends became strong allies and saved the squads from being abolished.

Even though we had the highest clearance rate for robberies in the city there were certain elements very high up in the Department that didn't like us because we weren't under their control. SCRUs reported to individual borough commanders and that meant fewer people under the command of the bosses at headquarters. The more people a boss had under him the more powerful he was, and power was an aphrodisiac.

One of the highest ranking chiefs at headquarters had tried several times to get rid of the SCRUs but a few well-placed phone calls to the heads of senior citizen organizations and his attempts would end in frustration. One time it looked like he might get his way so, in desperation, I called the president of a very large, very vocal, senior citizen group called the Gray Panthers. When I told him that we might be disbanded his comment was, "Jim, as soon as I hang up with you I'm going to call the mayor and the police commissioner and tell them if they even consider abolishing the Senior Citizen Robbery Squads I'll have twenty busloads of Gray Panthers picketing City Hall in the morning."

The shit must have hit the fan because the next morning I got a call from a captain in the commissioner's office stating, "I've been instructed to call every SCRU in the city and inform them that there will be no change in their status now or in the future." I never told anyone except Chief Henry that I was the one who called the Gray Panthers. I knew that some of those bastards in headquarters would come gunning for me if they ever found out the role I played in saving the SCRUs. By now George Roberts and I had become very good friends with the chief. We called him Charlie whenever the three of us were alone but in front of anyone else it was always Chief Henry. I loved the man and that's why I was saddened when he told me about his plan to retire.

He had the greatest retirement party I had ever attended and I threw myself into the revelry so hard that I missed the lieutenant's test the next day. It would be years before there would be another one but I didn't care. I loved what I was doing and there was always the possibility if I passed the test I would be transferred to a busy precinct as a desk officer and that scared the shit out of me.

About two months after Charlie Henry retired I called him at home to see how he was doing and invited him to dinner at Jack Donohue's—I'd spring for it. He accepted and asked me to bring along George Roberts.

The three of us had a good meal, then adjourned to the

bar. George and I were teasing him, saying, "Why don't you pull your retirement papers and come back to the job. Since you're gone we don't have a rabbi anymore."

We were laughing when Charlie said, "I do miss it. Three months ago I was the chief with thousands of men under my command. When I spoke everyone listened. When I snapped my fingers they jumped and now I'm nothing."

George said, "Charlie, you know we still love you."

"George, I know who my friends are, that's why I'm here. But as soon as I go outside do you know who I am? I'm just another black guy walking down a New York street."

A couple more drinks, a little more conversation, and as a vow to get together passed our lips we said good-bye.

A month later my home phone rang and when I pick it up I heard, "Jim, its Charlie, meet me at Jack Donohue's tonight around eight, there's something I have to tell you. This time I'll bounce for dinner."

"Okay, but George is working tonight so I'll be coming alone."

"That's okay, you can fill George in on most of what I'm going to tell you."

After he hung up, the question hung in the air: "What was it Charlie had to tell me that I couldn't share with George?"

Shortly after sitting down to dinner I asked Charlie, "What is it you have to tell me?"

"I pulled my papers and I'm coming back in the job as a deputy chief."

"Now that's great news, wait till I tell George. What's your assignment going to be?"

"I'm going to be liaison between the City Police and the Housing Authority Police."

"That sounds like a going-no-place job, why that?"

"Now comes the part you can't tell anyone, not even George. I have to tell someone or I'll bust and who better than a friend I know I can trust. Only three other people in the city know this—the mayor, the police commissioner, and Ben Ward, the Housing Police chief. And it's got to stay that way."

"It will, Charlie, it will."

"There's been some trouble in the Corrections Department and they're moving Ben Ward over as the new Corrections Commissioner to put out the fire. Ben and I have been close for years and he recommended me as his replacement. Jim, you're looking at a man with four stars on his shoulders and the next chief of the Housing Authority Police."

I couldn't have been happier and bought the next two rounds of congratulatory drinks. We went our separate ways and I couldn't wait to see George the next day and tell him that Charlie Henry was back in town.

When I told George, he was thrilled. He loved and respected Charlie as much as I did and would have been ecstatic had I told him everything I knew. But a promise is a promise and I kept my mouth shut.

Six weeks passed and I got a call from George, who said excitedly, "Jim, guess what, I just got an engraved invitation in the mail for Charlie's swearing-in ceremony at the Blue Room at City Hall. He's going to be the next chief of the Housing Authority Police."

"I know, I just got my invitation a little while ago," I told him.

The day of the ceremony George and I hooked up with Deputy Inspector Bill Conroy, Commanding Officer of the 24th Precinct and also a good friend of Charlie's. The three of us rode down to City Hall together. We were the only ones below the rank of chief in the entire place. There were stars and gold braid everywhere. George and I, in our suits and ties, stood out in contrast to all the other uniformed guests. Questioning glances shot our way as the few bosses, aware of who we were, filled in the rest.

Charlie Henry cut his way through the crowd, walked

up to the three of us, and said, "Come on, you guys are sitting in the first row with my family."

He escorted us through the sea of stars and gold braid and as we took our seats he quietly told us, "After the ceremony I want you to go uptown to the Housing Police Headquarters. I have them setting up a catered party with plenty of food and booze. Just you three, I don't want any of these humps to know."

Charlie left and I whispered to George, "Do you realize what Charlie just did for us? There isn't a chief in the job that would mess with us knowing that Charlie's our friend, and that he's packing four stars."

While Charlie Henry settled into his new job business began picking up at the MNSCRU. Most of my detectives were as competent, hardworking, and dedicated as George Roberts and the cases were getting solved at a fantastic rate.

Even when off duty my guys were always ready to help a senior in trouble. Dennis O'Sullivan wasn't a big guy but he had a quiet toughness about him. On one of his days off he was inhaling some suds at Ford's Bar in the Bronx when he happened to look out the window and see two elderly women being harassed by a couple of thugs. Abandoning his beer he walked outside, identified himself as a police officer, and told the two thugs, "Stop bothering these ladies and move along."

Instead of moving along they picked up some fallen tree branches. Swinging them, they advanced on Dennis and he drew his gun but continued to retreat from them. They backed him down the street, around the corner, and into an alley. As his would-be assailants backed him up to a garage door at the end of the alley they laughed saying, "What do you do now, big shit cop? We're going to hit a home run with your fucking head."

As they closed in, Dennis began firing until he had emptied his gun. Both assholes died in that alley shortly after, from gunshots to their fucking heads. As they spent their final moments on earth a MNSCRU detective's words echoed in their ears, "That's what I'm going to do, assholes."

The court ruled both shootings as justifiable homicide. Then the threats against Dennis and his family started coming in. The guys he killed were part of a Bronx gang who fancied themselves as real badasses. We couldn't stand for that so one night two carloads of us paid a little visit to the gang's hangout. We caught them by surprise and kicked the living shit out of them. The message was delivered to the beaten and bloodied badasses, "Anything happens to Dennis or his family and we'll be back. And next time you'll end up like your two buddies in the alley."

Dennis acted as an individual because he was on his day off, but when on duty we always worked in teams. John Mattias and his black partner, Jimmy McCoy, were a great team and had been partners since the beginning of the MNSCRU. When they sank their teeth into a case they were like two pit bulls on a bone. John was a Gunny, a chief warrant officer in the Marine Reserve, as well as the first vice-president of the Grand Council of Hispanic Societies in Public Service, which included Hispanic cops, firemen, correction officers, and others as members. Jimmy was six feet tall, intelligent, streetwise, and an excellent detective who gave his all to every investigation.

John lived close to me on Long Island so we started carpooling to work and eventually became good friends. We even socialized off duty and were known to stop for a few drinks now and then.

Like the rest of the detectives in the squad John and Jimmy worked like hell and never looked at the clock. They had worked, on their own time and with no pay, on countless cases. The more heinous the crime the more time and effort they were willing to devote to its solution.

There was a case of an eighty-nine-year-old woman being robbed and raped that incensed them to the point that they vowed to work around the clock if necessary to nail the guy. After the robbery, the perp attempted rape but was having a difficult time entering her so this lowlife piece of shit took a knife and cut her vagina, and then he raped the old woman. With a crime this horrific even the bad guys would come forward with information to help catch the scumbag who did it.

The depraved son of a bitch tried to sell some of the woman's belongings in the neighborhood. John and Jimmy worked the area in a feeding frenzy, knocking on doors and questioning people in the street. When word got out what the guy had done to his victim, everybody was looking for the bastard. Within six hours of commission of the crime they had a nineteen-year-old Peruvian seaman in custody. It seems that he had jumped ship right after the freighter he worked on pulled into port.

They spirited him away two steps ahead of a forming lynch mob. In liberal New York people had actually showed up with a rope and one fellow we knew as Joe "The Butcher" was wielding a knife threatening to castrate the bastard. The only reason my detectives didn't let the mob have him was because they knew what was waiting for him in jail would be far worse than what the mob wanted to do.

Even the most hardened criminals would be looking to get a piece of his ass when he got to the Big House. This type of crime was viewed the same as child molestation was and even murderers despised it. His life in jail would be a succession of beatings and gang rapes until an overzealous attacker finally killed him. Still too good for the Peruvian piece of shit, but hey this isn't a perfect justice system.

We ended his career before it got started but I have no doubt he would have committed similar crimes if we hadn't apprehended him so quickly. Most perps tend to repeat what has worked for them, until we discern their patterns and then the assholes get caught.

On the wall in my office I had a four-foot-high map of

Manhattan North. Using colored pins I kept track of the type of robbery, where it took place, and if there was more than one perp involved. In addition I read the details of every case that came in as well as the detectives' follow-up reports, looking for similarities between cases—things like the description of the perps, the time when the crime was committed, the day of the week, the MO, or the manner of escape if known. Proximity of public transportation was looked at. Had the perp said anything to the victim? As similarities turned into patterns the cases involved would be turned over to a team of two or more detectives to examine and analyze. The detectives in my squad were intelligent, analytical, hardworking, and relentless. I can't remember a pattern case that wasn't eventually solved. The good thing about solving the pattern cases was that when you made an arrest you ended up with multiple cases solved.

Almost all the bad guys were stupid and somewhere along the line they would make that one mistake and get caught. They might become complacent, or brag to friends and reveal the details of the crime. Most of them had been arrested previously for drugs or petty crimes before graduating to vicious robberies, and their mug shots were in our photo file. My detectives would aggressively work the cases until the bad guy screwed up and then he'd be "SCRU'd".

But we didn't stop there, aggressively staying involved until a tough ADA was assigned. There were three we liked working with: John Moscow, a tough son of a bitch, was at the top of our list along with Catherine "Katie" Law and John Payne. Katie was a white middle-aged woman from the Midwest and John was a flamboyant black man in his mid-thirties who preferred sporting a fawn-colored cape instead of the standard business overcoat. They were no-nonsense prosecutors who always went straight for the jugular. They loved it when they saw us coming because we always handed them perps wrapped up in neat little packages ready for a conviction. Our thoroughness didn't go unnoticed and soon the other ADAs complained about never getting any of our cases. The order came down that we had to accept whoever was catching when we got to court, unless there had been some prior consultation with a particular ADA. We threw a few bones to our less-favored prosecutors and made sure we consulted with Katie or the two Johns, prior to going to court, on pattern cases and ones involving savage attacks.

Whenever a victim had been beaten we would document the injuries on film as evidence for the upcoming trial. The trial date could be as long as ten months after the arrest and by then most of the victims would have recovered and would appear normal again. We had our photo unit blow up the picture to poster size so the judge and the jury could see how savage the attack was. There were cases where these photos had literally added years onto sentences. Hey, anything we could do to keep the scum off the streets longer was a good thing.

Whenever you deal with a violent crime against the elderly there's always the chance it could result in a homicide. Toward the end of 1980 we had several cases with a discernible pattern that hadn't yet involved a homicide, but if we didn't get a solution soon I was afraid the perp would end up killing one of his elderly victims. Men and women in their seventies were being attacked from behind and bludgeoned into unconsciousness. When they woke up in the hospital they had no idea what had happened and consequently were unable to provide a description of the attacker. The robberies all occurred around three in the afternoon and the proceeds were generally small with a wallet or a pocketbook being taken. Two of my detectives were able to ascertain that several victims were robbed shortly after leaving their bank. A couple of witnesses cooperating with the investigation agreed to view a collection of photos; unfortunately the effort proved unsuccessful.

My guys caught a break when a concerned citizen came forward claiming to know the perp and where he could be found. Within three hours he was picked up and brought into the squad. When I saw him as he sat handcuffed in a chair something about him tickled my memory. I was sure I had seen him before so I walked over and picked up the arrest report and there it was, a name I recognized, Willie Bosket. That incorrigible prick recently out of a juvenile facility, where he was sent for murdering Noel and Moises Perez, was back to his old habits.

Well this time he went to "Big Boys Court" where he was sentenced to a long prison term. Willie was pure evil and putting him away only brought about a pause in his vicious crimes. This jackal-like predator would be back on the streets again and no amount of jail time would change his criminal bent. He should be caged for life like any dangerous animal.

My suspicions about him would be confirmed twenty-five years later during hunting season in upstate Roscoe, New York. It was there while having a drink at Trinca's Bar, that I overheard several state correction officers talking about Willie Bosket, the most incorrigible inmate they had ever come across. It seems Willie had attempted to burn down the prison where he was incarcerated and in the process had stabbed a corrections officer. Several stabbings later and Willie got sentenced to life without parole and had earned the honor of being named the most violent criminal offender in New York State history. He is so dangerous that the corrections department holds him in a specially designed Hannibal Lecter-type cell made up from three normal sized cells, with a shower of its own. Willie only gets to leave it one hour a day and even then he has no contact with other prisoners. If you look him up on the Internet you will find over five thousand entries. When I mentioned that I had thrown Willie his first major collar each officer bought me a drink.

CHAPTER TWENTY-THREE

Civil Rights–What the Hell Are Those?

Willie Bosket was still a recent memory when we encountered what would become our most frustrating pattern case. Complaints began coming in about a few Hispanic males who would follow elderly women home and then rob them. They never took money, only diamond rings and earrings.

These guys hit all over the place on different days and at different times. Most of the robberies took place in Washington Heights but when we checked with the other SCRUs we found that our guys had also hit in Queens and the Bronx. Predicting their movements was impossible. Hell, we weren't even sure how many perps we were looking at.

The one thing that made them unique was the method they used when stealing earrings or when removing a ring that stubbornly refused to come off. After knocking an old lady to the ground they would bite the skin off her finger and then remove the ring. With earrings, they simply bit off earlobes, and with senior citizen flesh and aged diamonds in their mouths they fled.

After a year we had over ninety cases in Manhattan North alone and all we had to show for our efforts were a bunch of witnesses and complainants who had been unable to pick anybody out of our mug books. We didn't know it at the time but one of the perps had never been locked up in New York so we didn't have his picture. Back then I got little comfort from the realization that when we finally arrested these barbarians we would have plenty of people to ID them. We had been sucking wind on these cases for over a year before we caught a break.

In Queens some plainclothes cops interrupted two guys robbing an old woman. They were able to arrest one of the guys but the other one got away with an earlobe and an earring. Twenty-nine-year old Carlos Torres of 220 West 96th Street was under arrest but refused to give up his partner.

For some reason, after Torres's arrest, a lot of the robberies began to take place on the weekends and even though we didn't work Saturdays or Sundays some of the guys volunteered to come in for a couple of hours on their own time. I reminded them, "As much as I'd like to I can't authorize any overtime."

Their response was, "Fuck the overtime. We want these animals and we're going to keep the pressure on."

So now the MNSCRU was a seven-day-a-week operation. Up until now the procedure was that any cases coming in on the weekend were called into the borough office and would be picked up by the SCRU on Monday morning.

On a Sunday morning detectives Al Genova, Dennis O'Sullivan, and Harry Velez checked with our borough office and found no new cases, so they decided to call the Bronx borough office and see if anything had been called in. They were told that a new case had just come in the day before. There was a ring robbery in the hallway of one of a group of five-story private apartment buildings. Since it was a Sunday and no one was working the Bronx SCRU, my guys decided to go to the robbery scene and do a canvass.

They spent the next several hours knocking on every door in the apartment complex without any success. Not one of the sixty residents had seen or heard anything unusual or remembered seeing any strangers in the area. As they were leaving the complex they saw a man parking his car and approached him. Detective O'Sullivan identified himself and his partners as detectives and asked, "Did you see any strangers in the area yesterday?"

"Funny thing you should ask," the man answered. "I did see strangers yesterday and had a run-in with them. See, this is my reserved parking spot and these two young Spanish-looking men were parked in it. I asked them to move and they started giving me a hard time until I threatened to call the cops. That made them move but I was afraid they might come back after I went inside and damage my car, so I wrote down their license number." Reaching into his pocket he pulled out a piece of paper and handed it to Dennis, saying, "Here, I still have it."

The man went inside and left three very excited detectives standing in the parking lot. Al Genova said, "Guys, I think we got the bastards."

They ran the plate and it came back to an address in Yonkers, New York. Normally when a detective has to leave the city on Department business the regulations require a notification to the chief of detectives, but since they were on their day off that didn't apply. With O'Sullivan at the wheel they were off to Yonkers. Imagine their disappointment when they arrived at the address and found themselves staring at a vacant lot.

They sat in the car and mulled over their options, which were slim to none—they just hated to let go. Al Genova suddenly had a thought. "Remember a while back those cops in Queens arrested a guy named Carlos for a ring job and he lived on 96th Street off Amsterdam Avenue? It's a longshot but let's go peruse that periphery and see if we can spot the plate number over there."

They were off again with Dennis O'Sullivan still behind the wheel. They had only been on 96th Street a few seconds when Harry Velez called out, "Hey Dennis, stop the car, there's the plate."

"Look Harry, don't break my balls," Dennis said. "It's been a long disappointing day and I'm not in the mood for practical jokes."

"I'm not joking. Get the piece of paper out of your pocket and check it against the plate on that black Mustang."

Dennis compared the plate number on the paper to the one on the Mustang and did a double take. "Bingo, Harry," Dennis said. "That's it."

A million-to-one shot had just paid off. They backed the car down the street and waited. A half an hour passed and a tall Hispanic male entered the vehicle and drove away. They tailed the suspect to several locations for forty-five minutes hoping he would lead them to his partner. Finally, fearful of losing him in the Manhattan traffic, they jumped the car and arrested him at gunpoint.

I got the call at home from Al Genova, who said, "Jim, we just arrested a mutt named Tito Gonzales, we're positive he's one of the scumbags doing the ring and earring jobs."

"Good work, Al, and pass that on to Dennis and Harry."

"I will."

"I'm leaving in five minutes and I'll see you soon."

"Stay home, enjoy what's left of your Sunday. We have to get him ID'd on at least one of the robberies and then do all the paperwork. Ronnie D'Allesandro is on his way in to give us a hand and he'll help us convince Tito to give up his partner. That could take all night but we'll get what we want. Tito's not going anywhere, he'll still be here when you come in tomorrow morning."

"Okay, I'll see you in the a.m. and you can give me all the details. Hell of a job."

"Thanks, we got real lucky."

"Lucky my ass, perseverance breaks cases. You work hard enough and fate drops luck right in your lap."

When I got in the next morning I found out that Tito had played "let's make a deal" and easily gave up his partner in hopes of getting a lighter sentence. His partner was Simon

Bolivar Matos, a thirty-one-year-old native of the Dominican Republic, only five-five and one hundred and fifty pounds. Not a big guy, but how big do you have to be to terrorize elderly women?

Matos had a prior arrest in New York so we were able to get his mug shot for a photo array. The identifications began to pile up while Tito filled us in on his partner's routine. Matos was a full-time student at Hostos College in the Bronx and lived with his wife, Cynthia, at 12 Seamans Avenue in Washington Heights. He would leave his apartment at seven o'clock every morning, purchase a newspaper, and then go to school.

We staked out his building the next morning at six-thirty and at seven sharp he came out and walked down the stairs. Before he got to the bottom he spotted us and drew his gun. In the fourteen-shot gunfight that ensued Matos caught three shots—two before he bolted out a back door, down a narrow alley, and over a chain-link fence. The third hit him as he was going over the fence. He made his escape through Inwood Park and was patched up by a Peruvian immigrant doctor not licensed to practice in this country. His wounds were not life-threatening but the third bullet did managed to castrate him. At least there wouldn't be any little Simon Boilvar Matoses running around. Good news for the elderly and infirm women in the area.

We threw up a net around New York and had a hundred copies of his mug shot distributed to the New York Port Authority Police. They watched the planes, trains, buses, and boats. We also contacted the New Jersey Port Authority Police but not fast enough. He squeaked out of Newark Airport using his own passport and made it to Venezuela.

We figured him to end up in his native country and if we ever wanted to bring him to justice we needed to establish contact with law enforcement in the Dominican Republic. Fortunately one of the uniformed cops in the 24th Precinct, Lorenzo Almonte, was from the Dominican Republic and he had an excellent contact there. Lorenzo put me in touch with Colonel Gomez-Estrada of the Dominican Secret Police and that country's representative to the International Police Organization (INTERPOL).

When he heard how many muggings we had and how they were carried out he was outraged. He told me, "You know, Sergeant O'Neil, in this country we revere and respect our elderly. How could a native of this country turn into such an animal? You can be sure we will do everything we can to bring this excuse for a person to justice if he ever shows up here." I asked the colonel, "Are you sure you will be able to catch him if he returns to your country?"

He answered, "Unlike the U.S. there are no civil rights here. If I go to a village looking for someone and am told the person is not there, and subsequently find out he was, I burn the village. Rest assured that if he comes back to the Dominican Republic I will own him. Send me any pictures you have and keep me informed of any additional information you receive. I will track him through my counterparts in INTERPOL and keep you informed."

For several months, the way Matos moved through South and Central America indicated that he had plenty of money. We began canvassing the banks in the Washington Heights area looking for any accounts in his or his wife's name. We located a bank on Broadway where they had a joint account with a very large balance. Since Matos's escape there had been periodic withdrawals of several thousand dollars at a time. We figured Cynthia was sending him the money.

The bank manager was very cooperative and never even asked us if we had a subpoena before giving us information. I asked him to keep an eye on the account and give me a call if the wife ever made a large withdrawal. The periodic withdrawals continued for several months and then one morning the bank manager called to tell me the wife had made a $25,000 withdrawal.

We went to the bank and asked to speak with the teller who handled the transaction. The manager introduced us to Annie, a pleasant young woman in her early twenties. She told us, "I asked her if she was buying a car or a house and she told me that she wasn't. What she needed was a combination of cash and travelers' checks because she was going to meet her husband in Santo Domingo."

After thanking Annie, I headed straight for my office and within a half an hour I was talking to Colonel Gomez-Estrada. I filled him in on the latest information, and he said, "I'll alert my people at the airport to watch out for Matos and his wife."

A couple of days later he called to tell me, "I have Matos in custody. Are you aware there is no extradition treaty between our countries?"

"I know that but I hoped you could just tie him up and throw him on a plane bound for New York's Kennedy Airport. Then we would meet the plane when it arrived."

"I can't do that," the colonel told me, "but I will do something better. Make a package up with copies of all the crime reports and detectives' follow-up reports on every case, especially the ones where victims had picked Matos's picture out. There is a one-thirty afternoon flight of Air Dominica leaving Kennedy Airport every day. Have a detective hand-deliver the package to the pilot, with instructions to bring it to me personally the second he lands the plane in Santo Domingo."

"I can do that but what good will it do?"

"We are going to put him on trial down here for the crimes he committed up there."

"You can do that?"

"Sergeant O'Neil, I told you there are no civil rights here. We do what we want, when we want. This man is our sinner and we will take care of him. Besides I hear your jails are easy and the food is good. We don't have exercise rooms, or TV, or libraries in our jails and hard time here is very hard."

The next day the package was delivered to the pilot and he handed it over to Colonel Gomez-Estrada minutes after the plane touched Santo Dominican soil. Justice is swift in the Dominican Republic and two weeks later the colonel called and told me, "I am very pleased to tell you that Simon Bolivar Matos was tried for his terrible crimes and found guilty. This morning he was sentenced to thirty years hard labor and is already in prison. There will be no appeal and no parole. I am very pleased to have been able to assist you in this matter. If I can be of any help in the future please call me."

"Thank you for your assistance and please," I told him, "if there is ever anything I can do for you, Colonel, don't hesitate to call me."

The wheels of justice turned slower in the U.S. and it was ten months before Tito Gonzales was tried, found guilty, and sentenced to fifteen years.

CHAPTER TWENTY-FOUR

No More Easy Targets

We began getting a rash of street muggings in Washington Heights and since they were outside our specialized guidelines of indoor crimes against the elderly, we enlisted the aid of the Special Operations Division (SOD). I specifically asked for Mary Glatzle's undercover team, which I considered to be one of the best in the country. Mary was a rather ordinary looking thirty-something who was five-eight, and on the thin side with shoulder length mousy brown hair. Using makeup and costume she could appear to be anything from a young hooker to a helpless old woman. She worked with a backup team of two black guys and one white guy specializing in street crimes. Mary put herself at danger's doorstep constantly and had been mugged over a hundred times, earning her the nickname of "Muggable Mary" and a small place in literary history as the subject of a book and a TV movie. With her help, three days and two arrests later we had our guys, and a small piece of Washington Heights street crime ceased to exist.

Things in Manhattan North were getting better for the elderly. Crimes against senior citizens were being solved at a very fast rate and the scum who committed them were being convicted and given long sentences. The days were disappearing when a senior would bear the burden of being repeatedly victimized. Crimes that would have gone unreported three years ago were now being brought to our attention. The word was spreading that if you perpetrated a crime against a senior anywhere north of 59th Street you were going to get caught, and then prosecuted to the fullest extent of the law. Manhattan North seniors no longer presented an easy target and the lowlifes who preyed on them were heading for greener pastures outside the area policed by the MNSCRU.

Twenty-two years had flown by since that day in February when I stood at attention inside the old police academy with 144 strangers and swore to uphold the law. The time flew for me but not so for my Peggy and now she pleaded with me to retire. She felt I had been involved in too many gunfights, had attended too many cops' funerals, and had too many of my partners shot, most of them so badly injured that they were off the job collecting disability pensions.

It wasn't easy being a cop's wife, always wondering if your husband would live to retirement. No it wasn't easy, but being married to a cop's wife was just as hard. They wanted you to give up the very thing that made you feel alive, the thing that made you walk tall. They just didn't understand how being a policeman tugged at the sinewy fabric of your soul.

I loved her and I understood her concern, so after two weeks of agonizing over what to do I decided to inform my borough commander of my impending retirement. His response shocked me. "All right," he said. "I'll start looking for a replacement right away."

My heart sank. It was like his words, not mine, had sealed my fate. I added, "I would like to stay on until you find a suitable replacement, someone who will exemplify the high standards the MNSCRU demands of its members. I would hate to see someone replace me just to fill a contract."

"Sergeant O'Neil, what you and your men have done is nothing short of amazing and I promise you that whoever takes your place will have the ability and the dedication needed to continue the job you started. I'll see to it that you speak to every candidate and I assure you your recommendation will carry a lot of weight in determining who will be chosen."

Over the next month I spoke to a lot of good cops but one stood out. Sergeant Georgie Pagan had worked in busy houses his entire career and had earned several medals of valor and a stack of commendations. Here was a real cop's cop. During the conversation I was so impressed that I told him if he wanted the job I would do everything I could to see that he got it.

"I want it," was all he said.

On March 8, 1984, Georgie Pagan became the new boss in the MNSCRU.

Even though I knew the seniors of Manhattan North were being left in good hands I felt an unfamiliar sadness grab hold of me and like most things unfamiliar it made me uneasy. Maybe it was the thought that I still had so much more to give to those I had sworn to protect and serve, or perhaps it was just the stirrings of a dreaded return to a simpler, safer life. Gone was the thrill of the chase and with it went the camaraderie of those I served with.

CHAPTER TWENTY-FIVE

Oh To Be a Kid Again

I was sad about my career winding down but took heart in the fact that there was a whole crop of young dedicated cops coming up on the job—cops like Ronnie Bunde Jr.

I'd been friends with Ronnie Jr.'s father since 1957 and as our families grew Ronnie Jr. became very close to Peggy and me—it seemed so natural when he began calling us Aunt Peg and Uncle Jim. He was an all-around good kid, very personable and even at a young age driven to succeed. I still remember the day he made Eagle Scout. I was as proud of him as if he were my own son and when he joined the NYPD I felt a father's sense of pride.

He had a month to go in the academy when I put in a call to a friend of mine, Donnie Sommers, the personnel director for Manhattan North, and arranged for a contract to get Ronnie Jr. assigned to the 34th Precinct. It was the busiest of all of the seventy-six New York precincts and I figured it would give him the opportunity to make a lot of collars. After he got a few prerequisite years in the bag and built up a good arrest record, I would have no trouble getting him made a detective. There was something comforting in knowing that "Detective" Ronnie Bunde Jr. would be working the streets after my retirement.

Ronnie Jr. had distinguished himself in the 34th and I was ready to make the move on his behalf, but before I could he was gone. On a miserably cold, dark winter's day his car hit a patch of black ice and skidded off the road into a tree. Ronnie Jr. had died and with him a piece of his parents and his Aunt Peg and Uncle Jim also died. In the sea of blue at the wake I spotted his commanding officer, Deputy Inspector Mike Markman, whom I had known for a number of years.

"You know, Mike," I told him, "one day you were going to get a call from me asking you to assign Ronnie to the Precinct Robbery Investigation Program as a first step toward a gold shield."

"Jim, I have three hundred cops in my command and he was the best. There would have been no need for that call. In my estimation he had a hell of a career in front of him. It seems so inadequate to say under these circumstances but his parents should be proud of the way he lived his short life."

"I couldn't agree more."

Neither one of us said another word; we just shook our heads and walked away. Sometimes saying nothing speaks volumes.

The loss of Ronnie Bunde Jr. and the impending loss of my career weighed heavily on me. There I was, Sergeant James O'Neil, in the Pension Bureau office at One Police Plaza becoming "Mr." James O'Neil. With the paperwork finished I was asked to surrender my badge. I hesitated but did complete the ritual. As I handed it over I was impressed by the weight of it—funny that I had never noticed how heavy it was before. I walked out the door and counted the sixty-three steps to the elevator, got in and pushed the button for the first floor.

The numbers lit up one after the other in a descending fashion the way all elevators do when going down. I thought back over my career as all cops must when they realize the finality of retirement. Eighth floor—thoughts of the job as it was when I first signed up. Rampant corruption coursing through the department's veins like the plague. Seventh floor—fearful citizens scurrying cautiously through dangerous streets. Fifth floor–vicious predators seemingly unchecked as they preyed on victims of all ages. Fourth floor–the changes until the NYPD had become one of the cleanest departments in existence. Second floor—a rush of pride as I thought of my small contribution to the city's transformation from a dangerous place to live to one of the safest large cities in the country. First floor–the knowledge of the legacy I left the seniors of Manhattan North through the formation of the most successful senior citizen robbery unit in the country.

I left One Police Plaza and the shock of breathing civilian air for the first time in twenty-two years catapulted my thoughts back to when I was a kid.

Can you think back to what it was like playing cops and robbers? How it felt to strap on your six-shooter, the strings at the bottom of the holster tied around your leg to facilitate your lightning-fast draw? You were truly a scourge upon the unlawful and the mere mention of your name would send chills up and down their cowardly spines. There wasn't room in your town for any of them. Time and time again you put your adolescent life on the line and each time the rush of risking it all to protect the local citizenry made your chest swell with pride. Yes, you were awesome–you were *sheriff*.

I was blessed, being able to play those childhood games into my adult years. Oh yeah, I retired, but not a single day goes by I don't regret it. Even if the job had killed me that would have been okay, I loved it that much.

I hope there's such a thing as reincarnation because when I die I want to come back and do it all over again.

EPILOGUE

To those members of the law enforcement community both active and retired who have read this book I extend my salutations. As many of you know and others will someday realize, you may retire and leave the job but the job will never leave you. You will always look at people and situations differently and more keenly than those not part of your profession. You will always stand tall and proud knowing where you have been and what you have done. You will be thankful for the many opportunities you had to make people's lives a little better and safer. Thankful for the times you were able to render assistance to those persons who desperately needed help and had no one else to turn to.

To those of you not involved in law enforcement I extend my greetings and hope you enjoyed reading the book as much as I enjoyed living it. It was a pleasure and a privilege being afforded the opportunity to protect and serve my fellow human beings. While we never got rich monetarily we were abundantly rewarded spiritually. Our reward was found in the knowledge that "Blessed are the peacemakers, for they are the children of God," and that cops are part of the greatest fraternity in the world.

The years have gone by and the players in this tome have finished their active service and have gone on to other endeavors.

Wild Jimmy Crean retired as captain of a Bronx detective district and is now a successful lawyer.

Davy Katz spends his retired years out West. Peggy

and I had the pleasure to spend some time with him recently and he is still the crazy, funny partner I once had. His words to Peggy after kissing her on the cheek were, "Did the church canonize you yet?"

Eddie Schneider moved to Florida and is owner of that state's largest trailer and RV park as well as a thriving RV dealership. He was always adept at making lots of money and is now able to uphold the law just for the fun of it, as a part-time deputy sheriff.

Fred Lambert became the chief of security for a major bank in Manhattan and still resides in New York City.

Ed Bailey was a security chief at the Board of Education for many years until finally retiring for good. Ed passed away during the writing of this book and the fraternity lost a great brother.

Cleve Bethea retired on a disability pension after sustaining two gunshot wounds in the line of duty. After many surgeries to repair the shattered bone in his leg he regained his ability to walk unaided. He currently lives in a southern state tending to his chickens and using their egg production to supplement his pension.

George Roberts went into private investigation and is now deceased.

John Mattias died of cancer at the young age of forty-four and ended what would have been a brilliant investigative career.

Tricky Dick Lannon moved to New York's Catskill Mountains where he lives in a house atop a mountain road overlooking a beautiful valley.

Chief Charles O. Henry, my boss, my friend, and my mentor retired to Las Vegas where he passed away in February of 2006.

Time passes, but time can't dim the shining memories I treasure of a career spent with some of the finest cops and detectives on earth.

INDEX

OTHER BOOKS IN OUR BARRICADE CRIME SERIES

The Jews of Sing-Sing

Ron Arons

Besides famous gangsters like Lepke Buchalter, thousands of Jews committed all types of crimes--from incest to arson to selling air rights over Manhattan--and found themselves doing time in Sing-Sing.

$22.95 • Hardcover • 1-56980-333-1

The Mafia and the Machine

Frank R. Hayde

La Cosa Nostra reaches right into the heart of America. Nowhere is that more evident than in the "City of Fountains," where the Mafia held sway over the political machine.

$22.00 • Hardcover • 1-56980-336-6

Black Gangsters of Chicago

Ron Chepesiuk

Chicago's African American gangsters were every bit as powerful and intriguing as the city's fabled white mobsters. For the first time, Ron Chepesiuk chronicles their fascinating stories.

$22.00 • Hardcover • 1-56980-331-5

The Silent Don

Scott Deitche

A follow-up to Deitche's best-selling *Cigar City Mafia*, *The Silent Don* exposes the life of one of America's most powerful and feared mob bosses, Santo Trafficante Jr.

$22.00 • Hardcover • 1-56980-322-6
(coming soon in Paperback, December 2008)

Blood & Volume

Dave Copeland

Ron Gonen, together with pals Johnny Attias and Ron Efraim, ran a multi-million-dollar drug distribution syndicate in 1980s New York. But when the FBI caught up, Gonen had to choose between doing the right thing and winding up dead.

$22.00 • Hardcover • 1-56980-327-7

Gangsters of Harlem

Ron Chepesiuk

Veteran journalist Ron Chepesiuk chronicles the life and crimes of Harlem's gangsters, including "Nicky" Barnes, Bumpy Johnson, and the notorious Frank Lucas.

$22.00 • Hardcover • 1-56980-318-8

Cigar City Mafia: A Complete History of the Tampa Underworld

Scott M. Deitche

Prohibition-era "Little Havana" housed Tampa's cigar industry, and with it, bootleggers, arsonists, and mobsters—and a network of corrupt police officers worse than the criminals themselves. Scott M. Deitche documents the rise of the infamous Trafficante family, ruthless competitors in a "violent, shifting place, where loyalties and power quickly changed."

$22.95 • Hardcover • 1-56980-266-1

I'll Do My Own Damn Killin'

Gary W. Sleeper

A detailed look into the life of notorious casino owner Benny Binion, which looks into his life in Dallas before his infamous Las Vegas days.

$22.00 • Hardcover • 1-56980-321-8

Thief!

William "Slick" Hanner & Cherie Rohn
The true story of "Slick" Hanner and how he gained insider access to the Mafia, starting out as a Chicago street tough and workin his way to a friendship with Tony Spilotro, the Outfit's notorious frontman.

$22.00 • Hardcover • 1-56980-317-X

Gangster City: The History of the New York Underworld 1900–1935

Patrick Downey
From 1900 to 1935, New York City hosted more than 600 mob-land killings. No other book delivers such extensive detail on the lives, crimes, and dramatic endings of this ruthless cast of characters, including Jack "Legs" Diamond and the sadistic Dutch Schultz.

$23.95 • Hardcover • 1-56980-267-X
(coming soon in Paperback, March 2009)

Il Dottore

Ron Felber
By day, he was Dr. Elliot Litner, respected surgeon at Mount Sinai Hospital; by night, Il Dottore, a sex and gambling addict with ties to New York's reigning Mafia Dons. But when Attorney General Rudolph Guiliani stepped in, Litner had to decide where his loyalties lay: with La Cosa Nostra, or the Hippocratic oath.

$24.95 • Hardcover • 1-56980-278-5

Murder of a Mafia Daughter

Cathy Scott

Not until college did Las Vegas native Susan Berman learn her father had been a notorious leader of the local Mafia. Her life took an even more bizarre turn when the wife of her college friend, real estate heir Robert Durst, disappeared, leaving Durst a murder suspect. When Berman was found dead, shot execution-style, investigators wondered if she knew more about Durst than he could afford.

$23.95 • Hardcover • 1-56980-238-6

The Life and Times of Lepke Buchalter

Paul R. Kavieff
Lepke Buchalter had a stranglehold on the New York garment industry, rising from small-scale push-cart terrorism to leadership of Murder Inc.'s staff of killers-by-assignment, until an obscure murder ended his reign as America's most ruthless labor racketeer.

$22.00 • Hardcover • 1-56980-291-2

The Purple Gang

Paul R. Kavieff
This is the hitherto untold story of the rise and fall of one of America's most notorious criminal groups. The Purple Gang was a loosely organized confederation of mobsters who dominated the Detroit underworld and whose tentacles reached across the country.

$15.95 • Paperback • 1-56980-281-5
Hardcover

The Violent Years

Paul R. Kavieff
A follow-up to Kavieff's best-selling *The Purple Gang*, this book delves deeper

into the Prohibition-Era gangs of the Detroit area.

$22.00 • Hardcover • 1-56980-210-6

The Rise and Fall of the Cleveland Mafia

Rick Porrello
From obscurity, the Cleveland Mafia rose rapidly to power and position, taking its place as the third most powerful operation in the country. But the city's crime syndicates nearly decimated themselves during the Sugar War—"Big Ange" Lonardo's vendetta-driven play to control the lucrative bootleg liquor production racket.

$15.00 • Paperback • 1-56980-277-7 Hardcover

Lucky Luciano

Hickman Powell
Written by a top investigative reporter who covered Luciano's trial from beginning to end, *Lucky Luciano* is a detailed account of Luciano's intriguing life.

$23.95 • Hardcover • 1-56980-163-0

Mala Femina

Theresa Dalessio with Patrick W. Picciarelli
Theresa "Terri Dee" Dalessio was a Mafia daughter, pregnant teenager, barkeeper, heroin addict, murder witness, and twice-divorced mother of three. For a start.

$24.95 • Hardcover • 1-56980-244-0

Jailing the Johnston Gang

Bruce E. Mowday
Pennsylvania's Johnston Gang, led by Bruce Sr. and his brothers Norman and David, ran a prolific burglary ring during the 1960 and 1970s. But in 1978, fearing that younger members of the gang were going to rat them out, the brothers killed four teenagers and nearly killed Bruce Sr.'s own son.

$22.95 • Hardcover • 1-56980-363-3

Human Sacrifice: A Shocking Exposé of Ritual Killings Worldwide

Jimmy Lee Shreeve
Human sacrifice still goes on today, and uncomfortably close to home. Jimmy Lee Shreeve paints a horrifying picture of ritual killings around the world.

$15.95 • Paperback • 1-56980-346-3

Balls: The Life of Eddie Trascher, Gentleman Gangster

Scott M. Deitche with Ken Sanz
For 50 years, Eddie Trascher stole from mob-owned casinos, scammed gangsters, and was one of the top bookies in the country. He capped his career as an informant for Florida enforcement to get inside the Trafficante Mafia family.

$24.95 • Hardcover • 1-56980-366-8